Understanding
MP3

Understanding
MP3

Syntax, Semantics, Mathematics
Algorithms

MARTIN RUCKERT *Munich University of Applied Sciences*

Printed by CreateSpace, an Amazon.com Company

The author has taken care in the preparation of this book, but makes no expressed or implied warranty of any kind and assumes no responsibility for errors or omissions. No liability is assumed for incidental or consequential damages in connection with or arising out of the use of the information or programs contained herein.

```
Ruckert, Martin.
Understanding MP3
Includes index.
ISBN-13: 978-1541259331
ISBN-10: 1541259335
```

Internet page `http://www.cs.hm.edu/~ruckert/understanding_mp3/` contains current information about this book, downloadable software, and news.

Preface

This book started as a project to investigate "literate programming"[17], a programming style advocated by Donald E. Knuth. After meeting him in the Fall of 2000, I felt the desire to try this approach on an extensive example, and I chose the decoding of MP3 streams. My interest in MP3 decoding, at that time, was motivated by the search for a good project to use in teaching undergraduate classes in algebra using a novel, project oriented approach.

So from the outset, I wrote this book wearing two different hats. Wearing my software engineering hat, I tried to write efficient but well organized code. I focused on algorithms and data structures, investigating alternative ways to organize code. Wearing my hat as a mathematics educator, I tried to explain, comprehensively and thoroughly, the ideas and principles involved in MPEG audio coding and advertise the fine tools, provided by centuries of research in mathematics, that can be used to simplify and enhance the program. While I tried not to compromise at all in my role as a software engineer, I limited the treatment of mathematics to fit the prerequisites of the intended audience. To read this book, plain high school math ought to be more than sufficient

After the first chapters were written—implementing just MPEG Version 1, layer I— Reinald Klockenbusch from the Vieweg Verlag suggested to me the publication of this project as a book. I felt enticed by this proposal and signed the contract. Looking back, I must admit that I underestimated the difficulties. As the scope of the project grew to include an implementation of all three layers and the extensions for low sample frequencies, the complexity of the project multiplied.

It turned out to be much more difficult to produce a literate program than producing either a piece of literature or a program alone. It is easier to write only a book, because the author can easily decrease the level of detail in the exposition and resort to a more superficial description whenever desired. It is easier to write only a program, because the programmer can settle for correct and efficient code even if it is hard to understand. None of this is possible in literate programming. I found myself very often rewriting a correct and efficient piece of code just because I did not manage to explain it very well. And I had to think hard about extracting the interesting ideas from repetitive tasks, resorting to code and table generation instead of simple programming. On the positive side, while both activities—writing and programming—become harder, the quality increases too. Programs become more efficient, more reliable, and more readable; the documentation becomes comprehensive, detailed, and may be even enjoyable.

Considering it all, I still think it was work well spent. Writing this book, I learned immensely about programming, about mathematics, about efficiency, and about writing. I sincerely hope that the reader of this book can participate in this learning process and benefit from it as I did.

Depending on specific interests, reading this book can follow several paths. Chapters 1, 2, 3, and 4 give an introduction into the subject avoiding much of the technicalities. The more mathematically interested reader should consult Chapter 10 to find out how a signal can be disassembled into frequency components and how to put it back together again. Strictly necessary is the formalism explained there only for the understanding of Chapter 11. Some more interesting mathematics is incorporated into Appendix B.

The application programmer who just wants to use mp32pcm for decoding should consult Chapters 5 and 6. Chapters 7 and 8 contain the remaining details of layer I decoding, like the structure of frames and headers or the details of efficient bitwise reading.

The remaining chapters provide full details for the implementors of decoders. Chapter 9 explains the improvements that distinguish layer II from layer I. Chapters 11 to 13 discuss the features of layer III, with Chapter 12 entirely devoted to lossless compression using Huffman Coding. I have tried to expose the ideas involved so that the solutions presented here can be readily applied to similar problems found in many other audio or video compression schemes.

To conclude, I want to thank Reinald Klockenbusch and the Vieweg Verlag for suggesting and supporting this book project; Jeffrey Veit, for diligently and competently preparing the figures for print; my students at Munich University of Applied Sciences, for listening patiently, while I was test-teaching them the material presented in this book during the fall semester of 2004/2005; and Hans W. Britschgi, who generously let me use his beautiful house in the Swiss Alps, where I was able to find both quiet time and inspiration to complete this project.

Wolfgang, February 26, 2005   *Martin Ruckert*

Contents

List of Figures, Equations, and Tables

Figures

Equations

Tables

1 Introduction

MPEG audio coding became popular under the name "MP3". It is now the most important means of delivering high quality audio over the Internet and will play the lead role in digital movie sound as well as in digital audio broadcast. It is therefore of interest, for the audio engineer or for the educated movie-goer, to understand the basic principles of this exciting technology, or have enough background in technical details to write an audio decoder.

The purpose of this Project is twofold:

- to explain the syntax, the semantics, the mathematics, the software, and the purpose that is inherent in an MPEG audio bit stream, and

- to provide a highly efficient, general purpose implementation of a decoder, called mp32pcm, that can transform such a bit stream into an ordinary stream of PCM data.

The two goals of the project make it a prime candidate for an application of CWEB, the tool invented by D. Knuth to facilitate "literate programming", to produce a piece of software in the same fashion as one would produce a piece of literature. And as literature is intended to be read, understood, and enjoyed by ordinary human beings, I strive here to explain the transformation of a bit stream into music in a way that is not only understandable but even enjoyable.

This aim in front of me, I start with the question that seems the most interesting: How can there be music in a bit stream?

1.1 Encoding Music

The usual way to digitally encode music, or any kind of sound, is Pulse Code Modulation (PCM). After the microphone has converted sound to an analog electrical signal, the voltage level of this signal is measured in regular time intervals using an AD (Analog to Digital) converter and the results are stored as a sequence of numbers (Fig. 1). This process is called sampling. A typical format is 44100 measurements per second represented as 16 bit integer numbers. The number of measurements per second is called "sample rate". In our example, the sample rate is 44.1 kHz and each 16 bit number is called a sample. To reconstruct the music from the PCM code, the analog electrical signal is reconstructed using a DA (Digital to Analog) converter and fed to a loudspeaker.

This process has two main problems: A continuous change of voltage levels is reduced to a discrete number of measurements, and further, each measurement is rounded to the next possible value that can be represented as a 16 bit integer. The process of sampling inevitably introduces these errors. The first error is called "sampling error", the second is called "quantization error".

Fortunately, we can make these errors arbitrarily small by increasing the sample rate and using more bits to encode the voltage levels. For digital recordings on CD, it was decided that a PCM encoding using a sample rate of 44.1 kHz and 16 bit per sample is enough to render inaudible any errors introduced by the encoding.

It is interesting to note that there is a close connection between the sample rate and the highest frequencies that can be encoded, and the number of bits per sample and the dynamic range. We will see more of that later. For now, it may suffice to know what PCM code is and that it is straightforward to convert PCM code to audible sound using cheap hardware commonly called "sound cards".

Here immediately the next question comes up: If PCM is such a simple and convenient format, why do we need MPEG audio coding?

1.2 Audio Compression

The reason for MPEG audio coding is simply the following: PCM does take too much storage space. To record a single second of sound, the above mentioned PCM format requires $44100 \cdot 2 = 88200$ bytes, and a simple 5 minute song in stereo will take as much as $88200 \cdot 2 \cdot 60 \cdot 5 = 52920000$ bytes or approximately 50 Mbyte. While this is not too much for modern Computers and a CD can nicely store a whole collection of songs, the size is a problem when sending the song over a network connection like the Internet. Trusting the advertisement, a good modem connection is capable of transmitting up to 56000 bits per second. In a TCP/IP network, a certain amount of this raw data is needed for administrative overhead which leaves less than 50000 bits $= 6250$ bytes per second for the music. Transmitting the 5 minute song will then take $52920000/6250 = 8467.2$ seconds or 2 hours and 20 minutes. Who is willing to wait that long? Even worse, applications like Internet radio or Internet telephone rely on the ability to send sound data in "real time" that is, as fast as the sound data is produced. This requires a dramatic reduction in the size of the data used to encode the sound. MPEG audio coding is all about this: reducing the data needed to store sound to the bare minimum.

Before it is possible to listen to music coded as an MPEG bit stream, it is then necessary to convert the MPEG bit stream back to PCM data. The following will explain how this is done, and at the same time, why it works.

2 Digital Filters and Subband Synthesis

The PCM output of an MP3 decoder is computed from so called subbands. Each subband, there are 32 of them, contains the audible sound limited to a very narrow part of the frequency spectrum. Think of it as a kind of equalizer with 32 sliders; the first slider is for the lowest sounds and the last slider is for the highest tones. If we turn down all the sliders except one, we will hear only part of the music, namely the musical signal limited to a small part of the audible spectrum. This limited part of the spectrum is a subband. We will be able to hear the music as it was meant to be only if we open all sliders of our equalizer. This will combine all the signals of the different subbands and will yield the full spectrum.

The musical signal is split into subbands by a digital filter in the encoder and needs to be recombined in the decoder. To understand this process, we consider a simple example: We take a sine wave as input signal, were the amplitude at time t is given by the formula $f(t) = \sin(2\pi t)$. The signal is periodic with period length 1, i.e. the signal between 0 and 1 is repeated between 1 and 2 and so forth. This signal is periodically sampled with period length $1/10$, i.e. at $t = 0.0, 0.1, \ldots, 1.0$, which yields the values $x_i = f(i/10)$, that is $x_0 = 0.0$, $x_1 = 0.59$, $x_2 = 0.95$, $x_3 = 0.98$, $x_4 = 0.59$, $x_5 = 0.0$, $x_6 = -0.59$, $x_7 = -0.95$, $x_8 = -0.98$, $x_9 = -0.59$, and $x_{10} = x_0 = 0.0$, as shown in Figure 1.

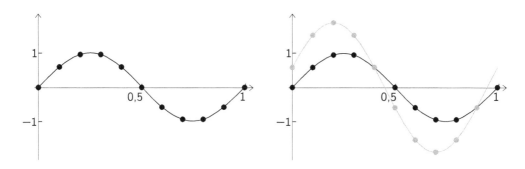

Fig. 1: The filter input   Fig. 2: The filter input and output

2.1 A Simple Filter

Now we examine the most simple digital filter: The output y_i of the filter is computed by $y_i = x_i + x_{i+1}$ from two successive input values. The filter's output is shown in Figure 2 together with its input.

It is immediately visible, that the output is again a sine wave of the same frequency but with a different gain (amplitude) and slightly shifted to the left (phase shift). Employing some useful 9th grade math, or equivalently a tool like Mathematica[28], one can show that in general

$$\sin(\omega t) + \sin(\omega(t + \delta)) = 2\cos(\omega\delta/2)\sin(\omega t + \omega\delta/2).$$

With $\omega = 2\pi$ and $\delta = 1/10$, $\sin(\omega t))$ corresponds to x_i and $\sin(\omega(t+\delta)$ corresponds to x_{i+1}, and we have $y_i = x_i + x_{i+1} = 2\cos(\omega\delta/2)\sin(\omega t + \omega\delta/2)$.

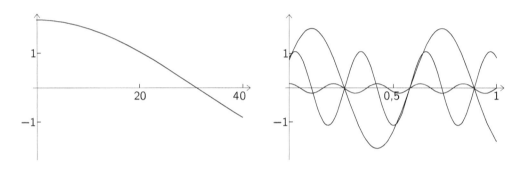

Fig. 3: The filter's frequency response   Fig. 4: Filter outputs for unit-gain inputs

The $\sin(\omega t + \omega\delta/2)$ term shows that the filter output is indeed a sine wave with the same frequency (given by ω) but shifted by $\omega\delta/2$ to the left. The factor $2\cos(\omega\delta/2)$, which does not depend on t, is the amplitude of the filter output. It depends on δ and ω. With a fixed sample rate, given by $\delta = 1/10$, the new amplitude depends only on the input frequency ω.

Plotting the filter's gain $2\cos(\omega\delta/2)$ against the frequency of the filter input, we obtain Figure 3, called the filter's frequency response. It shows that the filter amplifies low frequencies by almost a factor of two and mutes input signals with higher frequencies (ω close to 30). Figure 4 illustrates this effect. It shows the filter output for the three inputs $\sin(10t)$, $\sin(20t)$, and $\sin(30t)$.

2.2 The Complementary Filter

Next, we consider the complementary digital filter with output y_i' given by the formula $y_i' = -x_i + x_{i+1}$. Its filter gain is computed as before and turns out to be $2\sin(\omega\delta/2)$. Figure 6 shows the frequency response of both filters.

It is clearly visible how the new filter suppresses lower frequencies and boosts higher frequencies. Both filters together can now be used to separate any input signal into

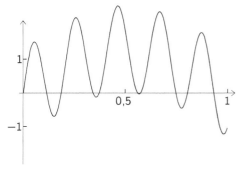

Fig. 5: The input signal to the left was created by adding a low frequency component and a high frequency component

$$\sin(1\pi t) + \sin(5\pi t).$$

This signal was then filtered by the simple low frequency filter and its complementary high frequency filter. The outputs are shown below.

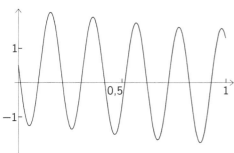

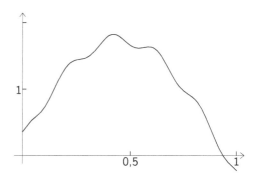

two subbands, one containing high frequency content and the other low frequency content. The input function $\sin(1\pi t) + \sin(5\pi t)$ is a good example (Fig. 5). While the separation of low and high frequencies in the output is clearly visible, it can also be seen that there is a wide overlap of both filters: the low frequency output still contains some significant high frequency content and vice versa.

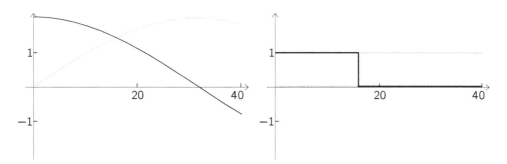

Fig. 6: Frequency response of both filters   *Fig. 7: Perfect frequency response*

Of course, much better filters can be constructed, as we will see, but for now, we stick to the simple filters and try to find out how the original signal can be restored from the output of the two filters. This is the same problem faced by the decoder, where the output must be computed from the subbands.

Recall that the filter outputs were given by $y_i = x_i + x_{i+1}$ and $y'_i = -x_i + x_{i+1}$. Therefore, we can compute x_i as

$$0.5y_i - 0.5y'_i = 0.5(x_i + x_{i+1}) - 0.5(-x_i + x_{i+1}) = x_i.$$

The formula $0.5y_i - 0.5y'_i$ is again a digital filter, the synthesis filter. We can, however, do more than just compute x_i. We can even compute x_{i+1} from y_i and y'_i by

$$0.5y_i + 0.5y'_i = 0.5(x_i + x_{i+1}) + 0.5(-x_i + x_{i+1}) = x_{i+1}.$$

This enables us to reduce the sample rate in the subbands to every second sample without loosing information. The 10 input samples can be fully reconstructed from two subbands with 5 samples each. This observation can be generalized: If a signal is carefully split into n subbands, the sample rate in each subband can be reduced by a factor of n without losing the ability to reconstruct the original signal from the subbands at the full sample rate. This process is called "decimating the subbands".

We have now a rough understanding of digital filters and will not further explore the art and science of digital filter design until we return to this topic in Chapter 10. The interested reader should consult a good book on digital signal processing, for example [24]. Here, some concluding remarks must suffice to bridge the remaining gap between the toy filters, studied so far, and the complex filters used in MPEG audio coding.

2.3 The Perfect Filter

A sequence of good digital filters to separate the input of an MP3 encoder into subbands, as required by the psychoacoustic compression, should have the following properties: It should not introduce a phase shift in the output signal, and adjacent subbands should have a minimal overlap.

The first requirement leads to symmetric filters, that is, filters where the dependency of the output value y_i on the input value x_{i+k} is the same as the dependency on x_{i-k}. For example $y_i = 0.5x_{i-1} + x_i + 0.5x_{i+1}$ would be such a filter.

Secondly, as one should expect, good filters need more information about the input signal. Using only two successive sample values, as our toy filters do, yields poor filters. Better filters can be constructed using longer sequences of input samples. If a filter output sample is computed from n input samples $x_k, \ldots, x_{k+n-1}$, we call it a filter of length n. The filter used in MPEG audio coding has a length of 512. The rest of the art is just choosing the right coefficients.

Now, one could aim at a perfect filter that cleanly cuts out a small part of the spectrum, with a frequency response similar to the one shown in Figure 7. Unfortunately, it turns out that perfect filters will require perfect information. One discovers that the perfect filter has the form

$$y_i = \sum_{k=-\infty}^{+\infty} \frac{\sin(k\omega_0)}{k\pi} x_{i+k} \qquad\qquad (Eq.\ 1)$$

where ω_0 is the cutoff frequency, that is the frequency where the response of the filter suddenly drops to zero.

While the coefficients get smaller and smaller when k progresses toward infinity, they never become exactly zero. Computing a sum with infinitely many coefficients, however, is immensely impractical, therefore a technique called "windowing" is employed: The perfect coefficients are multiplied by certain factors that reach zero outside a finite range. The resulting filter is not perfect, but nearly perfect. One such filter, obtained by numerical optimization, is used in MPEG audio coding and decoding.

2.4 Lapped Transforms

Before we can understand the filtering as prescribed by the standard, we have to consider another problem and its solution: lapped transforms.

As it is, the encoding is usually not invertible, that is: it is not possible to reconstruct the input exactly from the encoders output. The reconstruction is only a good approximation of the input. If we would just split the input samples in packets, each containing 512 samples, then encode the signal packetwise, and finally generate the output by decoding packet after packet, we would discover rough edges in the output signal where two packets are joined together. If the transition from one packet to the next is not smooth enough, the result will be audible distortion. The solution is to have the packets overlap generously and while we fade out one packet, we fade in the next packet in much the same way as a disk-jockey makes an (almost) inaudible transition from one piece of music to the next one. The overlapping packets (and the associated technique of splicing them together again) are known as lapped transforms. Now we are ready to look at the standard.

3 Standard Synthesis Subband Filter

The Standard ISO/IEC 11172-3: Information technology—Coding of moving pictures and associated audio for digital storage media at up to about 1,5 Mbit/s, Part 3, (from now on, we just call it "the standard"[1]) plainly states in Section 2.4.3.2.2 and the associated flow diagram figure A.2:

1. **Input**: *Take 32 new Subband samples y_k, $k = 0, \ldots, 31$.*

2. **Shifting**: *Move the contents of the vector v 64 places to the right. That is, for i=1023 down to 64 do $v_i = v_{i-64}$. The vector v is to be initialized with zeros during startup.*

3. **Matrixing**: *Calculate 64 new values*

$$v_i = \sum_{k=0}^{31} n_{ik} y_k \quad \text{with} \quad i = 0, \ldots 63 \text{ and } n_{ik} = \cos\big((16+i)(2k+1)\pi/64\big).$$

4. **Reduction**: *Build a vector u of 512 elements according to the formula*

$$u_{64k+j} = v_{128k+j} \quad \text{and}$$
$$u_{64k+j+32} = v_{128k+j+96} \quad \text{for } k = 0, \ldots, 7 \text{ and } j = 0, \ldots, 31.$$

5. **Windowing**: *Next, the elements of vector u are scaled by the elements of vector d (given by a large table) yielding a vector w with $w_j = u_j \cdot d_j$ for $j = 0, \ldots, 511$.*

6. **Calculate Samples**: *The vector x of 32 output samples is computed as*

$$x_k = \sum_{j=0}^{15} w_{k+32j} \quad \text{for} \quad k = 0, \ldots, 31.$$

It is not difficult to see that the computation of the decoded PCM samples in vector x from the input vector y of subband samples is split into several steps. This is done to achieve some basic optimizations. The Windowing step is applied once to 512 input values and should remind us to the input filter with "perfect" frequency response. Only by using so many input values, a high quality filter can be obtained.

It is preceded by some shuffling, called reduction, and an other filtering step, called matrixing. The matrixing step applies different filters, one for each of the 32 frequencies, to the subband samples y. Knowing already about decimation of subbands, we would have expected 32 output values from 32 subband samples, but here 64 values are computed and stored in the vector v. The vector v serves as a buffer of preprocessed input values such that the windowing step can take the necessary 512 values without repeating the preprocessing. And then, we see that indeed only 32 values, as expected, come out of the final sample calculation, which represents the overlapping of lapped transforms. While some of the details still need more exploration (see Chapter 10), the overall purpose of the process should be clear.

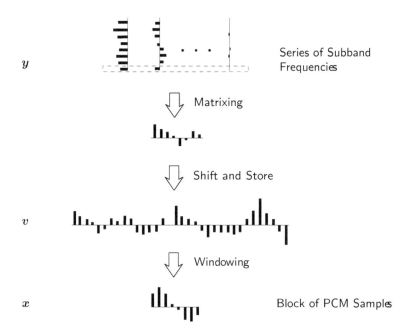

Fig. 8: Transforming series of subband frequencies to PCM samples

3.1 Computational Complexity

The computational complexity of the above procedure is $64 \cdot 31$ multiplications and $64 \cdot 32$ additions in step 3, 512 multiplications in step 5, and $32 \cdot 15$ Additions in step 6. This gives a total of 2569 multiplications and about the same number of additions.

To program the plain algorithm in C is straight forward. After compiling the code, it will need 12.58 μs to execute. About 13 % of the runtime is spent in the shifting loop, the matrixing loop takes 55 %, reduction needs 9 %, windowing 7 %, and sample calculation 16 %. Under identical conditions, a good implementation (like mpg123[22]) needs only 3.2 μs to complete the same job. How is this done?

First, the reduction step has no computational content. If the windowing step selects the right values directly from the vector v, step 4 can be eliminated completely. Second, the windowing step can be combined with the sample calculation into one loop where each value from v is multiplied by the appropriate constant from d just before it is added into the output vector x. This cuts down the number of load and store instructions by half and avoids copying and looping overhead. These changes bring the runtime down to 10.30 μs.

More can be gained from optimizing the matrixing step. If we look at the coefficients n_{ik}, we discover that $n_{ik} = -n_{(32-i)\,k}$ because

$$
\begin{aligned}
n_{ik} &= \cos\big((16+i)(2k+1)\pi/64\big) \\
&= \cos\big(-(16+i)(2k+1)\pi/64\big) \quad \text{using} \quad \cos(x) = \cos(-x) \\
&= \cos\big(-(16+i)(2k+1)\pi/64 + 2k\pi\big) \quad \text{using} \quad \cos(x) = \cos(x+2\pi) \\
&= -\cos\big(-(16+i)(2k+1)\pi/64 + (2k+1)\pi\big) \quad \text{using} \quad \cos(x) = -\cos(x+\pi) \\
&= -\cos\big((48-i)(2k+1)\pi/64\big) \\
&= -\cos\big((16+(32-i))(2k+1)\pi/64\big) = -n_{(32-i)\,k}.
\end{aligned}
$$

This means that the Matrixing computations for $i = 0, 1, \ldots, 15$ yield the same results as the computations for $i = 32, 31, \ldots, 17$, except for the sign. Similarly, we have $n_{(48-i)\,k} = n_{(48+i)\,k}$, and hence the computations for $i = 33, 34, \ldots, 48$ are repeated in reverse order for $i = 63, 62, \ldots, 48$. For $i = 16$, we have $n_{ik} = 0$ and we need no computation to conclude $v_{16} = 0$.

Our initial suspicion was justified: from 32 subbands, we can compute only 32 PCM samples—the rest is repetition. Of the 64 results in the matrixing step, we need only 32, from $i = 0$ to 15 and from $i = 33$ to 48. If we do the second batch of computations first, we can write these computations as

$$
v_i = \sum_{k=0}^{31} \cos\big(i(2k+1)\pi/64\big) y_k \quad \text{with } i = 0, \ldots 31.
$$

Here v is a vector of 32 elements, half the size of the old v, that contains all the elements of v except for the sign and some reordering. Steps 4, 5, and 6 can be done with the shorter vector using different indices and an occasional change in the sign of the coefficients. While this change cuts the number of operations in the matrixing step in half and reduces by the same amount the load and store instructions in the shifting loop, more improvement is still ahead.

3.2 The Discrete Cosine Transform

The matrixing transformation with the coefficients $\cos\big(i(2k+1)\pi/64\big)$ is known as 32 point Discrete Cosine Transform (DCT) and belongs to the class of Discrete Fourier Transforms. Very efficient methods are known to compute these transformations. The most common version will do the 32 point DCT with only 80 Multiplications and

209 Additions[19]. The algorithm used for instance in mpg123[22] requires exactly
this many operations. Here, we will not discuss how this method works, nor how one
would be able to find such a fast algorithm. We will deal with this in Chapter 10.

But progress does not stop here. It is long known[4], that even faster algorithms
are possible. If we do not insist on the exact output of the transformation but allow
a scaling step that multiplies the outputs of the transformation by fixed constants
to obtain the values of the DCT, we can use the so called Cosine Discrete Fourier
Transform (CosDFT) instead. The scaling step is then combined with the windowing
step and therefore can be performed without additional computational costs. The
code that we use in mp32pcm to compute the CosDFT is given in Appendix A.2.
It looks quite boring, needs only 49 Multiplications and 216 Additions and is not
written by hand, but is generated by an automatic tool called spiral[30]. In spite of
the significant reduction in the number of operations, the CosDFT algorithm does
not run much faster than the DCT algorithm. Obviously, the number of operations
is not the only factor that determines the execution speed of an algorithm.

3.3 Processor Architecture

The programming of modern processors faces two new challenges: memory latency
and pipeline stalls. The speed of processors has reached an incredible level, and as a
consequence, the transportation of data from off-chip memory to the processor takes
significantly more time than simple computations on the data. Therefore the number
of load and store instructions is an important factor in execution speed. To complicate
matters, processors use a technique called "caching", that allows the processor to
remember values instead of loading them from off-chip memory, and to proceed after
a store operation without waiting until it is completed. It is even possible to speculate
about the future and initiate the loading of values that might be needed soon.

In spite of all this, algorithms still tend to be faster, if the computations involve
only a small number of values that can be kept in registers, avoiding load and store
operations altogether.

There are, however, reasons that lead to a different conclusion: algorithms tend to
be faster if they involve sequences of mostly unrelated computations. Why that?

Today's general purpose processors use a technique called "pipelining" to speed
up computations. You can compare the pipeline of a processor to the assembly line
of a plant: Imagine a factory producing cars. You observe—somewhat simplified—
that every 20 minutes the raw material for one car enters the plant and one new
car exits the plant. The fact that every 20 minutes a new car leaves the plant does
not mean that we can produce the whole car in only 20 minutes. But from the
outside, it appears to be the speed of the plant. Inside the plant, we discover that
this speed is the result of working in parallel on many cars. Two different versions
of parallel work are possible: Many small but complete plants each work on a single
car from begin to finish. This type of parallelism is found in "vector processors".
Or the assembly line parallelism, where many specialized units work in sequence
to produce one car. Processors with this type of parallelism are called "pipeline
processors", because instructions pass through the assembly line like water through

a pipeline. Pipelining is the cheaper form of parallelism because expensive hardware, like a floating point multiplier, is needed only once, and therefore, pipelining is found in most general purpose processors. The regular flow of instructions through the pipeline, however, comes to a halt if the execution of an operation needs the result of a previous operation that is still in the pipeline and has not yet progressed to a stage where this result is already available. The instruction (and all that follow) is then delayed until the required operand is computed. This situation is called a "pipeline stall". It is best avoided by scheduling a mix of unrelated instructions for execution.

Producing fast code is a very hard problem. It requires finding a balance between contradicting requirements that depend very much on the target processor and its facilities for caching and pipelining. This task is best left to the compiler that generates the machine code and different compilers achieve different results.

We compare the GNU C compiler version 2.95.3[12], the Intel C Compiler version 7.0 [16], and the Optimizing Microsoft 32-Bit C/C++ compiler version 12.00.8804 [23], as well as four different implementations: The DCT used in mpg123 version pre0.59s[22], the DCT used in mad version 0.14.2b[21], the DCT derived with spiral (not used), and the CosDFT derived with spiral actually used with mp32pcm. In Table 1, the run times are given in μs. We postpone a complete discussion of performance until Section 3.6.

C Compiler	mad	mpg123	DCT	CosDFT
GNU	0.84 μs	1.47 μs	1.09 μs	1.13 μs
Intel	0.62 μs	0.43 μs	0.31 μs	0.31 μs
Microsoft	0.71 μs	0.79 μs	0.56 μs	0.49 μs

Tab. 1: Run time comparison for the DCT

3.4 Eliminating the Shifting

The vector v contains 16 blocks of 32 subband samples each. The shifting is needed because the windowing step uses each of these blocks successively in all 16 positions within v (Fig. 9). If we do not want to move the data, we can, instead, move the start point of v inside a larger vector w (Fig. 10). Of course, we can not move the start point indefinitely since the amount of memory available for w is limited. When we reach the left end of w, we have to start over at the right end and at this point, we have to make a copy of v, which is now at the left end, because next it will be needed at the right end of w (Fig. 11).

Increasing the storage by n blocks, therefore, implies that we can skip the copying n times before copying is necessary again. Any value of $n > 0$ is possible. With just one block more, we can cut the amount of copying in half. Another good choice could be 16 additional blocks—doubling the amount of memory. This reduces the time spent with copying quite drastically (to 1/16). For very different reasons—we want to keep a certain amount of "historic" data from the stream—as explained in Appendix A.1, we choose to have $n = 2 * 18 + 15 = 51$.

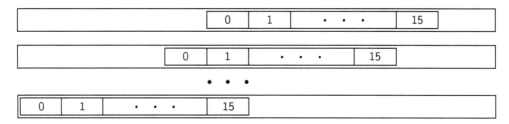

Fig. 9: Shifting a block of subbands through all positions

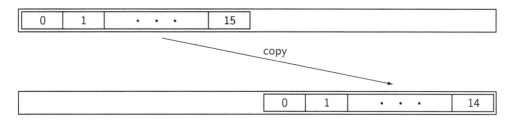

Fig. 10: Shifting the start point of **v**, keeping subbands in place

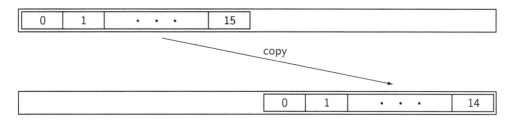

Fig. 11: Copy the subbands and start over at the right end

⟨ private declarations ₁ ⟩ ≡   (1)
#**define** WINDOWBLOCKS 16
#**define** SHIFTBLOCKS (2 ∗ BLOCKS + WINDOWBLOCKS − 1)
#**define** SHIFTSIZE (SHIFTBLOCKS ∗ SUBBANDS)
#**define** CHANNELS 2   Used in 6, 7, and 130.

⟨ stream data ₂ ⟩ ≡   (2)
  double **w**[CHANNELS][SHIFTSIZE];   Used in 42.

Now, instead of copying **v** each time, we need to copy it only every 36th time. The
shifting requires moving the beginning of **v** inside **w**. For this purpose, we store as
part of the ⟨ stream data ₂ ⟩ for each channel an *offset* that indicates the intended
start of **v** inside of **w**.

⟨ stream data ₂ ⟩ +≡   (3)
  int *offset*[CHANNELS];

In each shifting step, the intended beginning of v moves to the left to make space for new subband samples. If the *offset* becomes negative, we have to copy $16 - 1$ blocks and start over 16 blocks left of the right end of w. This is the C code to

⟨ shift vector v ₄ ⟩ ≡   (4)

```
s→offset[ch] = s→offset[ch] − SUBBANDS;
if (s→offset[ch] < 0)
{  s→offset[ch] = SHIFTSIZE − WINDOWBLOCKS * SUBBANDS;
   memmove(&(s→w[ch][s→offset[ch] + SUBBANDS]), &(s→w[ch][0]),
       sizeof(double) * (WINDOWBLOCKS − 1) * SUBBANDS);
}
v = s→w[ch] + s→offset[ch];                                    Used in 70, 75, and 408.
```

After that, v is shifted and ready to receive the next block of data.

3.5 The Core Algorithm

What remains, after the elimination of shifting, as the core of the algorithm is captured by the functions *dct32* and *windowing*.

⟨ private declarations ₁ ⟩ +≡   (5)

```
extern void dct32(const double *y, double *v);
extern void windowing(const double *v, mp3_sample *x);
```

dct32 takes a vector y of scaled samples performs the ⟨ 32 point CosDFT ₄₁₁ ⟩ on y, with the output ending up in vector v. The *windowing* function takes v and writes output samples to vector x. The code for the ⟨ 32 point CosDFT ₄₁₁ ⟩ can be found in Appendix A.2 and the code to ⟨ apply windowing ₄₁₂ ⟩ is in Appendix A.3.

Since the performance of the decoder depends largely on these two routines, they are written to a separate file, `perform.c`, to facilitate further optimization.

⟨ `perform.c` ₆ ⟩ ≡   (6)

```
#include "mp32pcm.h"
  ⟨ private declarations ₁ ⟩
  ⟨ conversion from double to mp3_sample ₁₃₈ ⟩

  void windowing(const double *v, mp3_sample *x)
  {  ⟨ apply windowing ₄₁₂ ⟩  }

  void dct32(const double *y, double *v)
  {  ⟨ 32 point CosDFT ₄₁₁ ⟩  }
```

3.6 Performance

After all these optimizations, we return to the question of performance. The distribution of the runtime of `mp32pcm` is shown in Table 2. The runtime is now dominated by the windowing step, which inevitably requires about 500 additions and multiplications, while the CosDFT needs only a reasonable fraction of the overall time. The reading of bits is only critical inside the main loop, where we read the subband samples. Decoding the header or reading the bit allocation and scalefactor information contributes almost nothing to the overall runtime. Still, the reading of the subband samples is surprisingly expensive, since apart from some bit manipulation and table lookup, only a single multiplication is required per sample.

Activity	Intel[16]	GNU[12]	References
read bit allocation	1 %	1 %	see Section 7.4
read scalefactors	1 %	1 %	see Section 7.9
read subband samples	15 %	25 %	see Section 7.6
CosDFT	25 %	30 %	see Appendix A.2
windowing	56 %	41 %	see Appendix A.3
rest	2 %	2 %	

Tab. 2: Distribution of runtime for different compilers

Table 3 presents the times in ms for running the different decoders on the layer I file `fl1.mpg`, provided with Part 4 of the standard[2].

	mad[21]	mpg123[22]	mp32pcm 32 bit	mp32pcm 16 bit
GNU[12]	5.83 ms	3.29 ms	3.11 ms	3.55 ms
Intel[16]	5.27 ms	3.23 ms	2.30 ms	2.70 ms
Microsoft[23]	6.02 ms	4.49 ms	4.39 ms	4.29 ms

Tab. 3: Run time comparison for layer I decoding

Some remarks may help to interpret this table:

- `mad` uses fixed point binary fractions with operations that can be implemented through integer arithmetic and shifting. Different formats of these numbers can be used to adjust the speed accuracy tradeoff. But even if optimized for speed, the decoder runs slower than `mpg123` or `mp32pcm`. Due to the extensive use of hand-optimized code, the differences between various compilers are relatively small.

- `mpg123` is commonly regarded as the fastest decoder available. Again there are various options to influence the speed/quality tradeoff. The influence of the compiler on the speed is minor because critical parts (the DFT) are written in assembly language.

- `mp32pcm` is slightly faster than `mpg123` when compiled with the Intel compiler and slower when compiled for 16 bit with the GNU compiler. The difference is due to the faster code that the Intel compiler produces for CosDFT and windowing. For this reason, the distribution of `mp32pcm` supplies the assembly output of the Intel compiler for these parts (in file `perform.s`) as an alternative to the C sources (in `perform.c`). If using the file `perform.s`, the GNU compiler will produce a decoder as fast as the Intel compiler.

4 Subbands, the Key to Audio Compression

Now that we understand how to produce music from subbands, we will learn why we produce music from subbands. The answer is simple: to produce music of the highest possible quality. The term "quality" is used here in a strictly technical sense. We will not discuss the differences between "Goldberg Variations" and "The Pizza Song" but simply define quality as the absence of noise.

Noise, however, is a subjective quantity. To the woman in the apartment next to me, both, the Goldberg Variations and the Pizza Song, will be pure noise when I play it loudly at three o'clock in the morning. To be precise, noise is the perceived difference between the desired signal, and the actual signal. The big problem is: what is the desired signal (as amply illustrated by the above example)? Technicians, as usual, avoid the big problems and solve the small problems. Here: How to minimize the perceived difference.

Traditional attempts to minimize audible differences between original and reproduced sound usually focus on the intermediate representation of sound, for instance as air waves, and try to reproduce this representation as accurate as possible. This is like storing computer programs as accurate photographs of the code listing. As an improvement, use digital photographs! Nobody does this, because this method of storing would preserve mostly unimportant details, like the particular font used to print the program, while sometimes confusing a zero and the letter "O". Modern storage technology should try to understand what is stored and store the relevant and not the accidental. Hence, we should focus on the ultimate goal, to recreate the original sensation of sound in the brain of the listener. To do so, we have to know what creates sensations of sound and to distinguish important aspects from irrelevant aspects of sound.

Before we study the process of hearing, we allow for a short detour and look at the process of seeing colors.

4.1 Seeing Colors

The interesting aspect of color vision is the fact that since ancient times artists—and later technicians—have used the imperfections of human vision to substitute recreated colors for original colors. When a painter paints a field of sunflowers, he will not attempt to extract the original yellow color, with its specific frequency spectrum, from the actual sunflower petals, but he will use the primitive colors on his palette and mix them to obtain a yellow that perfectly matches the color of the sunflowers in front of him in bright daylight. Some claim that a true artist can evoke the sensation of sunflower-yellow even better than any particular sunflower itself.

In our color television sets, all colors are mixed just from three colors—red, green, and blue—and when discussion comes to high quality color television, nobody talks about improving the color representation by adding a fourth color. Even expensive high quality color printing uses only three colors. (The fourth color of four color printing is actually black, the absence of color, since it is technically not possible to achieve a deep saturated black on white paper just by mixing other colors.)

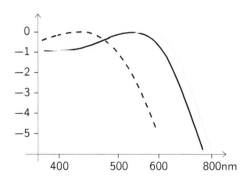

Fig. 12: Spectral sensitivity of the different receptor cells for blue (dashed), green (solid), and red (grey) in the eye.
The vertical axis shows the relative sensitivity to a photon on a logarithmic scale. The horizontal axis shows the wavelength in nm.

The reason is simply that the human eye features three different kind of light receptors (Fig.12), each with a different frequency dependent sensitivity to light. Any two light patterns that evoke the same stimulation in these three types of receptors will be indistinguishable. For instance, a pure yellow light at a wavelength of 580 nm can not be distinguished from a mixture of green light at 540 nm and red light at 620 nm. Different light spectrum—same sensation.

While it would be tempting to pursue this topic in greater detail—the interested reader is referred to the work of Baylor and Mollon in [18]—we have to get back to our main discourse and see what we can learn from this example: That one should spend the money where it really matters! It is of no importance to reproduce the exact light pattern emitted by a sunflower, it is important to evoke the same sensation in the eye of the beholder.

4.2 The Human Ear

Most of the things that really matter in respect to audible sound are consequences of the construction of the human ear and the complicated processes in our brain that interpret the stimuli originating from the ear. Here we can only give a simplified account of the most important aspects. A complete treatment of this issue can be found in [35].

The visible part of the ear collects sound and funnels it through the ear canal to the ear drum. The ear drum converts the vibrations of the air to mechanical vibrations of the ear bones. These, in turn, transport the vibrations to the "cochlea". The cochlea is a thin, fluid-filled tube, about 32 mm long, and shaped like a snail. When the ear bones impinge on the cochlea, the vibrations of the bones are transformed into vibrations of the fluid in the cochlea and waves that travel along the basilar membrane. The basilar membrane stretches from one end of the cochlea to the other, separating it into two distinct regions. Located on the basilar membrane is the organ of Corti containing sensory cells, called hair cells, that finally translate vibrations into a signal that can be processed by the nervous system.

Through experiments it could be determined, that low frequencies will cause excitations of the hair cells at one end of the cochlea and high frequency sounds are registered by the hair cells at the other end (Fig. 13).

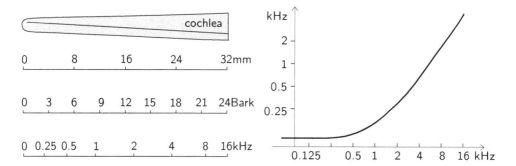

Fig. 13: Frequency resolution of the ear   *Fig. 14: Critical bandwidth versus frequency*

The signal of an individual hair cell, when it reaches its final destination in the brain, therefore contains information about the presence of a certain small frequency range and its strength in the sound that enters the ear. If our aim is to reproduce the sensation of a sound as perfect as possible, we have to consider its frequency representation.

4.3 Psychoacoustics

Psychoacoustics is the science that investigates the complex relation of sounds and hearing. Its results are used here to give an answer to two questions:

- How good is the frequency resolution of the ear? In other words: How many "colors" do we need to be able to mix any other shade of color?
- How good is the amplitude resolution of the ear? In other words: What is the minimum change in loudness that is still recognizable, either absolute or as a coloration of an other sound?

The concept of psychoacoustics that corresponds to colors is that of "critical bandwidth". There are many different methods to measure it, and consequently there are different scales. For practical purposes, however, these differences are negligible. The basic idea is, that two tones, or a tone and a narrow band noise, that are very close together are indistinguishable from a single tone. This effect is called masking. Increasing slowly the difference in frequency, the level of masking remains constant over a certain frequency range and then drops quickly. The frequency range with constant

masking level is called the critical band width. In summary: two frequencies that are
farther apart than the critical bandwidth count as different colors. The critical bandwidth depends on the absolute frequency (Fig. 14). For frequencies below 500 Hz,
it remains constant at about 100 Hz. Then the critical bandwidth increases and is
roughly about 20 % of the center frequency. It is possible to subdivide the audible
frequency spectrum from 0 Hz to 16 kHz into 24 small bands that are as wide as the
critical band for the center frequency. Starting the first band at 0 Hz with a center
frequency of 50 Hz and a width of 100 Hz up to the last band ending at 16 kHz.
Because the critical-band concept is so important in describing hearing sensations,
it was used to define a new unit, 1 Bark (named after the scientist Barkhausen), to
measure frequencies. The Bark scale starts at 0 Hz = 0 Bark, with 100 Hz = 1 Bark,
and so on until 24 Bark. Not surprisingly, as illustrated in Figure 14, the Bark scale
is nicely aligned with the geometry of the cochlea.

Using this result, an audio coder could restrict itself to representing 24 different
"colors". Because the requirement of variable bandwidth is often inconvenient, an
alternative is the use of more filters with a bandwidth that is always below the critical
bandwidth; or to make a compromise, as MPEG version 1, layer I and II do, to have
a constant bandwidth, slightly larger than 1 Bark for low frequencies and slightly
smaller for high frequencies.

We turn now to the amplitude resolution of the ear. A simple idea is to measure
the lowest amplitude of a pure tone before it becomes inaudible (Fig. 15). This value
can be determined quite precisely. It shows that the amplitude resolution depends on
frequency and, unfortunately, also on age.

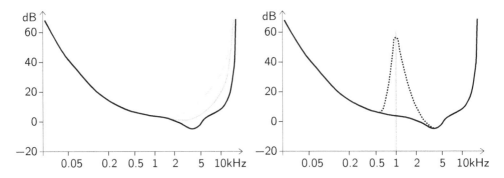

Fig. 15: Absolute threshold of hearing   Fig. 16: Masking threshold for a pure tone

While this result gives some indication as to what the ear can and what it doesn't,
this is by no means enough. The typical situation in audio coding is not a pure
tone—and the rest is silence—, but typical is a complicated mixture of tones and
noise. Now we can subdivide the whole sound into 24 bands of critical width, and ask
what is the amplitude resolution in band i given the excitation levels in all the other
bands. For actual measurements, a simpler scenario is needed. For instance (Fig. 16),
the threshold of hearing of a pure tone at frequency f can be determined given a

second pure tone at a fixed frequency and fixed amplitude. In spite of the simplified scenario, useful conclusions about the capabilities of the human auditory system can be drawn. For instance, a high level of excitation in one band will diminish the amplitude resolution in the adjacent bands. The situation, however, remains complex. Many other effects—for instance the occurrence of temporal masking, where a loud signal will render inaudible another signal occurring shortly after the loud—have to be taken into account to construct a good MPEG encoder. Today good encoders are still fine-tuned with extensive listening tests.

4.4 Minimizing Noise

We return to the initial problem of minimizing the perceived difference between the original signal and the encoded signal. Assume that we have devised a digital filter system that splits an input signal into a series of subbands, none of them wider than the critical bandwidth of its center frequency. Then we have the equivalent of a painters palette, with all the primitive colors available to mix any color desired.

Assume further that we apply this filter system to an input signal and obtain a precise representation of the signal in terms of pure colors, which, when remixed, reproduce the exact same sensation as the original signal. Of course, there is no absolute precision, neither analog nor digital. But we can use, for instance, a 64 bit floating point numbers and are far beyond the precision of earlier stages in the sound processing, like microphones and amplifiers.

For permanent storage or transmission, this ultimate precision is however neither practical nor necessary. Floating point numbers combine a large range with excellent precision by using two quantities to represent a number: exponent and mantissa. For example, the floating point number $0.123\,456\,789\,012\,345 \cdot 10^{200}$ uses a fifteen digit mantissa and a three digit exponent to represent a 200 hundred digit number with a precision of fifteen leading digits (this is approximately the precision of a 64 bit floating point number using the IEEE standard representation).

In MPEG audio coding, the role of the exponent is taken by the scalefactors. Scalefactors are stored as 6 bit quantities (layer I and II) or as 4 bit quantities combined with an 8 bit global gain (layer III). This is a slightly smaller range, but the limits of the dynamic range of audio signals are well known.

Removing the leading decimal point from the mantissa, it becomes just an integer quantity. The number of bits used to store this mantissa determines the accuracy of the representation. Reducing the number of bits from 52, as required in the IEEE floating point standard for 64 bit integers, to something like 16, 13, 6—or even only 2, 1, or 0—as done in the MPEG encoder, reduces the accuracy and requires rounding the long mantissa to a short mantissa. This rounding operation reduces the bit requirements and at the same time introduces a rounding error. This is the source of differences between the original signal and the encoded signal. Here we produce noise.

This is an important point: The noise is not introduced by the signal representation as subbands; the CosDFT is a completely invertible transformation. It is not introduced by a finite digital representation, in contrast to analog representation, because digital representation can be far more precise than analog representation. The noise is introduced deliberately, controlled, and—unlike the noise that is introduced by other stages of the sound processing—informed, by a psychoacoustic model, about the consequences.

A good psychoacoustic model can, for each subband, predict the required accuracy, such that a listener can not tell the original signal from the decoded signal. It can make sure that the noise introduced by the rounding errors is below the threshold of hearing.

4.5 The Quality of MPEG Audio Coding

Among the audiophile community, MP3 encoding often has a bad reputation. This is largely due to two reasons:

First, the psychoacoustic models of ten years ago where not as good as they are today, and therefore, encoders based on these models would fail to allocate bits where they would be required. These missing bits will inevitably lead to audible artifacts. Still today, there is a wide range of encoders on the market. For instance, encoders used in portable devices are restricted by the available battery resources that determine the speed of the processor. With limited computational resources, these encoders must settle for simpler models and can not produce the same quality as encoders without such restrictions. While the decoding process is completely determined by the MPEG standard, the encoding process is not standardized. While all compliant decoders should be equal, encoders are not.

Second, the MPEG standard specifies a parameterized encoding process. Encoding is possible with different sample rates, different layers, different stereo modes, and most importantly, different bit rates. Unlike the audio-CD specification, which requires a fixed sample rate of 44.1 kHz and 16 bit per sample, or Sony's ATRAC standard for minidisks, with a sample rate of 44.1 kHz and a fixed bit rate of 256 kbit/s, the encoding according to the MPEG standard is adaptable to fit different usage scenarios, from telephone to recording studio. While it is possible to asses the quality of CD audio or ATRAC, there is no such thing as "the quality of MPEG audio coding". It depends largely on the parameters.

It is possible to compare CD Audio to MPEG version 1, layer III, joint stereo, 32 kbit/s or to MPEG version 1, layer III, stereo, 320 kbit/s. While the first comparison turns out to be disappointing, the latter will be satisfactory at least. The MPEG audio bit stream at 32 kbit can be fairly compared with a regular telephone line, and in this comparison the MPEG bit stream will do very good. The strength of the MPEG coding schema, its wide adaptability, turned out to be a disadvantage in the market.

One can think of the psychoacoustic model as a kind of cost function. It tells for each bit how much sound quality one can buy with it. The encoder can then spend the available bits where they buy the most quality. If we give the encoder a sufficient bit rate to spend, it can produce an excellent encoding. If you are a miser, what do you expect?

5 How To Use mp32pcm

mp32pcm is basically a big file of C code, containing

⟨ header files ₉ ⟩   (7)
⟨ private declarations ₁ ⟩
⟨ private types ₄₂ ⟩
⟨ global variables ₄₃ ⟩
⟨ auxiliary functions ₆₉ ⟩

and

⟨ functions ₃₉ ⟩   (8)

as most C programs do. It is possible to produce a library or object file from it that can be linked with your favorite application. Any sensible use of mp32pcm is not possible, however, without some information on how to use the code that comprises mp32pcm. This chapter provides informally all the information that a programmer will need to use mp32pcm. The formal aspects of this information, needed by the C compiler, are provided in the file mp32pcm.h, the header file.

5.1 Header File

The header file mp32pcm.h will be included in the C files. To make sure that the implementation obeys the formal requirements spelled out in the header file, even the implementation includes mp32pcm.h. It enables the C compiler to cross-check the implementation against this part of the specification.

⟨ header files ₉ ⟩ ≡   (9)
#include "mp32pcm.h"   Used in 7.

Together with the information provided below—the semantic specification—this is all you need to use mp32pcm.

   The header file has the following layout:

⟨ mp32pcm.h ₁₀ ⟩ ≡   (10)
#include <stdlib.h>
  ⟨ public declarations ₁₅ ⟩

  ⟨ type definition of **mp3_sample** ₁₄ ⟩
  ⟨ type definition of **mp3_info** ₂₃ ⟩
  ⟨ type definition of **mp3_options** ₁₉ ⟩

  ⟨ definition of *mp3_open* ₁₁ ⟩;

⟨ definition of *mp3_read* ₁₃ ⟩;
⟨ definition of *mp3_close* ₁₆ ⟩;

You might observe that all the identifiers defined in the header file start with "mp3_"
or "MP3_". This is done to help avoiding name conflicts with other identifiers used by
the application.

5.2 Streams

The basic concept of mp32pcm is that of a stream. Picture the decoding as an
input stream of MPEG audio data flowing into the mp32pcm decoder, producing an
output stream of PCM data. Several such streams might coexist at the same time,
representing e.g. several tracks of a mixing application. A stream is created by a call
to the function *mp3_open*, used with *mp3_read*, and destroyed with *mp3_close*.

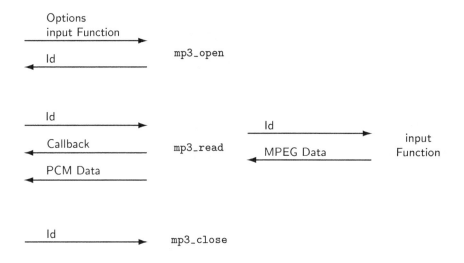

Fig. 17: Using mp32pcm

After successful completion, *mp3_open* will not return an internal data structure
representing such a stream, but only a small, non negative integer, called a "handle" or
an "id". This technique provides an absolute separation between data that belongs
to the application and data that belongs to mp32pcm. This separation will allow
upgrades in mp32pcm without affecting in any way existing applications, an advantage
that makes programming with handles very common. For instance, the Windows API
or the UNIX file handling primitives work with such handles in a very similar fashion.

5.3 Creating Streams with *mp3_open*

The function *mp3_open* will create a stream. Upon successful completion, *mp3_open* will always return the smallest non-negative number that is not yet associated with an open stream. E.g. opening five streams will return the numbers 0, 1, 2, 3, and 4, in that order. Then, after closing stream 2, the next call to *mp3_open* will return 2. The stream id may be used by an application as an index into an array containing application-specific supplemental information for the stream. On failure, *mp3_open* will return a negative value.

mp3_open needs two parameters, a function to read the input and a pointer to options.

$\langle$ definition of *mp3_open* $_{11}$ $\rangle \equiv$ (11)
   extern int *mp3_open*(
     $\langle$ definition of *input_read* $_{12}$ $\rangle$,
     $\langle$ definition of *option_pointer* $_{18}$ $\rangle$)   Used in 10 and 39.

Only the first parameter is mandatory, the second parameter may be NULL, in which case some reasonable defaults will be used.

5.4 Demand-Driven Decoding

Streams work demand-driven. That means, decoding is initiated by requesting some decoded output samples. This request is made by calling the function *mp3_read*, which in turn might need some input data to work on. It will therefore retrieve the *input_read* function that was provided in the *mp3_open* call. This function is then used repeatedly to obtain the input needed.

$\langle$ definition of *input_read* $_{12}$ $\rangle \equiv$ (12)
   int (*input_read*)(**int** *id*, **void** *buffer*, **size_t** *size*)   Used in 11 and 50.

Each call of *input_read* has three parameters, the *id* of the stream, the pointer to a *buffer*, and the buffer's *size* in byte. The application that provides this function should fill the *buffer* with up to *size* bytes and then return. The return value should give the exact number of bytes written to the *buffer*, or zero if no more input is available. If an error occurs while the application is processing the input function, a negative value should be returned. As indicated before, the application might use the given *id* to distinguish between several streams and access stream-specific information maintained by the application.

In the simplest form (see Section 5.7), where a program uses just one single stream that reads data from the standard input, it is possible to make a single call to *mp3_open* (*read*, NULL) providing the standard UNIX function *read* as the input function. The assigned stream id will be zero which matches the file handle for the standard input, producing valid calls to *read*(**int** *fd*, **void** *buffer*, **size_t** *size*).

5.5 Reading Streams with *mp3_read*

Decoded PCM data can be obtained by calling the function *mp3_read*.

⟨ definition of *mp3_read* ₁₃ ⟩ ≡   (13)
    extern int *mp3_read*(**int** *id*, **mp3_sample** *buffer, **int** *size*)   Used in 10 and 55.

It needs three arguments: The *id* of a stream that was returned by a successful call
to *mp3_open* and was not closed by *mp3_close* in the meantime. Further, a pointer
to a *buffer* suitably aligned to receive the PCM samples, and the *size* of the buffer in
samples.

The **mp3_sample** type is a signed integer type. To obtain a standard compliant
decoder, it must have at least 16 bit. On my machine, with my compiler, this is a
short int. You can get higher precision output by providing a larger integer type, for
instance a plain **int**, to obtain 32 bit output. You may then post-process the output
and round or dither it as desired.

⟨ type definition of **mp3_sample** ₁₄ ⟩ ≡   (14)
    typedef short int mp3_sample;   Used in 10.

Due to the internal format of the bit stream, which is organized in frames, PCM data
is produced in large chunks. Each chunk containing the data from one frame. Using
layer I, a frame contains 384 samples, using layer II or layer III, a frame contains
1152 samples—twice this many samples are used for a stereo signal. It is mandatory
to use a buffer containing at least `MP3_MIN_BUFFER` samples of type **mp3_sample**
(approximately 4 kbyte).

⟨ public declarations ₁₅ ⟩ ≡   (15)
#**define** `MP3_MIN_BUFFER` $(2 * 1152)$ Used in 10 and 130.

Note that even a single channel stream has the same minimum buffer requirements,
since it will use, at least temporarily, the same buffer space as a stereo signal.

   mp3_read will attempt to read *size* decoded samples from the given stream to the
buffer. On success, it will return the number of samples read. The return value zero
indicates the end of the stream. A negative value indicates an error. It is not an error
if the number returned is smaller than *size*.

5.6 Closing the Stream with *mp3_close*

After having read enough PCM data, or if the call to *mp3_read* returns zero, indicating
that the end of the stream has been reached, the stream should be closed by calling
the function *mp3_close*.

⟨ definition of *mp3_close* ₁₆ ⟩ ≡   (16)
    extern int *mp3_close*(**int** *id*)   Used in 10 and 53.

This function will close the stream and return all data structures associated with the
stream to free storage. It returns zero on success and a negative value if an error
occurred. After closing a stream, its *id* must no longer be used in a call to *mp3_read*.
A later call to *mp3_open* might return again the same *id* for a new stream.

5.7 A Simple Application

The most simple, but still useful application reads MPEG audio data from the standard input and outputs PCM data to the standard output. It looks like this:

⟨ example.c   17 ⟩ ≡   (17)
```
#include <unistd.h>
#include "mp32pcm.h"
#define BUFSIZE  (4 * MP3_MIN_BUFFER)
  int main(void)
  { int id;
    mp3_sample buffer[BUFSIZE];
    int size;

    id = mp3_open(read, NULL);
    if (id < 0) return 1;
    while ((size = mp3_read(id, buffer, BUFSIZE)) > 0)
      write(1, buffer, size * sizeof(mp3_sample));
    if (mp3_close(id) < 0) return 1;
    return 0;
  }
```

An other sample application can be found in Appendix D.

5.8 Options

It is often necessary to tailor the behavior of the decoder to specific needs. For this purpose, options can be passed to the stream as part of the *mp3_open* call by supplying a pointer to a structure, called **mp3_options**.

⟨ definition of *option_pointer* 18 ⟩ ≡   (18)
  mp3_options *option_pointer*   Used in 11.

If the pointer is NULL, the decoding engine will use reasonable default values. The application may deallocate the option structure after the *mp3_open* call or reuse it at will. The *mp3_open* function will make copies of all the data found in the **mp3_options** structure.

⟨ type definition of **mp3_options** 19 ⟩ ≡   (19)
```
  typedef struct mp3_options {
    ⟨ options  20 ⟩
  } mp3_options;
```
                                                                   Used in 10.

Some options are just *flags*, that switch on certain features.

⟨ options 20 ⟩ ≡   (20)
  int *flags*;   Used in 19.

One such feature is for instance "two channel mono". Usually, the decoder will output two channel 16 bit (or 32 bit) interleaved samples. That is, the samples of the two channels alternate in the output and each sample is 16 bits long. If the input is only a single channel stream (mono), the decoder will output only one channel, where each

16 bit sample is immediately followed by the next sample. If instead, the application prefers to get two interleaved channels, that happen to be equal, it should set a flag by OR-ing *flags* with this constant:

⟨ options ₂₀ ⟩ +≡   (21)
#**define** MP3_TWO_CHANNEL_MONO #0100

More flags and further options are explained below. A complete list of all options can be found in Table 4.

Option	Page
flags MP3_TWO_CHANNEL_MONO	27
flags MP3_DONT_FLUSH	41
flags MP3_SYNC_1	33
flags MP3_SYNC_2	33
flags MP3_SYNC_3	33
flags MP3_INFO_NEVER	30
flags MP3_INFO_IGNORE	30
flags MP3_INFO_ONCE	30
flags MP3_INFO_FRAME	30
flags MP3_INFO_READ	30
flags MP3_INFO_PCM	30
flags MP3_INFO_MPG	30
flags MP3_INFO_CRC	30
flags MP3_INFO_RESERVED	30
flags MP3_NO_PARTIAL_FRAME	170
info_callback	28
equalizer	229

Tab. 4: All options

5.9 Information Retrieval

When decoding a stream, not only the generated PCM data is of interest, but also other information like the sampling frequency, the number of channels, whether there is a copyright on the stream, and more such details. To store this information inside the stream, the stream is structured as a sequence of frames, where each frame stores the necessary information in a frame header. Whenever a header has been decoded, this information is available and can be passed to the application. To receive the information, the application specifies an *info_callback* function as part of the options.

⟨ options ₂₀ ⟩ +≡   (22)
    int (*info_callback*)(**mp3_info** *p*);

If NULL is supplied instead of a function, no callback will occur. The argument of the callback function is a pointer to an **mp3_info** structure containing the most recent information on the decoded stream—fresh from the header— and some other useful data like e.g. the *id* of the stream and the header itself.

⟨ type definition of **mp3_info** ₂₃ ⟩ ≡   (23)
   typedef struct mp3_info {
     int *id*;
     unsigned int *header*;

     ⟨ infos ₃₁ ⟩
   } **mp3_info**;   Used in 10.

   Each stream maintains its own *info* data structure

⟨ stream data ₂ ⟩ +≡   (24)
   mp3_info *info*;

where its *id* is stored.

⟨ initialize *s* ₂₅ ⟩ ≡   (25)
   s→*info.id* = *id*;   Used in 39.

   After inspecting the information provided, the *info_callback* function can alter the behavior of the decoder by specifying an appropriate return value. The most common return value is MP3_CONTINUE. Receiving it, the decoder will just do that, continue decoding. Alternatively, the callback function can return MP3_SKIP to skip the decoding of the current frame, return MP3_REPEAT to repeat the last frame, return MP3_REPAIR to reconstruct the frame from the last frame, or return MP3_MUTE to insert one frame of silence.

⟨ public declarations ₁₅ ⟩ +≡   (26)
#**define** MP3_CONTINUE   0
#**define** MP3_SKIP   #0100
#**define** MP3_REPEAT   #0200
#**define** MP3_MUTE   #0400
#**define** MP3_REPAIR   #0800

The return value MP3_SKIP can be combined, using a bitwise OR operator, with either MP3_REPEAT, MP3_REPAIR, or MP3_MUTE effectively replacing the current frame. By returning MP3_SKIP for every frame, an application can collect all the information about the stream without incurring the computational cost of decoding it.

   Another possible return value is MP3_BREAK

⟨ public declarations ₁₅ ⟩ +≡   (27)
#**define** MP3_BREAK   #1000

If used, the current frame will not be decoded; instead, the *mp3_read* function will return immediately delivering all the samples decoded so far—may be none. The next call to *mp3_read* will then resume decoding with the current frame which might cause a second callback to occur, if the *flags* that control the callback mechanism permit.

The effect of returning MP3_ERROR, or any other negative value, is similar to returning MP3_BREAK. Instead of returning the number of decoded samples, however, the function *mp3_read* will just pass through to its caller the return value from the information callback.

⟨ public declarations $_{15}$ ⟩ +≡   (28)
#**define** MP3_ERROR − 1

5.10 Controlling *info_callback* and *mp3_read*

The application can control exactly when a callback will occur by OR-ing together the following values and storing them in the *flags* field.

⟨ options $_{20}$ ⟩ +≡   (29)
#**define** MP3_INFO_NEVER   #00   /* call *info_callback* never */
#**define** MP3_INFO_IGNORE   #01   /* flag is ignored */
#**define** MP3_INFO_ONCE   #02   /* call *info_callback* once at the very beginning */
#**define** MP3_INFO_FRAME   #04   /* call *info_callback* for each frame, */
#**define** MP3_INFO_READ   #08   /* ... for each call to *mp3_read* */
#**define** MP3_INFO_PCM   #10   /* ... for each PCM parameter change, */
#**define** MP3_INFO_MPG   #20   /* ... for each MPEG parameter change, */
#**define** MP3_INFO_CRC   #40   /* ... if a CRC error occurred. */
#**define** MP3_INFO_RESERVED   #80   /* for future use */

A change in the PCM format means either the sample rate or the mode, determining the number of channels, has changed. A change in the MPEG format could be a change in the version, the layer, the bit rate, the CRC protection, the mode, the copyright state, the original state, or the emphasis.

After a callback has occurred, the application can change the settings for the next callback using a simple mechanism: a non zero low order byte of a non negative return value will be used to set the corresponding *flags*. This means that, unless the application uses a negative return value, it can simply OR the new flags with the usual return value. There is only one exception to this rule: If the new value is supposed to be MP3_INFO_NEVER, the low order byte would be zero and the old value would remain untouched. In this case the application has to use MP3_INFO_IGNORE to achieve the desired effect.

Since the interpretation of the data that is returned by *mp3_read* depends on the information obtained through *info_callback*, it is often necessary to control the synchronization between the two functions. As a general rule, the application will call *mp3_read*, then receives an *info_callback*, and finally *mp3_read* returns the PCM data. The information presented by the *info_callback* should then be valid for the PCM data returned by *mp3_read*. It is, however, possible that some information is valid at the beginning of the data returned by *mp3_read*, but then, it changes and is not longer valid at the end of the returned data. This might be no problem—for instance in a variable bit rate stream, the bit rate changes, but this change has no influence on any further processing of the decoded data—or this might as well be a big problem—if for instance the sample rate of the output data changes in the middle of the stream (which is not quite conforming to the standard, but happens anyway).

In all these cases, you might get several information callbacks before the *mp3_read* function returns, depending on the setting of the *flags*. This is sometimes not desirable, because it is then difficult to correlate the change in information with the data returned. By returning the value `MP3_BREAK` from the *info_callback*, an application can achieve complete synchronization of information and PCM data.

A special case occurs, if *mp3_read* is called with the *size* parameter set to zero, the *buffer* set to `NULL`, and a nonzero *info_callback* function. We call this the

$\langle$ callback exception $_{30}$ $\rangle \equiv$ (30)
$\quad$ ($buffer \equiv$ `NULL` $\land size \equiv 0 \land s{\rightarrow}options.info\_callback \neq$ `NULL`)   Used in 56 and 61.

In this case, the next frame header in the stream is analyzed and the *info_callback* function is invoked, but no attempt is made to decode the data inside the frame. In other words, calling *mp3_read* this way implies a callback with an implicit return value of `MP3_BREAK`. This can be used at the beginning of the decoding process to advance the stream to the first frame and to extract information from the first frame without starting the decoding.

5.11 MPEG Format Information

mp32pcm can decode streams for three different MPEG versions. MPEG Version 1 is described by ISO/IEC 11172-3, and MPEG Version 2 is described by ISO/IEC 13818-3. MPEG Version 2.5 is a later extension of Version 2 to include lower sample rates and is not an ISO/IEC standard.

In addition to the different versions, the standard specifies three different layers of increasing complexity and performance. Layer III became very popular and is widely known as "MP3". The layer information, 1, 2, or 3, is given as a plain integer, the version information has three possible values listed below.

$\langle$ infos $_{31}$ $\rangle \equiv$ (31)
$\quad$ **int** *version*;   /* can be one of */
#**define** MP3_V1_0 $^{\#}$00   /* MPEG Version 1 (ISO/IEC 11172-3) */
#**define** MP3_V2_0 $^{\#}$01   /* MPEG Version 2 (ISO/IEC 13818-3) */
#**define** MP3_V2_5 $^{\#}$02   /* MPEG Version 2.5 (later extension of MPEG 2) */
$\quad$ **int** *layer*;   Used in 23.

MPEG frames provide more information that is specific to the MPEG format.

$\langle$ infos $_{31}$ $\rangle +\equiv$ (32)
$\quad$ **int** *crc_protected*;   /* can be TRUE or FALSE */
$\quad$ **int** *bit_rate*;   /* the frame's bit rate */
$\quad$ **int** *frame_size*;   /* the byte size of this frame */
$\quad$ **int** *frame_position*;   /* the byte position of this frame in the stream */
$\quad$ **int** *samples*;   /* the number of samples decoded so far */
$\quad$ **int** *private*;   /* a bit of privacy */
$\quad$ **int** *mode*;   /* *mode* can be one of the following */
#**define** MP3_STEREO $^{\#}$00

```
#define MP3_JOINT_STEREO  #01
#define MP3_DUAL_CHANNEL  #02
#define MP3_MONO  #03
  int copyright;                              /* can be TRUE or FALSE */
  int original;                               /* can be TRUE or FALSE */
  int emphasis;                               /* can be 0,1,2 or 3 */
  int frame;                                  /* counts the frames */
```

5.12 PCM Format Information

In regard to the PCM data, there are only three aspects of interest: the number of bits per sample, the number of samples per second (the sample frequency or sample rate) and the number of channels, either 1 for mono or 2 for stereo. Normally these parameters should not change within a single stream.

$\langle$ infos $_{31}$ $\rangle$ $+\equiv$ (33)
```
  int sample_rate;                            /* the frequency in Hz */
  int channels;                    /* the number of channels 1=mono 2=stereo */
  int bit_per_sample;
```

The bit_per_sample is determined by the decoder, not by the stream. We have invariably:

$\langle$ initialize s $_{25}$ $\rangle$ $+\equiv$ (34)
```
  s→info.bit_per_sample = sizeof(mp3_sample) * 8;
```

5.13 Stream Synchronization

MPEG streams are defined as streams of bit containing MPEG audio data packaged in so called frames. In practice, other data often is also part of the stream.

Sometimes, so called tags (see Section 5.14), contain supplemental information, like the name of the song writer, the album, the track number, or even a picture of the performer. In other cases, especially if MPEG streams are transmitted over an unreliable medium like the Internet, part of the stream is just garbage, e.g. it consists of partial or corrupted frames. In all these cases, it is necessary to find a valid frame in the stream before decoding can begin. This is called synchronizing the stream. To help with synchronizing, every frame starts on a byte boundary with twelve (or eleven) consecutive 1-bits. This is called the "syncword". In the simplest case, synchronization means skipping input bytes until twelve, consecutive, byte-aligned 1-bit are found.

This simple synchronization is, however, not very reliable. Even in a random bit stream, roughly every 2000 bytes will contain such a syncword. The same 2000 bytes taken from an MPEG stream might contain in addition only 4 to 5 true syncwords. Therefore, if we start decoding a valid MPEG bit stream somewhere in the middle, as it is the case if we switch On an Internet radio station, false synchronization is quite likely.

To improve synchronization, the decoder can determine the frame length from the suspected frame header and check, if after the current frame there is a second frame exactly at the position predicted. Doing this for two or even three frames, makes synchronization more and more secure. On the other hand, if the input contains many errors, it might be impossible to find enough correct frames in a row, and synchronization might fail completely. (Whether it is worth listening to such a stream is a different question altogether.) By default, synchronization requires checking two consecutive syncwords.

The following values can be used to set the right *flags* to alter this behavior.

⟨ options $_{20}$ ⟩ +≡   (35)
#**define** MP3_SYNC_1   #0400   /* ... trust a single syncword */
#**define** MP3_SYNC_2   #0000   /* ... trust two syncwords (default) */
#**define** MP3_SYNC_3   #0800   /* ... trust three syncwords */

Once the stream is synchronized, the decoder will predict the next syncword from past information and trust a single syncword if found at the predicted location.

5.14 Tags

Tags are considered a valid part of an MPEG stream. Since there are different tag formats and the interpretation of tags is highly application dependent, mp32pcm will not do anything with tags, except to detect them and forward them to the *tag_handler*. The *tag_handler* is a function, that can be provided as part of the options.

⟨ options $_{20}$ ⟩ +≡   (36)
    ⟨ definition of *tag_handler* $_{37}$ ⟩;

It is called whenever the decoding engine detects data in the stream that is not a valid frame. Because there is no absolute criteria to distinguish tags from plain garbage, even garbage is forwarded to the *tag_handler*. In case the value supplied for the tag handler is NULL, tags are just skipped.

⟨ definition of *tag_handler* $_{37}$ ⟩ ≡   (37)
    void (*_tag_handler_)(**int** *id*, ⟨ *tag_read* function $_{38}$ ⟩)   Used in 36.

The first parameter of the *tag_handler* identifies the stream that contains the tag. The next parameter is the ⟨ *tag_read* function $_{38}$ ⟩. The *tag_handler* should use it to read whatever it needs from the stream.

⟨ *tag_read* function $_{38}$ ⟩ ≡   (38)
    int *tag_read*(**int** *id*, **void** *_buffer_, **int** *count*)   Used in 37, 175, and 176.

The function *tag_read* must identify the stream by the parameter *id*, and it is mandatory to use the *id* that was given as first argument to the *tag_handler*. It further provides a *buffer* to be filled with *count* bytes from the MPEG stream. The function will return the actual number of bytes read, which will be less or equal to *count*. The function will return 0 if the end of the MPEG stream is reached. If an error occurs while reading, the function returns a negative value.

Normally the parameter *count* will be positive and the corresponding number of bytes will be removed from the input and put into the buffer. Conveniently, the *tag_read* function is reversible (to a large degree). If *count* is negative, as one should expect, the corresponding number of bytes are taken from the buffer and put back into the input. This feature can be used to push back bytes into the input, allowing the tag reader some look ahead.

A simple tag handler can look like this:

#**define** LOOKAHEAD 10

```
  void tag_handler(int id, int tag_read(int id, void *buffer, int count))
  { unsigned char lookahead[LOOKAHEAD];
    int count;
    count = 0;
    while (count < LOOKAHEAD)
    { int k = tag_read(id, lookahead + count, LOOKAHEAD − count);
      if (k≤ 0) break;
      else count = count+k
    }
    if (count < LOOKAHEAD)
    { tag_read(id, lookahead, −count);
      return;
    }
    inspect the lookahead
    if (there is a tag) read further input and process the tag
    else tag_read(id, lookahead, −count);
  }
```

The above code reads a fixed amount of look ahead into a buffer. If there is insufficient input, the tag handler is not interested in this tag any more and writes the partial look ahead, obtained so far, back to the stream. Otherwise, it can inspect the look ahead and possibly process the tag. If no tag was found, again the tag handler returns the look ahead.

The code illustrates how to read data from the stream, and how to write excess data back to the stream. The push back will work under two conditions.

- The *tag_handler* must not push back more bytes than it has read.
- It must not push back more than BUFFERSIZE − MAX_RESERVOIR bytes.

6 How mp32pcm Works

We have seen how *mp3_open*, *mp3_read*, and *mp3_close* are used. Now, we take a deep breath, dive into the internals of these functions, and explore step by step how the decoding is done.

6.1 The Function *mp3_open*

The first thing an application will do is calling *mp3_open* to obtain the stream *id*. There is one required parameter, the *input_read* function, and if it is there, all the decoding engine will have to do is finding the next unused *id*, allocating the internal data of the stream, and initializing it.

⟨ functions $_{39}$ ⟩ ≡   (39)
```
  ⟨ definition of mp3_open 11 ⟩
  { int id;
    stream *s;

    if (input_read ≡ NULL) return MP3_ERROR_NO_INPUT;
    ⟨ set id to the next available id 44 ⟩
    ⟨ allocate s 46 ⟩ ⟨ zero s 48 ⟩ ⟨ initialize s 25 ⟩
    return id;
  }
```
                                                          Used in 8.

⟨ public declarations $_{15}$ ⟩ +≡   (40)
#**define** MP3_ERROR_NO_INPUT − 2

The data for a stream is allocated dynamically and the pointer to it is stored in *streams*, a global array indexed by stream ids.

⟨ private declarations $_1$ ⟩ +≡   (41)
#**define** STREAMS 512

⟨ private types $_{42}$ ⟩ ≡   (42)
```
  typedef struct {
    ⟨ stream data 2 ⟩
  } stream;
```
                                                          Used in 7.

⟨ global variables $_{43}$ ⟩ ≡   (43)
  static stream *∗streams*[STREAMS] = { NULL} ;   Used in 7.

To find the next available id, we just search the array *streams* for an empty slot.

⟨ set *id* to the next available id ₄₄ ⟩ ≡   (44)
  id = 0;
  while (*streams*[*id*] ≠ NULL)
  { *id*++;
    if (*id* ≥ STREAMS) **return** MP3_ERROR_TOO_MANY;
  }   Used in 39.

⟨ public declarations ₁₅ ⟩ +≡   (45)
#**define** MP3_ERROR_TOO_MANY − 3

To ⟨ allocate *s* ₄₆ ⟩, we call *malloc*.

⟨ allocate *s* ₄₆ ⟩ ≡   (46)
  s = (**stream** ∗) *malloc*(**sizeof**(**stream**));
  if (*s* ≡ NULL) **return** MP3_ERROR_MEMORY;
  streams[*id*] = *s*;   Used in 39.

⟨ public declarations ₁₅ ⟩ +≡   (47)
#**define** MP3_ERROR_MEMORY − 4

Before we start to initialize the new data structure, we fill it completely with zeros.

⟨ zero *s* ₄₈ ⟩ ≡   (48)
  memset(*s*, 0, **sizeof** (∗*s*));   Used in 39.

Most values of the stream data are chosen in such a way, that 0 is a reasonable default.
For *memset* to work, we need

⟨ header files ₉ ⟩ +≡   (49)
#**include** <string.h>

Specific initialization is needed for the *input_read* function and the *option_pointer*.

⟨ stream data ₂ ⟩ +≡   (50)
  ⟨ definition of *input_read* ₁₂ ⟩;

  mp3_options *options*;

⟨ initialize *s* ₂₅ ⟩ +≡   (51)
  s→*input_read* = *input_read*;
  if (*option_pointer* ≠ NULL) *s*→*options* = ∗*option_pointer*;

6.2 The Function *mp3_close*

The function *mp3_close* is quite simple. We

⟨ retrieve the stream ₅₂ ⟩ ≡   (52)
  if (*id* ≥ STREAMS ∨ *id* < 0) **return** MP3_ERROR_NO_ID;
  s = *streams*[*id*];
  if (*s* ≡ NULL) **return** MP3_ERROR_NOT_OPEN;   Used in 53, 55, and 176.

and free the allocated data.

⟨ functions ₃₉ ⟩ +≡   (53)
  ⟨ definition of *mp3_close* ₁₆ ⟩

```
{ stream *s;
  ⟨ retrieve the stream  52 ⟩
  free (s);
  streams [id] = NULL;
  return 0;
}
```

⟨ public declarations 15 ⟩ +≡   (54)
#**define** MP3_ERROR_NO_ID − 5
#**define** MP3_ERROR_NOT_OPEN − 6

6.3 The Function *mp3_read*

The function *mp3_read* will retrieve the stream, check the parameters, and enter the main loop.

⟨ functions 39 ⟩ +≡   (55)
```
  ⟨ definition of mp3_read  13 ⟩
  { stream *s;
    ⟨ retrieve the stream  52 ⟩
    ⟨ check parameters  56 ⟩
    s→info.changes |= MP3_INFO_READ;
    s→info.samples = 0;
    do { ⟨ prepare the frame for decoding  62 ⟩
      ⟨ handle the info_callback  61 ⟩
      switch (output_mode)
      { ⟨ generate output data  66 ⟩ }
    } while (s→info.samples + MP3_MIN_BUFFER ≤ size);
    return s→info.samples;
  }
```

How the parameters are checked is important for the main loop:

⟨ check parameters 56 ⟩ ≡   (56)
```
  if (s→state & END_OF_OUTPUT) return MP3_ERROR_DONE;
  if (¬⟨ callback exception  30 ⟩)
  { if (buffer ≡ NULL) return MP3_ERROR_NO_BUFFER;
    if (size < MP3_MIN_BUFFER) return MP3_ERROR_NO_SIZE; }
```
                                                                         Used in 55.

⟨ public declarations 15 ⟩ +≡   (57)
#**define** MP3_ERROR_DONE − 7
#**define** MP3_ERROR_NO_BUFFER − 8
#**define** MP3_ERROR_NO_SIZE − 9

Together with the initialization of *s→info.samples*, it establishes the loop invariant for the main loop: We are not at the END_OF_OUTPUT, we have a buffer, and enough space in it to ⟨ generate output data 66 ⟩.

Conditions, like END_OF_OUTPUT, are stored in the streams *state*.

⟨ stream data $_2$ ⟩ +≡   (58)
  int *state*;

The *state* is a bit vector, that can be tested, set, or reset using

⟨ private declarations $_1$ ⟩ +≡   (59)
#**define** END_OF_OUTPUT   #0001
#**define** END_OF_INPUT   #0002

Within the loop, at any time, we can

⟨ terminate decoding $_{60}$ ⟩ ≡   (60)
  s→state = *s→state* | END_OF_OUTPUT;
  return *s→info.samples*;   Used in 62.

This will exit the loop once and for all.

Relying on the loop invariant, we do not need to watch the existence and size of the *buffer* inside the loop. To maintain the loop invariant, we check the remaining space upon reentry to the loop.

We will eventually exit the main loop, because when we ⟨ generate output data $_{66}$ ⟩, usually the number of *samples* increases. "Usually" means always with one exception: we might skip a frame (sorry, no output) but this will advance the input stream. The input stream will eventually end and this will inevitably ⟨ terminate decoding $_{60}$ ⟩.

Last not least, we have to take precautions because of the ⟨ callback exception $_{30}$ ⟩, when we

⟨ handle the *info_callback* $_{61}$ ⟩ ≡   (61)
  if (*s→options.info_callback* ≠ NULL)
  { **if** (⟨ callback exception $_{30}$ ⟩) { ⟨ process callback exception $_{180}$ ⟩ **return** 0; }
    ⟨ issue *info_callback* $_{186}$ ⟩
  }   Used in 55.

While the ⟨ callback exception $_{30}$ ⟩ prevents a use of the *buffer* in the first part of the main loop—where we don't need it—the above code establishes the loop invariant, without exception, for the second part of the loop.

Before we can think about generating output, we have to do some preparations. An MPEG stream is organized as a sequence of frames, and we have to

⟨ prepare the frame for decoding $_{62}$ ⟩ ≡   (62)
  if (*s→frame* ≡ NULL)
  { *s→frame* = *synchronize*(*s*);
    if (*s→frame* ≡ NULL) { ⟨ flush the stream $_{72}$ ⟩ ⟨ terminate decoding $_{60}$ ⟩ }
  }
  ⟨ position the stream past the header $_{156}$ ⟩
  ⟨ derive further information $_{65}$ ⟩
  ⟨ perform additional checks $_{99}$ ⟩   Used in 55.

The variable *frame* is supposed to point to a frame. If it is NULL, it means that the decoder does not know where the frame is, and it will try to *synchronize* the stream.

If, after searching, *frame* is still NULL, the decoder gives up. Otherwise, for the rest of the main loop, we have a valid *frame* pointer. We use it to position the input stream at the beginning of the frame, and start to decode the frame header. There we find most of the information we must provide for the *info_callback*; some further information is derived from it. Derived information is for example the *output_mode* or the *frame_size*. Once we know the *frame_size*, we load the entire frame, if this succeeds, we can perform some additional checks to make sure nothing serious can go wrong later. When we generate output, we will omit all error checks in order to obtain best performance.

If, after these checks, the processing of the *info_callback* does not advise the decoder otherwise, it will proceed with the last part of the main loop. It starts with a multiway branch according to the *output_mode*.

⟨ global variables ₄₃ ⟩ +≡   (63)
    static int *output_mode*;

Three rather obvious possible values for the *output_mode* are the different layers.

⟨ private declarations ₁ ⟩ +≡   (64)
#**define** LAYER_I   1
#**define** LAYER_II 2
#**define** LAYER_III 3

The output mode is set when we

⟨ derive further information ₆₅ ⟩ ≡   (65)
    output_mode = *s*→*info.layer*;   Used in 62.

Other *output_mode*'s will follow. For now, we focus on layer I. (We will deal with layer II in Chapter 9 and with layer III in Chapter 11). As a general rule, the audio data is separated in two parts: The side information tells the decoder how to read and interpret the subband samples that follow.

⟨ generate output data ₆₆ ⟩ ≡   (66)
case LAYER_I:
    ⟨ decode layer I side information ₁₀₄ ⟩
    layer_I_decode_samples(*s*);
    output_blocks(*s*, *buffer* + *s*→*info.samples*, 12);
    s→*frame* = *next_frame*(*s*);
    break;   Used in 55.

A layer I frame contains 12 blocks with 32 subband samples for each channel. The subband samples are stored in the array **y**.

⟨ global variables ₄₃ ⟩ +≡   (67)
    static double y[BLOCKS][CHANNELS][SUBBANDS];

As we know already, the maximum number of CHANNELS is 2 and the number of SUBBANDS is 32, the maximum number of BLOCKS for this implementation will be 18, which is the same as the number of SUBFREQUENCIES needed for layer III.

⟨ private declarations ₁ ⟩ +≡   (68)

```
#define SUBBANDS   32
#define SUBFREQUENCIES   18
#define BLOCKS   SUBFREQUENCIES
```

The function *output_blocks*, which we discuss in detail in the next section, takes n blocks of subband samples from the vector $\boldsymbol{y}$ and writes PCM data in the output *buffer*. It increments the value of *info.samples* to reflect the number of samples written to the buffer.

6.4 Output Blocks of Samples

The main job of the decoder, which consumes about 70 % of the total runtime, is packaged into the function *output_blocks*.

$\langle$ auxiliary functions $_{69}$ $\rangle \equiv$ (69)

```
    static void output_blocks(stream *s, mp3_sample *buffer, int n)
    { int i;
        for (i = 0;  i < n;  i++) ⟨output a single block of samples 70 ⟩
        if (s→options.flags & MP3_TWO_CHANNEL_MONO)
            s→info.samples += n * 2 * SUBBANDS;
        else  s→info.samples += n * s→info.channels * SUBBANDS;
    }
```
                                                                    Used in 7.

The core of the function is the code to $\langle$ output a single block of samples $_{70}$ $\rangle$. Due to Chapter 3, we are well prepared for this step: We start with the left channel ($ch = 0$). After shifting vector $\boldsymbol{v}$, we use the function *dct32* to perform a 32 point CosDFT on a block of $\boldsymbol{y}$ values and put the results into $\boldsymbol{v}$. Then the *windowing* function will take the data from $\boldsymbol{v}$ and store the PCM data in the *buffer*.

If there is a second channel, we repeat the process, otherwise, we $\langle$ post-process single channel output $_{71}$ $\rangle$. In both cases, the *buffer* pointer is updated accordingly.

$\langle$ output a single block of samples $_{70}$ $\rangle \equiv$ (70)

```
    { double *v;
        { int ch = 0;
            ⟨shift vector v 4 ⟩
            ⟨equalize 445 ⟩
            dct32(y[i][ch], v);
            windowing(v, buffer);
        }
        if (s→info.channels > 1)
        { int ch = 1;
            ⟨shift vector v 4 ⟩
            ⟨equalize 445 ⟩
            dct32(y[i][ch], v);
            windowing(v, buffer + 1);
            buffer = buffer + 2 * SUBBANDS; }
```

else ⟨ post-process single channel output ₇₁ ⟩
}   Used in 69.

So far, the decoder performs only those steps, that are strictly necessary to conform to the standard. But here, it is just too tempting to put in some extra code to ⟨ equalize ₄₄₅ ⟩ the output. An equalizer is a nice thing to have when adapting the sound of music to special listening conditions, by means of a frequency dependent gain. This ordinarily requires splitting a signal into different frequencies, scaling them, and putting them together again. In the above code, we are in the fortunate situation that the individual frequencies are readily available, and the synthesis is about to occur. It would be a pity to miss this opportunity. The details of equalization are found in Appendix C.

The *windowing* function is optimized for interleaved stereo signals. It writes the PCM samples into every second *buffer* element. If we have only a single channel stream, we have to ⟨ post-process single channel output ₇₁ ⟩: Either duplicating the samples for the second channel or condensing the samples to eliminate the holes in the output buffer that were left for the second channel.

⟨ post-process single channel output ₇₁ ⟩ ≡   (71)
  { **int** *sb*;
    if (*s*→*options.flags* & MP3_TWO_CHANNEL_MONO)
    { **for** (*sb* = 0; *sb* < SUBBANDS; *sb*++) *buffer*[2 ∗ *sb* + 1] = *buffer*[2 ∗ *sb*];
      buffer = *buffer* + 2 ∗ SUBBANDS; }
    else
    { **for** (*sb* = 0; *sb* < SUBBANDS; *sb*++) *buffer*[*sb*] = *buffer*[2 ∗ *sb*];
      buffer = *buffer* + SUBBANDS; }
  }   Used in 70, 75, and 408.

6.5 Terminating *mp3_read*

In case no frame can be found for decoding, we can still produce meaningful output because the vector *v* possibly still contains 15 blocks of valid data. Unless the *flag* MP3_DONT_FLUSH is set in the *options*, we shift zeros into the vector *v* and

⟨ flush the stream ₇₂ ⟩ ≡   (72)
  if (¬(*s*→*options.flags* & MP3_DONT_FLUSH))
  { **int** *n*; ⟨ determine the number *n* of non zero blocks in *v* ₇₆ ⟩
    output_silence(*s*, *buffer* + *s*→*info.samples*, *n*); }   Used in 62.

⟨ options ₂₀ ⟩ +≡   (73)
#**define** MP3_DONT_FLUSH #0200

The function *output_silence* is very similar to the *output_blocks* function of the previous section.

⟨ auxiliary functions ₆₉ ⟩ +≡   (74)
  static void *output_silence*(**stream** ∗*s*, **mp3_sample** ∗*buffer*, **int** *n*)
  { **int** *i*;

    for $(i = 0;\ i < n;\ i{+}{+})$ ⟨output a single block of silence ₇₅⟩
    if $(s{\rightarrow}options.flags$ & `MP3_TWO_CHANNEL_MONO`$)$
      $s{\rightarrow}info.samples\ {+}{=}\ n * 2 *$ `SUBBANDS`;
    else $s{\rightarrow}info.samples\ {+}{=}\ n * s{\rightarrow}info.channels *$ `SUBBANDS`;
    }

The difference between ⟨output a single block of samples ₇₀⟩ and ⟨output a single block of silence ₇₅⟩ is the replacement of the *dct32* function by a loop to put zeros into v. There is no equalization of the zeros either.

⟨output a single block of silence ₇₅⟩ ≡   (75)
    { **double** $*v$;
      { **int** $sb,\ ch = 0$;
        ⟨shift vector v ₄⟩
        for $(sb =$ `SUBBANDS` $- 1;\ sb \geq 0;\ sb{-}{-})\ v[sb] = 0.0$;
        $windowing(v, buffer)$;
      }
      if $(s{\rightarrow}info.channels > 1)$
      { **int** $sb,\ ch = 1$;
        ⟨shift vector v ₄⟩
        for $(sb =$ `SUBBANDS` $- 1;\ sb \geq 0;\ sb{-}{-})\ v[sb] = 0.0$;
        $windowing(v, buffer + 1)$;
        $buffer = buffer + 2 *$ `SUBBANDS`; }
      else ⟨post-process single channel output ₇₁⟩
    }
                                                  Used in 74.

This section closes with the code to

⟨determine the number n of non zero blocks in v ₇₆⟩ ≡   (76)
    { **double** $*v$;
      int $i,\ ch,\ sb$;
      for $(n = 0, ch = 0;\ ch < s{\rightarrow}info.channels;\ ch{+}{+})$
      { $v = s{\rightarrow}w[ch] + s{\rightarrow}offset[ch]$;
        for $(i = n;\ i <$ `WINDOWBLOCKS` $- 1;\ i{+}{+})$
          for $(sb = 0;\ sb <$ `SUBBANDS`; $sb{+}{+})$
            if $(v[i *$ `SUBBANDS` $+ sb] \neq 0.0)$ { $n = i + 1$; **break**; }
      }
    }
                                                  Used in 72.

We start with $n = 0$ and loop over all channels. We locate the vector v inside the larger vector $s{\rightarrow}w$ and search within all but the last block (it would be shifted out immediately) for a nonzero subband value. If one is found, we update n and immediately advance to the next block. For the second channel, we can start searching with the value of n found for the first channel.

7 Unpacking the Frame

We have seen how to generate PCM samples from blocks of subband samples, which are packaged inside frames in an MPEG audio stream, but we still need to see the details. This chapter will explain most of them.

Each frame has four parts: the header, the optional CRC field for error checking, then the audio data, which is split into side information and subband samples, and finally there might be ancillary data. Let's examine these parts one after the other.

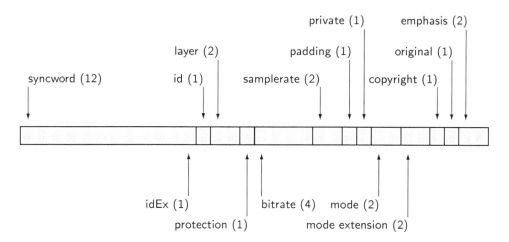

Fig. 18: The header layout

7.1 Header

The first four bytes of a frame are the header.

⟨ private declarations $_1$ ⟩ += (77)
#**define** HEADER_SIZE 4

It serves two purposes: synchronization, that is finding the beginning of a frame— we deal with that later—, and providing information on the stream. The function *decode_header* will extract this information into *info* and return 1. If *frame* does not point to a valid header, *decode_header* will return 0.

⟨ auxiliary functions $_{69}$ ⟩ +≡   (78)
    static int *decode_header*(**mp3_info** *∗info*, **unsigned char** *∗frame*)
    { **unsigned int** *header*;
        header = (((((*frame*[0] ≪ 8) | *frame*[1]) ≪ 8) | *frame*[2]) ≪ 8) | *frame*[3];
        info→header = *header*;
        ⟨ decode the header $_{79}$ ⟩ ⟨ determine *frame_size* $_{90}$ ⟩
        if (*info→frame_size* > MAX_FRAME) **return** 0;
        return 1;
    }

According to the MPEG standard, the first 12 bits of the header are 1111 1111 1111. They are called the "syncword" and help us to *synchronize* the stream. Later versions (see Chapter 14) use, however, only 11 bits for the syncword. Once we found the syncword, we do not need to keep it.

⟨ decode the header $_{79}$ ⟩ ≡   (79)
    { **int** $n = 11$; ⟨ get the next n header bits $_{80}$ ⟩
        if (*bits* ≠ $^\#$7FF) **return** 0;
    }   Used in 78.

We read n bits from the *header* by shifting it to the right until only n bits remain and assign the result to *bits*. Then we discard these n bits from the header by shifting the header to the left.

⟨ get the next n header bits $_{80}$ ⟩ ≡   (80)
    int *bits* = *header* ≫ (32 − n);

    header = *header* ≪ n;   Used in 79, 81, 82, 83, 85, 87, 88, 92, 94, 95, and 98.

We use the 12th bit of the header, also called the ID extension bit, and the next bit of the header, the ID bit, to determine the MPEG *version*.

Constant	ID ext.	ID	Version
MP3_V2_5	0	0	MPEG Version 2.5
MP3_V2_0	1	0	MPEG Version 2 (ISO/IEC 13818-3)
MP3_V1_0	1	1	MPEG Version 1 (ISO/IEC 11172-3)
	0	1	reserved

Tab. 5: Version

⟨ decode the header $_{79}$ ⟩ +≡   (81)
    { **int** $n = 2$; ⟨ get the next n header bits $_{80}$ ⟩
        if (*bits* ≡ 0)   *info→version* = MP3_V2_5;
        else if (*bits* ≡ 2) *info→version* = MP3_V2_0;
        else if (*bits* ≡ 3) *info→version* = MP3_V1_0;
        else return 0;
    }

The next two bits indicate the layer.

⟨ decode the header $_{79}$ ⟩ +≡   (82)
```
{ int n = 2; ⟨ get the next n header bits 80 ⟩
  if (bits ≡ 0) return 0;
  info→layer = 4 − bits;
}
```

Bit	Layer
11	Layer I
10	Layer II
01	Layer III
00	reserved

Tab. 6: Layer

Next comes the protection bit. If it is 1 then there is no CRC field for error checking; if it is 0 there is a CRC error check (see Section 7.2).

⟨ decode the header $_{79}$ ⟩ +≡   (83)
```
{ int n = 1; ⟨ get the next n header bits 80 ⟩
  info→crc_protected = (bits ≡ 0);
}
```

The next four bits indicate the bit rate. Table 7 gives the possible version 1 bit rates in kbit/s. This bit rate is the total bit rate irrespective of the mode, be it mono or stereo, joint stereo or dual channel. The value 1111 is not allowed. The value 0000 indicates a "free format" stream (see Section 8.4). In this case, the variable *free_format* is set to 1 to mark the stream as free format stream.

⟨ infos $_{31}$ ⟩ +≡   (84)
```
  int free_format;
```
Free format streams have a fixed but otherwise arbitrary bit rate. (With the restriction that even then, the decoder is not required to support bit rates larger than the maximum bit rates of 448 kbit/s, 384 kbit/s, or 320 kbit/s in the respective layer.) If the stream is not a free format stream, the bit rate can vary from frame to frame. The *bit_rate_table* can be found in Appendix A.6.

⟨ decode the header $_{79}$ ⟩ +≡   (85)
```
{ int n = 4; ⟨ get the next n header bits 80 ⟩
  if (bits ≡ 0) info→free_format = 1;
  else if (bits ≡ #F) return 0;
  else
  { info→free_format = 0;
    info→bit_rate = bit_rate_table[info→version][info→layer − 1][bits];
  }
}
```

Bit	Layer I	Version 1 Layer II	Layer II
0000	free	free	free
0001	32	32	32
0010	64	48	40
0011	96	56	48
0100	128	64	56
0101	160	80	64
0110	192	96	80
0111	224	112	96
1000	256	128	112
1001	288	160	128
1010	320	192	160
1011	352	224	192
1100	384	256	224
1101	416	320	256
1110	448	384	320
1111	—	—	—

Tab. 7: Version 1 bit rate index

The next two bits are the *frequency_index*.

$\langle$ infos $_{31}$ $\rangle$ +≡   (86)
  int *frequency_index*;

It encodes the sample rate. Any change in the sample rate should be important for the application that uses the decoded stream.

Bit	Sample Rate in Hz
11	reserved
10	32000
01	48000
00	44100

Tab. 8: Version 1 sample rates

$\langle$ decode the header $_{79}$ $\rangle$ +≡   (87)
  { **int** $n = 2$; $\langle$ get the next n header bits $_{80}$ $\rangle$
    if (*bits* ≡ 3) **return** 0;
    info→*frequency_index* = *bits*;

$info \rightarrow sample\_rate = frequency\_table\,[info \rightarrow version\,][info \rightarrow frequency\_index\,];$
}

The *frequency_table* can be found in Appendix A.7 on page 211.
Next is the padding bit.

⟨decode the header ₇₉⟩ +≡   (88)
    { **int** $n = 1$; ⟨get the next n header bits ₈₀⟩
    $info \rightarrow padding = bits;$
    }

We store this bit in

⟨infos ₃₁⟩ +≡   (89)
    int *padding*;

If this bit is 1, the frame contains an additional slot. The standard uses the term
"slot" to mean four bytes in layer I and one byte in layers II and III. With padding,
the encoder can achieve an exact average bit rate. The standard requires, that the
accumulated length of any sequence of audio frames does not deviate more ±1 slot,
from

$$\sum \text{samples per frame} \cdot bit\_rate\,/\,sample\_rate,$$

where a layer I frame contains 384 samples, and a layer II or III frame contains 1152
samples. We add *padding* when we determine the *frame_size* from the *bit_rate*.

⟨determine *frame_size* ₉₀⟩ ≡   (90)
    { **if** $(info \rightarrow layer \equiv 1)$ $info \rightarrow frame\_size =$
            $4 * (info \rightarrow padding + (384/(8*4)) * info \rightarrow bit\_rate\,/info \rightarrow sample\_rate\,);$
        else $info \rightarrow frame\_size =$
            $info \rightarrow padding + (1152/8) * info \rightarrow bit\_rate\,/info \rightarrow sample\_rate;$
    }
                                                                        Used in 78 and 171.

Using the same formula, we compute the *bit_rate* from the *frame_size* in case of free
format streams.

⟨determine free format *bit_rate* ₉₁⟩ ≡   (91)
    { **if** $(s \rightarrow info.layer \equiv 1)$ $s \rightarrow info.bit\_rate =$
            $((s \rightarrow info.frame\_size\,/4 - s \rightarrow info.padding\,) * s \rightarrow info.sample\_rate + 11)/12;$
        else $s \rightarrow info.bit\_rate =$
            $((s \rightarrow info.frame\_size - s \rightarrow info.padding\,) * s \rightarrow info.sample\_rate + 143)/144;$
    }
                                                                              Used in 171.

The above code adds 11 respectively 143 to round up the result to the next whole
number. The rounding might cause an error of $0 \leq \epsilon < 1$ in the bit rate. The only
use the decoder makes of the *bit_rate* is the reverse computation of the *frame_size* for
free format bit streams. This computation will not propagate the error to its result
because it involves a division by the *sample_rate*, which is at least 8000. The division
will truncate the result towards zero and thereby remove the error completely.

The private bit is next. This bit is used for whatever the encoder needs the bit.

⟨ decode the header $_{79}$ ⟩ +≡   (92)
  { **int** $n = 1$; ⟨ get the next n header bits $_{80}$ ⟩
    $info{\rightarrow}private = bits$;
  }

The mode is determined by the following two bits.

Symbolic constant	Bit	Mode
MP3_MONO	11	one mono channel
MP3_DUAL_CHANNEL	10	two independent channels
MP3_JOINT_STEREO	01	intensity stereo or mid/side stereo allowed
MP3_STEREO	00	two stereo channels

Tab. 9: Mode bit

Mid/side stereo is only an option in layer III, otherwise joint stereo always is intensity stereo.

⟨ decode the header $_{79}$ ⟩ +≡   (94)
  { **int** $n = 2$; ⟨ get the next n header bits $_{80}$ ⟩
    $info{\rightarrow}mode = bits$;
    if ($info{\rightarrow}mode \equiv$ MP3_MONO) $info{\rightarrow}channels = 1$;
    else $info{\rightarrow}channels = 2$;
  }

The mode extension is in the next two bits.

⟨ decode the header $_{79}$ ⟩ +≡   (95)
  { **int** $n = 2$; ⟨ get the next n header bits $_{80}$ ⟩
    ⟨ process the mode extension bits $_{97}$ ⟩
  }

The only use we make of the mode extension bits in layer I is the computation of the *bound*.

⟨ infos $_{31}$ ⟩ +≡   (96)
  int *bound*;

The *bound* determines which subbands are coded in intensity stereo. Intensity stereo is a more compact coding than normal stereo, because both channels carry the same signal only with different intensity. That means that we have different scalefactors for both channels but can reuse the sample data. The difference between true stereo and intensity stereo is less audible at higher frequencies. Hence, subbands below *bound* are coded with true stereo, and subbands at or above *bound*, with intensity stereo. Of course, the *bound* can be used only in joint stereo mode.

⟨ process the mode extension bits $_{97}$ ⟩ ≡   (97)
   $info{\rightarrow}bound = bits * 4 + 4;$
   if $(info{\rightarrow}mode \neq$ `MP3_JOINT_STEREO`) $info{\rightarrow}bound = 32;$ Used in 95.

More about *bound* or *mode_extension* can be found in Section 7.4 and Section 11.10.

The header ends with the copyright bit (1 means copyright protection), the original bit (1 means it's an original, not a copy), and the two emphasis bits (00 means no emphasis, 01 means 50/15 μs, 10 is reserved, and 11 means CCITT J17 (whatever that is)).

⟨ decode the header $_{79}$ ⟩ +≡   (98)
   { **int** $n = 1$; ⟨ get the next n header bits $_{80}$ ⟩
     $info{\rightarrow}copyright = bits;$
   }
   { **int** $n = 1$; ⟨ get the next n header bits $_{80}$ ⟩
     $info{\rightarrow}original = bits;$
   }
   { **int** $n = 2$; ⟨ get the next n header bits $_{80}$ ⟩
     $info{\rightarrow}emphasis = bits;$
   }

7.2 Error Protection with the CRC Field

After the header there may be two bytes containing the CRC field for error protection. The CRC, short for Cyclic Redundancy Check, is then compared to the CRC as computed from the actual frame. As long as there is no transmission error, both numbers are equal. If they are different, we can conclude that the data in the frame is corrupted.

⟨ perform additional checks $_{99}$ ⟩ ≡   (99)
   if $(s{\rightarrow}info.crc\_protected)$
   { **if** $(getbit(s, 16) \neq crc\_check(s))$
     { $output_mode = $ `REPAIR | SKIP`;
       $s{\rightarrow}info.changes \mathrel{|=}$ `MP3_INFO_CRC`;
     }
   }   Used in 62.

The CRC is used only on part of the frame, mainly because evaluating the CRC involves some computational cost. So only the "important" bits are protected by the CRC. Let's review the VIBs (the very important bits) starting with the header. The first two bytes of the header, while important, are not included in the CRC. If these are wrong, there is no hope anyway. Only the two last header bytes are checked. Two CRC bytes follow and, obviously, are skipped.

⟨compute the CRC for the header $_{100}$⟩ ≡   (100)
   $byte\_pointer = s{\rightarrow}frame + 2$;
   ⟨compute the CRC for one byte $_{441}$⟩;
   ⟨compute the CRC for one byte $_{441}$⟩;
   $byte\_pointer{+}{+}$;
   $byte\_pointer{+}{+}$;   Used in 101.

The algorithm to ⟨compute the CRC for one byte $_{441}$⟩ and the necessary mathematics are explained in Appendix B. What remains to be checked in layer I are $4 \cdot 32\,\text{bit} = 16\,\text{byte}$ for the bit allocation data of channel one and $4 \cdot bound\,\text{bit} = bound/2\,\text{byte}$ for channel two (see Section 7.4).

⟨auxiliary functions $_{69}$⟩ +≡   (101)
   static short unsigned int crc_check(**stream** $*s$)
   { **short unsigned int** crc;
     unsigned char $*byte\_pointer$;
     int n;

     $crc = {^\#}\mathtt{FFFF}$;
     ⟨compute the CRC for the header $_{100}$⟩
     if $(s{\rightarrow}info.layer \equiv 1)$
     { $n = 16$;
       if $(s{\rightarrow}info.channels > 1)$ $n = n + s{\rightarrow}info.bound/2$;
       while $(n{-}{-} > 0)$ ⟨compute the CRC for one byte $_{441}$⟩;
     }
     else if $(s{\rightarrow}info.layer \equiv 2)$ ⟨compute the CRC for layer II $_{215}$⟩
     else
     { $n = s{\rightarrow}info.fixed\_size - \mathtt{HEADER\_SIZE} - 2$;
       while $(n{-}{-} > 0)$ ⟨compute the CRC for one byte $_{441}$⟩;
     }
     return crc;
   }

The standard requires ${^\#}\mathtt{FFFF}$ as initial value for the crc.

We postpone the details for layer II until Section 9.4, but include, because it is so simple, the code for layer III where we need to check the so called "fixed part" of the frame (see Appendix A.11) less the four header bytes and the two CRC bytes.

7.3 Side Information

The header and the CRC field are followed by the side information. We store it in a global variable $side\_info$ indexed by the subbands.

⟨global variables $_{43}$⟩ +≡   (102)
   static side_information $side\_info$[SUBBANDS][CHANNELS];

We will define the type of $side\_info$ incrementally, as needed. For now it is sufficient to know that it is a structure containing ⟨side information $_{105}$⟩.

⟨ private types ₄₂ ⟩ +≡   (103)
  typedef struct {
   ⟨ side information ₁₀₅ ⟩
  } **side_information**;

The primary components of layer I side information are the bit allocation and the scalefactors.

⟨ decode layer I side information ₁₀₄ ⟩ ≡   (104)
  { ⟨ read the *bit_allocation* ₁₀₆ ⟩
   ⟨ read the scalefactors ₁₁₁ ⟩
  }
                           Used in 66.

Both components are described in detail in the next two sections.

7.4 Bit Allocation

We have 32 subbands, and for each subband, we need to know the number of bits used for coding the subband sample. This part of the side information is called the *bit_allocation*.

⟨ side information ₁₀₅ ⟩ ≡   (105)
  char *bit_allocation*;   Used in 103.

The bit allocation is provided by 4 bits for each channel and subband below *bound*.

⟨ read the *bit_allocation* ₁₀₆ ⟩ ≡   (106)
  { **int** *sb*, *ch*;
    for ($sb = 0$; $sb < s{\to}info.bound$; $sb{+}{+}$)
      for ($ch = 0$; $ch < s{\to}info.channels$; $ch{+}{+}$)
      { **int** *n*;
        ⟨ read bit allocation *n* ₁₀₈ ⟩
        side_info[*sb*][*ch*].*bit_allocation* = *n*;
      }
  }
                          Used in 104.

For the remaining subbands, we share the same 4 bits for both channels.

⟨ read the *bit_allocation* ₁₀₆ ⟩ +≡   (107)
  { **int** *sb*;
    for ($sb = s{\to}info.bound$; $sb < $ SUBBANDS; $sb{+}{+}$)
    { **int** *n*;
      ⟨ read bit allocation *n* ₁₀₈ ⟩
      side_info[*sb*][0].*bit_allocation* = *n*;
      side_info[*sb*][1].*bit_allocation* = *n*;
    }
  }

To ⟨ read bit allocation *n* ₁₀₈ ⟩, the next 4 bits in the stream are interpreted as an unsigned 4 bit integer *a* in the range from 0 to 15. The value 0 indicates that no bits are allocated for this subband. There is no signal in this subband and consequently there will be no scalefactors and no samples for this subband. Any other value $0 < a < 15$ indicates that there will be $n = a + 1$ bits per sample. The value $a = 15$ (binary 1111) is not allowed, since three such values in a row could easily be taken for a syncword.

⟨ read bit allocation n ₁₀₈ ⟩ ≡   (108)
  { **int** $a = getbit(s, 4)$;

    if $(a \equiv 15)$
    { $s \rightarrow state = s \rightarrow state$ | `BITALLOCATION_ERROR`;
      $a = 14$;
    }
    if $(a > 0)$ $n = a + 1$;
    else $n = 0$;
  }   Used in 106 and 107.

⟨ private declarations ₁ ⟩ +≡   (109)
#**define** `BITALLOCATION_ERROR`   #0008

7.5 Scalefactors

Ordinarily, large quantities are coded by large numbers and small quantities by small numbers. If bits are an expensive resource and quality is our foremost concern, we have to rethink this correlation. In fact, large numbers with many digits are necessary only for precision; for large quantities, we can as well use large units of measure. For example, we can say 1 hour instead of 3600 seconds. For the encoder, it is best to choose the number of bits for encoding a sample value on the basis of the required precision, and then to choose the correct "unit of measure" in order to be able to code the given value. The decoder has to reverse this process. Before any computations can be performed on the sample values, they need to be converted to the same standard unit of measure. This conversion, called requantization, is done by multiplying the raw sample value by an appropriate scalefactor. A slightly modified (see Section 7.9) version of the scalefactor is stored as

⟨ side information ₁₀₅ ⟩ +≡   (110)
  double $mfactor$[GROUPS];

Since in layer II we will need the $mfactor$ three times, once for each group, we define the side information here appropriately. Note, however, that in layer I, we will use only $mfactor$[0] To save bits, scalefactors (that is units of measure) are transmitted only once per frame, subband, and channel.

⟨ read the scalefactors ₁₁₁ ⟩ ≡   (111)
  { **int** sb, ch;
    for $(sb = 0;\ sb < $ SUBBANDS$;\ sb++)$
      for $(ch = 0;\ ch < s \rightarrow info.channels;\ ch++)$
      { **side_information** $*si$;
        $si = \&(side\_info[sb][ch])$;

⟨ read one scalefactor 112 ⟩
        }
    }
                                                                Used in 104.

All sample values that belong to one frame, the same channel, and the same subband
share the same scalefactor—unless we have no bits allocated for a subband in which
case we need no scalefactor either.

⟨ read one scalefactor 112 ⟩ ≡   (112)
    { int $n = si \rightarrow bit\_allocation$;
        if $(n \neq 0)$
        { int i;
            ⟨ read scalefactor index i 113 ⟩
            ⟨ assign scalefactor 115 ⟩
        }
    }
                                                                Used in 111.

Scalefactors are not provided directly, instead the input stream contains 6 bits for each
scalefactor, and these are used as an index into an array of precomputed scalefactors.
The value 63 (in binary 111111) is not allowed, since two of them could be confused
with a syncword.

⟨ read scalefactor index i 113 ⟩ ≡   (113)
    $i = getbit(s, 6)$;
    if $(i \geq 63)$
    { $s \rightarrow state = s \rightarrow state$ | SCALEFACTOR_ERROR;
        $i = 62$;
    }
                                                            Used in 112 and 205.

⟨ public declarations 15 ⟩ +≡   (114)
#define SCALEFACTOR_ERROR #0010

Since the only purpose of these indices is to look up factors when processing the
subband samples, and the same factors are shared for a whole sequence of subband
samples, it is obviously more efficient to do the table lookup only once and store
the factors instead of the index for later use. As we will see in Section 7.9, we take
the correct factor from a precomputed global table called *mfactors* and store the
particular *mfactor* as side information.

⟨ assign scalefactor 115 ⟩ ≡   (115)
    $si \rightarrow mfactor[0] = mfactors[n][i]$;
                                                                Used in 112.

7.6 Subband Samples

In this section, we describe how we decode layer I subband samples. In layer I,
each frame contains 12 blocks and for each block and each channel, we need to read
and store subband samples. For efficiency, we have two separate loops: One for two
channel streams, the other for single channel streams.

⟨ layer I subband samples loop $_{116}$ ⟩ ≡   (116)
  { int i;
    if ($s{\rightarrow}info.channels > 1$)
      for ($i = 0$; $i < 12$; $i{+}{+}$) ⟨ read and store stereo subband samples $_{120}$ ⟩
    else
      for ($i = 0$; $i < 12$; $i{+}{+}$) ⟨ read and store mono subband samples $_{117}$ ⟩
  }
                                                                   Used in 122.

The simpler case first: For a single channel, we iterate over all subbands, as follows:

⟨ read and store mono subband samples $_{117}$ ⟩ ≡   (117)
  { int sb;
    for ($sb = 0$; $sb < $ SUBBANDS; $sb{+}{+}$)
    { ⟨ read one scaled subband sample $_{118}$ ⟩ }
  }
                                                                   Used in 116.

To ⟨ read one scaled subband sample $_{118}$ ⟩, we retrieve the number n, of bits to read, using the side information, then we ⟨ read one n bit $sample$ $_{121}$ ⟩, scale it with the $mfactor$, and store it in the vector $\boldsymbol{y}$, ready for the CosDFT.

⟨ read one scaled subband sample $_{118}$ ⟩ ≡   (118)
  int $sample$;
  { int $n = side\_info[sb][0].bit\_allocation$;
    ⟨ read one n bit $sample$ $_{121}$ ⟩
    $\boldsymbol{y}[i][0][sb] = sample * side\_info[sb][0].mfactor[0]$;
  }
                                                          Used in 117 and 120.

For two channels, we simply

⟨ read the second scaled subband sample $_{119}$ ⟩ ≡   (119)
  { int $n = side\_info[sb][1].bit\_allocation$;
    ⟨ read one n bit $sample$ $_{121}$ ⟩
    $\boldsymbol{y}[i][1][sb] = sample * side\_info[sb][1].mfactor[0]$;
  }
                                                                  Used in 120.

Even a two channel stream has only a single subband sample for subbands above the $bound$. It is then used for both channels. Different scalefactors, however, can be used to obtain intensity stereo.

⟨ read and store stereo subband samples $_{120}$ ⟩ ≡   (120)
  { int sb;
    for ($sb = 0$; $sb < s{\rightarrow}info.bound$; $sb{+}{+}$)
    { ⟨ read one scaled subband sample $_{118}$ ⟩
      ⟨ read the second scaled subband sample $_{119}$ ⟩
    }
    for (; $sb < $ SUBBANDS; $sb{+}{+}$)
    { ⟨ read one scaled subband sample $_{118}$ ⟩

$\boldsymbol{y}[i][1][sb] = sample * side\_info[sb][1].mfactor[0];$
   }
}
Used in 116.

If n is zero, is pretty easy to ⟨ read one n bit *sample* 121 ⟩.

⟨ read one n bit *sample* 121 ⟩ ≡   (121)
   if $(n \equiv 0)$ *sample* = 0;
   else ⟨ read the *sample* 125 ⟩   Used in 118 and 119.

Before we tackle the more complex problem of how to ⟨ read the *sample* 125 ⟩ from the stream, we summarize our results and put the code into a function. We use a function not only for structural reasons but also for improved efficiency. The ⟨ layer I subband samples loop 116 ⟩ is embedded within two code fragments to localize and to globalize the bit stream. This allows a more efficient low level access to the bit stream as we will see in Chapter 8.

⟨ auxiliary functions 69 ⟩ +≡   (122)
   static void *layer_I_decode_samples*(**stream** *s)
   { ⟨ localize the bit stream 146 ⟩
     ⟨ layer I subband samples loop 116 ⟩
     ⟨ globalize the bit stream 147 ⟩
   }

Now back to the problem of how to ⟨ read the *sample* 125 ⟩ from the stream.

7.7 Reading a Sample

The n bits obtained from the stream need to be converted to a sample value. The ISO standard specifies that after

> *inverting the first of these bits, they should be interpreted as a two's complement fractional number s''', where the most significant bit represents the value -1. From s''' the value s'' is computed according to the formula:*
>
> $$s'' = \frac{2^n}{2^n - 1}(s''' + 2^{-n+1}).$$
>
> *where n is the number of bit allocated for this sample.*
> *This is called requantization.*
> *After requantizing, the numbers need to be scaled by a factor f found in a table of scalefactors (see ...). The table is indexed by the so called scalefactor index, which is stored in the stream. We obtain the final value of the subband sample s' as $s' = fs''$.*

Everything clear? Here, we observe, as we do at several other places, that the ISO standard is written with two objectives in mind: to be precise, while still preserving the challenge of writing a decent decoder. For a good book that unveils some of the mysteries of the standards genesis, see [5].

7.8 Requantization

Let's consider an example. Assume that the number of bits to read is $n = 4$ and that we read 1110. After inverting the first bit we have 0110. As a binary number it has the value $0 \cdot 2^3 + 1 \cdot 2^2 + 1 \cdot 2^1 + 0 \cdot 2^0 = 6$. The two's complement is a method of representing negative values with fixed length bit strings using the fact that most hardware will cause "wrap around" when large numbers are added. For instance, when we add to 0110 (representing 6) the binary number 1110, representing the value $1 \cdot 2^3 + 1 \cdot 2^2 + 1 \cdot 2^1 + 0 \cdot 2^0 = 14$, we get 10100, representing the value 20. If our hypothetical hardware is limited to bit strings of length 4, it will throw away the leading digits and retain only the last four bits 0100, representing the value 4. Adding two numbers, we obtained a result that is smaller than the first operand. Such a behavior of addition is expected only if we add negative numbers, and indeed, this property of addition with fixed bit length, called wrap around, is used to implement negative numbers. If we ignore the leading digits, a number like 0100 might represent many different values; it could be 0100 (=4) or 10100 (=20) or 100100 (=36). The same trailing four bits are used over and over as the representation of different integer values, and it is possible, of course, to extend this pattern also to negative values. Addition with fixed bit length is correct only in so far as it derives a correct representation of the sum of the values. Mathematically, all values that share the same representation have the property that they yield the same remainder when divided by $2^4 = 16$. Here, we will not enter into the theory of finite Rings (see Appendix B.1) but conclude the explanation of two's complement by stating that

- we regard a number as negative if the leading bit is 1 and positive otherwise, and

- we assume that any bit string represents the value with the smallest absolute value.

Hence, 0110 represents 6, 1110 is negative and represents -2, the result of the addition is 0100 and correctly represents 4.

There is an easy way to negate binary numbers in two's complement, which we will need later. Just observe that when all the bits of a number are inverted, we almost get the negative number, there is just a displacement of one. Hence, negating a number in two's complement is the same as inverting all bits and adding 1 to the result. This schema works in both directions.

Now we turn to binary fractions. We are used to decimal fractions having a decimal point, like in 3.1415 for example. Shifting the decimal-point one place to the left means division by 10, shifting it to the right means multiplication by 10. In our example, 3.1415 represents the value $31415/1000$, as expected. With binary fractions, shifting the binary-point one place to the left means division by 2 and shifting it to the right means multiplication by 2. For example 0110 represents 6, 011.0 represents $6/2 = 3$, 01.10 represents $6/4$, and 0.110 represents $6/8$.

What is now the value of the most significant bit if we place a binary-point directly after the leading digit? 1000 is negative, it represents -8, therefore 1.000 represents $-8/8 = -1$. And this is the interpretation of the bit strings required by the ISO standard.

To continue our example, the bit string 0110 is positive, it is interpreted as 0.110, and represents the value $6/8$. Next, according to the ISO standard, we have to add $2^{-4+1} = 2^{-3} = 1/2^3 = 1/8$, in binary notation 0.001, and obtain $0.110+0.001 = 0.111$ representing $7/8$, the largest value that can be represented in this fashion as a four bit binary fraction. And here, we start to understand why we had to invert the most significant bit and add the extra bit. As the ISO standard hints in Appendix C, Section C.1.5.1.7, this is done to avoid the bit string 1111, because a sequence of 1's is used as syncword. With ordinary coding, the bit string 1111 represents $-1/8$, it is in the middle of the possible value range and quite common, so it should not be excluded. If we invert the most significant bit, the code 0111 becomes critical. This code, however, is at the very end of the value range. This is better but not optimal. The range of possible values is not symmetric, we have only 7 positive values (1 to 111), but 8 negative values(1000 to 1111), including -1. Since the encoding process chooses scalefactors so that after scaling the input values v are all in the range $-1 < v < +1$, it is best to avoid the value -1. If this is done, by subtracting 0001 while encoding and adding it while decoding, we can represent the range from $-7/8$ to $+7/8$ without using the code 1111 at all.

7.9 Modified Factors

What remains to complete the requantization is the multiplication with $2^n/(2^n-1)$ and the multiplication with the factor f from the scalefactor table. But before we can do the multiplication, we have to convert the encoded values from the special n bit two's complement binary fraction format to some standard format in order to use the usual multiplication hardware. We will convert the values to regular signed integers (for almost all processors just another word for two's complement representation). To do so, we shift the n bit binary fractions by $k - n$ bits to the left, where k is the number of bits of a regular **int**.

This gives us k bit binary fractions instead of n bit binary fractions. Then, we remove the (invisible) binary-point, which corresponds to a multiplication by 2^{k-1}, and have signed k bit integers.

There is still one tiny improvement possible: the addition can be eliminated by using binary negation (as explained above). Instead of inverting the most significant bit, we invert all the other bits and negate the result. The negation can be combined with other multiplications at no extra computational cost and only the inversion operation remains.

Now the code: After we ⟨ get n bits $_{142}$ ⟩ from the input—they are already aligned to the left as k bit integers in the variable *bits*—, we invert all but the leading bit by computing the bitwise XOR with a mask that has a leading 0-bit and the other bits set to 1. We construct the mask by taking -1, which is the value having all bits set to one, making it an **unsigned int**, and shifting it to the right by 1 bit.

⟨ inversion mask $_{123}$ ⟩ ≡   (123)

   (((**unsigned int**) -1) ≫ 1)   Used in 125.

To set to zero all but the first n bits, we do a bitwise AND with the

$\langle$ allocation mask $_{124}$ $\rangle \equiv$ (124)
$\quad \sim(((\mathbf{unsigned\ int})\ -1) \gg n)$ Used in 125.

It is constructed similar to the $\langle$ inversion mask $_{123}$ $\rangle$ and uses bitwise negation.

Now, we can easily

$\langle$ read the *sample* $_{125}$ $\rangle \equiv$ (125)
$\quad \{$ **unsigned int** *bits*;

$\qquad \langle$ get n bits $_{142}$ $\rangle$
$\qquad bits = bits \oplus \langle$ inversion mask $_{123}$ $\rangle$;
$\qquad bits = bits\ \&\ \langle$ allocation mask $_{124}$ $\rangle$;
$\qquad sample = (\mathbf{int})\ bits$;

$\quad \}$ Used in 121 and 201.

Next, we consider the scaling with the factor f. For the scaling with f, the standard contains a big table of factors, and the bit stream provides for each subband an index i into this table. A closer inspection of the table reveals that the numbers given there are just powers of $\sqrt[3]{2}$. That is, f_i is nothing but $2 \cdot (\sqrt[3]{2})^{-i} = 2^{1-i/3}$.

$\langle$ f_i $_{126}$ $\rangle \equiv$ (126)
$\quad pow(2, 1 - i/3.0)$ Used in 127, 208, and 209.

Because multiplication with 2 corresponds to shifting by one bit, one can think of multiplication with $\sqrt[3]{2}$ as "shifting by 1/3 bit to the left". Doing it three times gives $(\sqrt[3]{2})^3 = 2$ which is shifting by one bit. Using scalefactors, binary numbers can be "shifted" precisely the right amount to obtain good resolution without overflow.

When we $\langle$ read the scalefactors $_{111}$ $\rangle$ from the stream, it is more efficient if we combine all the necessary scaling operations into one multiplication with a $\langle$ modified factor $_{127}$ $\rangle$. This $\langle$ modified factor $_{127}$ $\rangle$ is taken from a global table *mfactors*, once for each subband and channel, and stored in a local *mfactors* table that is part of the stream data. After the sample value is converted to an **int**, all we need to do is multiply it by this precomputed factor.

The $\langle$ modified factor $_{127}$ $\rangle$ combines the multiplication by -1 (because of the negation trick), the multiplication with $\langle$ f_i $_{126}$ $\rangle$, the division by 2^{k-1} (to undo the cast to an **int**), and the multiplication by $\frac{2^n}{2^n-1}$ into one single multiplication.

$\langle$ modified factor $_{127}$ $\rangle \equiv$ (127)
$\quad -1 * \langle$ output scalefactor $_{136}$ $\rangle * \langle$ f_i $_{126}$ $\rangle /$
$\qquad (((1 \ll n) - 1) * (((\mathbf{int})\ 1) \ll ((\mathbf{sizeof}\,(\mathbf{int}) * 8) - 1 - n)))$ Used in 134.

There is only one surprise in the above code, the multiplication with the $\langle$ output scalefactor $_{136}$ $\rangle$. This factor is explained in the next section. Basically, it scales the floating point output of the CosDFT and the windowing step back to the representation as k bit binary fractions, as required for the final conversion to the **mp3_sample** type. But since CosDFT and windowing are linear operations, the multiplication with the $\langle$ output scalefactor $_{136}$ $\rangle$ can, at no extra cost, also be done before these operations.

Back to the global table of *mfactors*. It is contained in the file **tables.h** which is a container for all kinds of tables that we will need. We include it to be able to use these tables.

⟨ header files ₉ ⟩ +≡   (128)
#include **"tables.h"**

The tables in this header file are not written "by hand", they are the output of the program **mktables** which must be redirected to the file **tables.h**.

⟨ **mktables.c**   ₁₂₉ ⟩ ≡   (129)
#include **<stdio.h>**
#include **<math.h>**
#include **"mp32pcm.h"**
  ⟨ printing prerequisites ₁₃₀ ⟩
  ⟨ print element ₁₃₂ ⟩

  int *main*(**void**)
  { ⟨ print table ₁₃₅ ⟩
    return 0;
  }

The ⟨ printing prerequisites ₁₃₀ ⟩, mentioned above, include definitions and auxiliary functions needed for printing tables. First and before all these are

⟨ printing prerequisites ₁₃₀ ⟩ ≡   (130)
  ⟨ public declarations ₁₅ ⟩
  ⟨ private declarations ₁ ⟩   Used in 129.

In addition, there is a generic function to print C-style arrays.

⟨ printing prerequisites ₁₃₀ ⟩ +≡   (131)
  void *print_array*(**char** *declaration*, **int** *size*, **void** *print_element*(**int** *i*))
  { **int** *i* = 0;

    if (*declaration*) *printf*("%s[%d]=", *declaration*, *size*);
    printf("{\n");
    while (1)
    { *print_element*(*i*);
      if (++*i* ≥ *size*) **break**;
      printf(",");
      if (*i* % 3 ≡ 0) *printf*("\n");
      else *printf*("␣");
    }
    printf("}");
    if (*declaration*) *printf*(";\n");
  }

It prints commas, line breaks, opening and closing braces, even the declaration, if desired. Only the output of the array elements is delegated to a function *print_element*, which is passed as a parameter.

Two such functions are for instance

$\langle$ print element $_{132}$ $\rangle \equiv$ (132)

  void *mfactors0* (**int** i)

  { *printf* ("%.16e", $\langle$ layer II modified factor for $n = -10$ $_{208}$ $\rangle$); }   Used in 129.

and

$\langle$ print element $_{132}$ $\rangle$ $+\equiv$ (133)

  void *mfactors1* (**int** i)

  { *printf* ("%.16e", $\langle$ layer II modified factor for $n = -7$ $_{209}$ $\rangle$); }

A bit different, because it needs two parameters, is

$\langle$ print element $_{132}$ $\rangle$ $+\equiv$ (134)

  void *mfactors* (**int** i, **int** n)

  { *printf* ("%.16e", $\langle$ modified factor $_{127}$ $\rangle$); }

With these preparations, we can print our first table:

$\langle$ print table $_{135}$ $\rangle \equiv$ (135)

  { **int** n, i;

    printf ("static␣const␣double␣mfactors[17][64]␣=␣{");

    print_array (NULL, 64, *mfactors0*);

    printf (",\n");

    print_array (NULL, 64, *mfactors1*);

    printf (",\n");

    for ($n = 2$; $n \le 16$; n++)

    { *printf* ("{\n");

      for ($i = 0$; $i < 64$; i++)

      { *mfactors* (i, n);

        if ($i < 63$) *printf* (",");

        if ($i \% 3 \equiv 2$) *printf* ("\n");

        else *printf* ("␣");

      }

      printf ("}\n");

      if ($n < 16$) *printf* (",\n");

    }

    printf ("};\n");

  }   Used in 129.

A word on the indexing of the global *mfactors* table may be appropriate. Observe that the $\langle$ modified factor $_{127}$ $\rangle$ depends only on the number of bits n and the index i. The range of n is $2 \le n \le 15$ and i is in the range $0 \le i \le 62$. Even if the range of i comprises only 63 values (the value 111111 is not used), it is better to include an additional value and have a table with 64 different entries per row. This enables faster table access: To load the element in column i and row n from a table that is stored row by row in memory, the computer takes the starting address of the table, adds n times the size of one row, and finally adds i times the size of one element. If the size of one row is a power of 2, multiplication can be replaced by shifting, which is significantly faster. The extra values that we put into the table for $n = 0$, $n = 1$, and $n = 16$ will come in handy later, in Chapter 9, when we deal with layer II.

7.10 Scaling the Output

After having performed the CosDFT and the windowing, we obtain PCM samples x as floating point values in the range $-1 < x < +1$. These are then multiplied by the $\langle$ output scalefactor $_{136}\rangle$ to get values in the range $-\langle$ output scalefactor $_{136}\rangle$ to $+$ $\langle$ output scalefactor $_{136}\rangle$. Provided the $\langle$ output scalefactor $_{136}\rangle$ was correct, one can then obtain **mp3_samples** with a simple cast.

$\langle$ output scalefactor $_{136}\rangle \equiv$ (136)
    ((**double**)((**unsigned**) $1 \ll$ OUTPUT_EXPONENT))   Used in 127, 138, 208, 209, and 410.

where the OUTPUT_EXPONENT depends on the number of bits in the **int** data type.

$\langle$ private declarations $_1\rangle +\equiv$ (137)
#**define** OUTPUT_EXPONENT (**sizeof**(**int**) $* 8 - 1$)

Unfortunately, a simple cast does not always perform proper rounding, which is important especially if the **mp3_sample** type has only 16 bits. Just dividing the sample value—or rather shifting it— would round down the **int** value. To obtain proper rounding, we first add half of the dividend. Since the rounding is surprisingly expensive, we avoid it for producing 32 bit output.

$\langle$ conversion from **double** to **mp3_sample** $_{138}\rangle \equiv$ (138)
#**include** <math.h>
  static mp3_sample *mk_sample*(**register double** x)
  { **if** (*fabs*(x) $\leq \langle$ output scalefactor $_{136}\rangle$)
    { **if** (**sizeof**(**mp3_sample**) $\equiv$ **sizeof**(**int**)) **return** (**mp3_sample**) x;
    else
    { **const int** $d =$ (**sizeof**(**int**) $-$ **sizeof**(**mp3_sample**)) $* 8$;
      return ((**int**) $x + (1 \ll (d - 1))) \gg d$;
    }
    }
    else if ($x > 0$) **return** $\langle$ maximum **mp3_sample** $_{140}\rangle$;
    else return $-\langle$ maximum **mp3_sample** $_{140}\rangle - 1$;
  }
                                    Used in 6.

The *fabs* function requires the inclusion of math.h. The function also checks if the output value is indeed in the expected range. If this is not the case, the output signal is clipped. The function returns the

$\langle$ maximum **mp3_sample** $_{140}\rangle \equiv$ (140)
  ((**signed int**)
  (((((**unsigned int**) 1) $\ll$ (**sizeof**(**mp3_sample**) $* 8 - 1$)) $- 1$))   Used in 138.

7.11 Ancillary Data

After the end of the audio data, there might be ancillary data. Mostly this is just a few unused bits that are here to fill up the frame up to the next byte boundary where the next frame starts. It might be a good idea to pass them to the tag handler so that the application could get access to these bits. The current implementation ignores them.

⟨ process ancillary bits $_{141}$ ⟩ ≡   (141)

   ;

                                                 Used in 362 and 399.

8 Reading the Bit Stream

Up to now, we considered the input of the decoder as a stream of bits that are extracted using "⟨get n bits $_{142}$⟩" or the *getbit* function. While bytewise access to the input is needed now and then, e.g. for synchronization or tag handling, the efficiency of the decoder depends largely on the ability to read individual chunks of bits. Of course, reading a single bit from a disk is not possible, and even from main memory, one can read only bytes.

8.1 Reading Bits

To ⟨get n bits $_{142}$⟩, with $n \leq 16$, from main memory—where we have only bytewise access—, we simply copy three consecutive bytes, containing the n bits, into a local variable *bits*.

⟨get n bits $_{142}$⟩ ≡ (142)
    $bits$ = ((**unsigned int**) *byte_pointer*[0]) ≪ (**sizeof** ($bits$) * 8 − 8);
    $bits$ |= ((**unsigned int**) *byte_pointer*[1]) ≪ (**sizeof** ($bits$) * 8 − 16);
    $bits$ |= ((**unsigned int**) *byte_pointer*[2]) ≪ (**sizeof** ($bits$) * 8 − 24);

Used in 125, 144, 212, and 424.

We used a variable *byte_pointer*, pointing to the position in memory where we take out the next byte. The variable *bit_offset* indicates where inside the 24 bits the desired n bits start. To complete the reading of n bits, we shift the bits to the left, to compensate for the *bit_offset*, and adjust *byte_pointer* and *bit_offset* according to n. This leaves the desired n bits aligned to the left in the variable *bits*.

⟨get n bits $_{142}$⟩ +≡ (143)
    $bits$ ≪= *bit_offset*;
    bit_offset += n;
    byte_pointer += (*bit_offset* ≫ 3);
    bit_offset = *bit_offset* & $^\#$07;

This is the fast and low level access to the input. Often, we do not need the bits aligned to the left, but aligned to the right, as an **unsigned int**. This type of access is provided by the function *getbit*.

⟨auxiliary functions $_{69}$⟩ +≡ (144)
    static unsigned int *getbit*(**stream** *$*s$, **const int** n)
    { **unsigned int** $bits$;

⟨localize the bit stream ₁₄₆⟩
⟨get n bits ₁₄₂⟩
$bits = (bits \gg (\textbf{sizeof } (bits) * 8 - n));$
⟨globalize the bit stream ₁₄₇⟩
return $bits$;
}

The variables bit_offset and $byte\_pointer$ are naturally part of the

⟨stream data ₂⟩ +≡   (145)
  char bit_offset;
  unsigned char $*byte\_pointer$;

The above function uses two code fragments, one to

⟨localize the bit stream ₁₄₆⟩ ≡   (146)
  register char $bit\_offset = s{\rightarrow}bit\_offset$;
  register unsigned char $*byte\_pointer = s{\rightarrow}byte\_pointer$; Used in 122, 144, and 217.

and one to

⟨globalize the bit stream ₁₄₇⟩ ≡   (147)
  $s{\rightarrow}bit\_offset = bit\_offset$;
  $s{\rightarrow}byte\_pointer = byte\_pointer$;   Used in 122, 144, and 217.

They copy the two variables $byte\_pointer$ and bit_offset from the stream into local variables and back, suggesting to the compiler to use registers if possible. While a perfect compiler should do such an optimization anyhow, real compilers do better if such hints are given by the programmer.

Before a function uses "⟨get n bits ₁₄₂⟩" to read directly from the bit stream, it should ⟨localize the bit stream ₁₄₆⟩ first and ⟨globalize the bit stream ₁₄₇⟩ before it returns—except if the function wants to hide its reading activities from the stream.

8.2 Reading Decoder Input

To read the decoder input into main memory, we use the $input\_read$ function from the $mp3\_open$ call to get bytes into an input $buffer$.

⟨private declarations ₁⟩ +≡   (148)
#**define** BUFFERSIZE $(2 * \text{MAX\_FRAME} + \text{HEADER\_SIZE} + \text{MAX\_RESERVOIR})$

⟨stream data ₂⟩ +≡   (149)
  unsigned char $buffer[\text{BUFFERSIZE}]$;

We have already encountered the variable $byte\_pointer$, giving the position where we take out the next byte. It is initialized to point to the beginning of this buffer.

⟨initialize s ₂₅⟩ +≡   (150)
  $s{\rightarrow}byte\_pointer = s{\rightarrow}buffer$;

We have to keep track not only were we take out bytes and bits, but we also need to know the possible range of valid bytes. For this purpose, we maintain two pointer $start$ and $finish$. $start$ points to the first valid byte in the buffer; $finish$ points right after the last valid byte that we may take out of the *buffer* and may possibly point even past the end of the buffer itself.

⟨ stream data ₂ ⟩ +≡   (151)
   unsigned char ∗*start*;
   unsigned char ∗*finish*;

⟨ initialize *s* ₂₅ ⟩ +≡   (152)
   s→*start* = *s*→*buffer*;
   s→*finish* = *s*→*buffer*;

Further, we want to know what is the current *buffer_position*, that is the position of the first byte in the buffer counted from the beginning of the stream starting with 0.

⟨ stream data ₂ ⟩ +≡   (153)
   int *buffer_position*;

The *buffer_position* makes it possible to convert relative positions inside the *buffer* into absolute byte positions inside the whole stream. For example, the position where the current frame starts is in the variable *frame*.

⟨ stream data ₂ ⟩ +≡   (154)
   unsigned char ∗*frame*;

The value of *frame* can be converted to the *frame_position*, the absolute position of the frame in the stream.

⟨ derive further information ₆₅ ⟩ +≡   (155)
   s→*info*.*frame_position* = *s*→*buffer_position* + (*s*→*frame* − *s*→*buffer*);

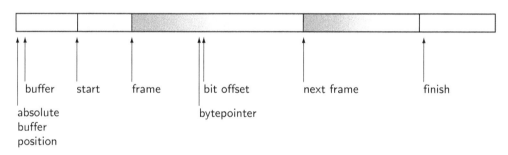

Fig. 19: Access to the input buffer

The *frame* variable was used already much earlier to ⟨ prepare the frame for decoding ₆₂ ⟩. There, we had to

⟨ position the stream past the header ₁₅₆ ⟩ ≡   (156)
   s→*byte_pointer* = *s*→*frame* + HEADER_SIZE;
   s→*bit_offset* = 0;   Used in 62.

This is quite simple using *frame*.

But now it is time to see how the input data actually gets into the *buffer*. To fill the input *buffer*, we determine how many bytes are still in the *buffer* and move them to the beginning of the *buffer*. Then we call *input_read* to fill the remaining *buffer* space. Afterwards, we adjust *finish* and, on occasion, the stream *state*.

⟨ auxiliary functions $_{69}$ ⟩ +≡   (157)
  static void *fill_input_buffer*(**stream** *∗s*)
  { **int** *size* = *s*→*finish* − *s*→*start*;

    ⟨ move buffer content left $_{158}$ ⟩
    size = *s*→*input_read*(*s*→*info.id*, *s*→*finish*, BUFFERSIZE − *size*);
    if (*size* ≤ 0) *s*→*state* = *s*→*state* | END_OF_INPUT;
    else *s*→*finish* = *s*→*finish* + *size*;
  }

When we move buffer data, we have to update *start*, *frame*, *byte_pointer*, *finish*, and *buffer_position*.

⟨ move buffer content left $_{158}$ ⟩ ≡   (158)
  if (*size* > 0)
  { **int** *distance* = *s*→*start* − *s*→*buffer*;

    if (*distance* > 0)
    { *memmove*(*s*→*buffer*, *s*→*start*, *size*);
      s→*start* = *s*→*buffer*;
      if (*s*→*frame* ≠ NULL) *s*→*frame* = *s*→*frame* − *distance*;
      s→*byte_pointer* = *s*→*byte_pointer* − *distance*;
      s→*finish* = *s*→*finish* − *distance*;
      s→*buffer_position* = *s*→*buffer_position* + *distance*;
    }
  }
                                         Used in 157 and 178.

The decoder can not fill the input buffer repeatedly unless, once in a while, it will also release buffer space. Discarding data in the buffer is done by moving the *start* pointer forward. This is done frame by frame, just when the decoder is about to advance to the next frame.

⟨ release the *buffer* for current frame $_{159}$ ⟩ ≡   (159)
  if (*s*→*info.layer* ≠ 3) *s*→*start* = *s*→*frame*;   Used in 166.

Layer III streams keep a reservoir of bytes, preceding the current frame (see Section 13.1). To be on the save side, we make sure that even a layer III stream never buffers more than it possibly needs for this reservoir.

⟨ release the *buffer* for current frame $_{159}$ ⟩ +≡   (160)
  else
    if (*s*→*frame* − *s*→*start* > MAX_RESERVOIR)
      s→*start* = *s*→*frame* − MAX_RESERVOIR;

8.3 Synchronization

The searching for the start of a frame is called "synchronizing". When we try to synchronize the stream, we use bytewise access to the input, because frames always start on a byte boundary. After we skipped the remaining bits in the current byte, we assume that the next thing in the input is a new frame. Therefore, we ensure that the complete frame header is in the buffer and try to decode it. If the decoding was successful, we ⟨ verify the frame $_{164}$ ⟩. If the decoding of the header did not work, we suspect a tag, and process it. In case nothing works, we probably found some garbage in the stream and start over. (We should not forget to discard some of the garbage in the buffer unless we want to get stuck on it.)

The function *synchronize* returns NULL if unable to synchronize the stream. Otherwise it will ⟨ verify the frame $_{164}$ ⟩ (which involves computing all *info*'s and loading the entire frame into the *buffer*) and return a valid *frame* pointer.

⟨ auxiliary functions $_{69}$ ⟩ +≡   (161)
  static unsigned char *∗synchronize*(**stream** *∗s*)
  { **if** (*s→bit_offset* > 0)
    { *s→byte_pointer* ++;
      s→bit_offset = 0;
    }
    do { **while** (*s→byte_pointer* + HEADER_SIZE > *s→finish*)
        if (*s→state* & END_OF_INPUT) **return** NULL;
        else *fill_input_buffer*(*s*);
      if (*decode_header*(&*s→info*, *s→byte_pointer*))
      { *s→frame* = *s→byte_pointer*;
        ⟨ verify the frame $_{164}$ ⟩
      }
      else ⟨ process tags $_{172}$ ⟩
      if (*s→byte_pointer* − *s→start* > MAX_RESERVOIR)
        s→start = *s→byte_pointer* − MAX_RESERVOIR;
    } **while** (1);
    return NULL;
  }

Before we can verify a frame, we make sure it is completely in the buffer.

⟨ load the entire frame $_{162}$ ⟩ ≡   (162)
  while (*s→frame* + *s→info.frame_size* > *s→finish*)
    if (*s→state* & END_OF_INPUT) ⟨ unexpected end of input $_{163}$ ⟩
    else *fill_input_buffer*(*s*);   Used in 164 and 166.

If, while loading the frame, unexpectedly, we encounter the end of the input, we return NULL. Only layer III frames (because of the reservoir) can sometimes work with a partial last frame.

⟨ unexpected end of input $_{163}$ ⟩ ≡   (163)
  { **if** (*s→info.layer* ≡ 3 ∧ ⟨ partial last frame $_{331}$ ⟩) **return** *s→frame*;

else return NULL;
}

Used in 162.

If we do not have a free format stream (we postpone this until the next section) and are not required to check for multiple syncwords, the verification of a frame looks like this:

⟨ verify the frame $_{164}$ ⟩ ≡   (164)
  { **if** $(s{\rightarrow}info.free\_format)$ ⟨ verify free format frame $_{167}$ ⟩
  else
  { ⟨ load the entire frame $_{162}$ ⟩
    if $(s{\rightarrow}options.flags$ & MP3_SYNC_1) **return** $s{\rightarrow}frame$;
    else ⟨ check multiple syncwords $_{165}$ ⟩
  }
  $s{\rightarrow}frame$ = NULL;
  $s{\rightarrow}byte\_pointer$ ++;
  }

Used in 161.

In case we were unlucky, we reset the *frame* pointer to NULL and advance the stream.

If more than one syncword is required, we load the next header and try to decode it. If a third syncword is required, we repeat this step. While doing this, we have to cope with two possible exceptions: We might encounter the end of the file, and we regard this as if the additional syncword had been found. Or we encounter a sudden switch to a free format bit stream. This is not valid according to the standard, but might happen if two MP3 files are just concatenated. Hence, we regard this case as an other form of "file end" and accept the frame.

⟨ check multiple syncwords $_{165}$ ⟩ ≡   (165)
  { **mp3_info** i = { 0 } ;
    while $(s{\rightarrow}frame + s{\rightarrow}info.frame\_size$ + HEADER_SIZE $> s{\rightarrow}finish)$
      if $(s{\rightarrow}state$ & END_OF_INPUT) **return** $s{\rightarrow}frame$;
      else $fill\_input\_buffer(s)$;
    if $(decode\_header(\&i, s{\rightarrow}frame + s{\rightarrow}info.frame\_size))$
    { **if** $(s{\rightarrow}options.flags$ & MP3_SYNC_3)
      { **while** $(s{\rightarrow}frame + s{\rightarrow}info.frame\_size + i.frame\_size$ + HEADER_SIZE $>$
            $s{\rightarrow}finish)$
        if $(s{\rightarrow}state$ & END_OF_INPUT) **return** $s{\rightarrow}frame$;
        else $fill\_input\_buffer(s)$;
      if $(i.free\_format)$ **return** $s{\rightarrow}frame$;
      else if $(decode\_header(\&i, s{\rightarrow}frame + s{\rightarrow}info.frame\_size + i.frame\_size))$
        return $s{\rightarrow}frame$;
      }
      else return $s{\rightarrow}frame$;
    }
  }

Used in 164.

Once the stream is synchronized, and we have a valid frame pointer, we need not go through all the effort of synchronization to get to the next frame. If we can rely on the current *frame*, we know its size and can figure out where the next frame is about to start. If we find at the predicted location a valid header, we accept this location as the start of the next frame.

⟨ auxiliary functions ₆₉ ⟩ +≡   (166)
  static unsigned char *∗next_frame*(**stream** *∗s*)
  { **int** *previous_free_format*;

    s→frame = *s→frame* + *s→info.frame_size*;
    s→info.frame++;
    while (*s→frame* + `HEADER_SIZE` > *s→finish*)
      if (*s→state* & `END_OF_INPUT`) **return** `NULL`;
      else *fill_input_buffer*(*s*);
    previous_free_format = *s→info.free_format*;
    if (¬*decode_header*(&*s→info*, *s→frame*)) **return** `NULL`;
    s→byte_pointer = *s→frame*;
    s→bit_offset = 0;
    if (*s→info.free_format* ∧ ¬*previous_free_format*) **return** `NULL`;
    ⟨ release the *buffer* for current frame ₁₅₉ ⟩
    ⟨ load the entire frame ₁₆₂ ⟩
    return *s→frame*;
  }

The above function will advance the stream to the next frame, update the *info*'s, load the complete frame into the *buffer*, and returns the pointer to the new frame. If anything goes wrong, it returns `NULL`. The main decoding loop, calling this function, will then resort to the more powerful function *synchronize* to get back on track.

8.4 Free Format Bit Streams

Free format bit streams specify the bit rate only indirectly through the size of the frame, and once the bit rate is determined, it remains constant. The size of the frame is again given only indirectly by the distance of two syncwords. Hence for these streams, the problem of synchronization is closely connected to the problem of determining the bit rate. To verify a free format stream, we start with a tentative *frame_size*—the size of the header is certainly a lower bound—and increase it until we find a matching free format header.

⟨ verify free format frame ₁₆₇ ⟩ ≡   (167)
  { **int** *frame_size* = `HEADER_SIZE`;

    do { **if** (++*frame_size* > `MAX_FRAME`) **break**;
      ⟨ find a matching header ₁₆₉ ⟩
      ⟨ verify the matching header ₁₇₁ ⟩
    } **while** (1);
  }

Used in 164.

A matching header should

- start with a byte of all 1-bits, of course,
- should match in the second byte seven bits of the previous header—syncword, version, and layer—followed by a protection bit, that we do not care for,
- and should then match in the third byte an other six bits of the previous header—bit rate and sample rate.

We test this by combining the individual header bytes with a mask, to suppress all bits we do not care for, and then test for equality.

⟨ matching free format header ₁₆₈ ⟩ ≡   (168)
　(s→frame[frame_size] ≡ #FF ∧
　　　(s→frame[frame_size + 1] & #FE) ≡ (s→frame[1] & #FE) ∧
　　　(s→frame[frame_size + 2] & #FC) ≡ (s→frame[2] & #FC))   Used in 169.

Once we know what we are looking for, we just make sure that we have enough bytes in the buffer and keep on looking as long as we have not found it. Only in case of an end of input, we give up.

⟨ find a matching header ₁₆₉ ⟩ ≡   (169)
　while (s→frame + frame_size + HEADER_SIZE > s→finish)
　　if (s→state & END_OF_INPUT) **return** NULL;
　　else fill_input_buffer(s);
　if (¬⟨ matching free format header ₁₆₈ ⟩) **continue**;   Used in 167.

In spite of the good intentions, the first version of this code produced an infinite loop. In one instance, the frame plus reservoir did not fit into the buffer, so there was no matching header and no end of file either...

A simple calculation gives us the maximum frame size. It is reached in layer 2 for the maximum bit rate of 384 kbit/s and the minimum sample rate 32 kHz, inclusive padding. While the standard specifies a slightly smaller maximum size (for layer III and 48 kHz), we stay on the save side. This calculation is based on the bit rate table, but the decoder is not required to support larger bit rates even when in free format mode.

⟨ private declarations ₁ ⟩ +≡   (170)
#**define** MAX_FRAME 1729

This constant is used to determine the size of the input buffer.

After we found the matching header, we verify it.

⟨ verify the matching header ₁₇₁ ⟩ ≡   (171)
　{ **mp3_info** i = { 0 }, *info = &i;

　　if (¬decode_header(info, s→frame + frame_size)) **continue**;
　　s→info.frame_size = frame_size;
　　⟨ determine free format bit_rate ₉₁ ⟩
　　if (s→options.flags & MP3_SYNC_3)
　　{ info→bit_rate = s→info.bit_rate;

$\langle$ determine *frame_size* $_{90}$ $\rangle$
while ($s{\rightarrow}frame + s{\rightarrow}info.frame_size + info{\rightarrow}frame_size + $ `HEADER_SIZE` $>$
        $s{\rightarrow}finish$)
    if ($s{\rightarrow}state$ & `END_OF_INPUT`) **return** $s{\rightarrow}frame$;
    else *fill_input_buffer*(s);
    if (*decode_header*(*info*, $s{\rightarrow}frame + s{\rightarrow}info.frame\_size + info{\rightarrow}frame\_size$))
        return $s{\rightarrow}frame$;
    else break;
}
else return $s{\rightarrow}frame$;
}
                                                                Used in 167.

The code is lengthy, but not too complicated. First, we decode the matching header, which should succeed. Then, we set the frame size for the current frame and determine the bit rate. If we need to check a third header, we copy the bit rate into the matching header and determine its frame size (which might change because of a different padding bit). We load enough bytes and try to decode a header at the precomputed position.

8.5 Tags

The processing of tags is part of the stream synchronization. If a tag handler exists, it is called, otherwise one byte is skipped before synchronization proceeds.

$\langle$ process tags $_{172}$ $\rangle$ $\equiv$ (172)
    { **if** ($s{\rightarrow}options.tag\_handler \neq$ `NULL`) { $\langle$ call the *tag_handler* $_{174}$ $\rangle$ }
    else $s{\rightarrow}byte\_pointer$ ++;
    }
                                                                Used in 161.

The tag handler needs a way to distinguish tags from garbage, or to say it more politely, known tags from unknown tags. For this purpose, the tag handler uses the *tag_read* function. It can read the initial part of the suspected tag into a buffer, examine the buffer and push the bytes back into the buffer if they can not be processed (for an example see page 34). To keep track of the number of bytes that the tag handler reads, the variable *tag_size* is used.

$\langle$ stream data $_2$ $\rangle$ $+\equiv$ (173)
    int *tag_size*;

We set it to zero, and then

$\langle$ call the *tag_handler* $_{174}$ $\rangle$ $\equiv$ (174)
    $s{\rightarrow}tag\_size = 0$;
    $s{\rightarrow}options.tag\_handler$($s{\rightarrow}info.id$, *tag_read*);
    if ($s{\rightarrow}tag\_size \leq 0$) $s{\rightarrow}byte\_pointer$ ++;
    else $\langle$ remove the tag from the input $_{179}$ $\rangle$ Used in 172.

If nothing was read from the stream, the stream is advanced by one byte, otherwise remainders of the tag are removed from the input buffer.

The function that the tag handler must use to read any data from the input is the *tag_read* function.

⟨ private declarations $_1$ ⟩ +≡   (175)
    static ⟨ *tag_read* function $_{38}$ ⟩;

The *tag_read* function will retrieve the stream and then give the tag handler what ever it needs.

⟨ auxiliary functions $_{69}$ ⟩ +≡   (176)
    static ⟨ *tag_read* function $_{38}$ ⟩
    { **stream** *∗s*;

      if (*buffer* ≡ NULL) **return** MP3_ERROR_NO_BUFFER;
      ⟨ retrieve the stream $_{52}$ ⟩
      if (*count* > 0) ⟨ read tag $_{177}$ ⟩
      else if (*count* < 0) ⟨ push back tag $_{178}$ ⟩
      s→tag_size = *s→tag_size* + *count*;
      return *count*;
    }

As long as bytes are available in the streams input buffer, they are taken from there, otherwise they come directly from the input.

⟨ read tag $_{177}$ ⟩ ≡   (177)
    { **int** *available* = *s→finish* − *s→byte_pointer* − *s→tag_size*;

      if (*available* > 0)
      { **if** (*count* > *available*) *count* = *available*;
        memmove(*buffer*, *s→byte_pointer* + *s→tag_size*, *count*);
      }
      else *count* = *s→input_read*(*s→info.id*, *buffer*, *count*);
    }
                                                    Used in 176.

As long as reading and writing happens in the streams input buffer, returning bytes reverses the reading process. If the tag is larger, we first move the data preceeding the tag in the input buffer entirely to the left. Now at least BUFFERSIZE − MAX_RESERVOIR bytes can be written back into the input buffer. To push back bytes into the input, we take them from the buffer and move them to the streams input buffer.

⟨ push back tag $_{178}$ ⟩ ≡   (178)
    { **int** *available* = *s→finish* − *s→byte_pointer* − *s→tag_size*;

      if (*available* > 0)
      { **if** (*s→tag_size* + *count* < 0) *count* = −*s→tag_size*;
        memmove(*s→byte_pointer* + *s→tag_size* + *count*, *buffer*, −*count*);
      }
      else
      { **int** *size* = *s→byte_pointer* − *s→start*;

        ⟨ move buffer content left $_{158}$ ⟩

```
    if (s→tag_size > BUFFERSIZE − size)
    {  s→buffer_position = s→buffer_position + s→tag_size − (BUFFERSIZE − size);
       s→tag_size = BUFFERSIZE − size;
    }
    s→finish = s→byte_pointer + s→tag_size;
    memmove(s→byte_pointer + s→tag_size + count, buffer, −count);
  }
}
```
Used in 176.

Once the tag handler returns, we need to remove the tag from the input. If there is valid data before and after the tag in the input buffer, we close the gap between both data areas by moving the data preceeding the tag forward. If there is no data after the tag, we adjust *finish*.

⟨ remove the tag from the input $_{179}$ ⟩ ≡   (179)
```
  {  int post = s→finish − s→byte_pointer − s→tag_size;
     int pre = s→byte_pointer − s→start;

     if (post > 0)
     {  if (pre > 0) memmove(s→start + s→tag_size, s→start, pre);
        s→byte_pointer = s→byte_pointer + s→tag_size;
        s→start = s→start + s→tag_size;
        if (s→frame ≠ NULL) s→frame = s→frame + s→tag_size;
     }
     else  s→finish = s→byte_pointer;
  }
```
Used in 174.

8.6 Information Callbacks and Breaks

Before thinking about how to make an information callback, we should consider whether to make it at all. In the simplest case, we have a callback exception (see page 31) which implies an unconditional callback.

⟨ process callback exception $_{180}$ ⟩ ≡   (180)
```
  int result = s→options.info_callback(&(s→info));

  if (result < 0) return result;
```
⟨ update *flags* $_{181}$ ⟩   Used in 61.

The *result* may specify either a negative return value for *mp3_read* or a modification of the *flags*.

⟨ update *flags* $_{181}$ ⟩ ≡   (181)
```
  if (result & #FF)
  {  s→options.flags = (s→options.flags & ~#FF) | (result & #FF);
     result = result & ~#FF;
  }
```
Used in 180 and 188.

The general case is more complex. Invocation of the callback depends on the *flags* and the *changes* in the new frame. The *flags* are under the control of the application, the *changes* are initialized and maintained by the decoder.

⟨ infos $_{31}$ ⟩ +≡   (182)
   int *changes*;

⟨ initialize *s* $_{25}$ ⟩ +≡   (183)
   s→*info*.*changes* = MP3_INFO_FRAME | MP3_INFO_ONCE;

Changes for MP3_INFO_FRAME, MP3_INFO_ONCE, MP3_INFO_CRC, and MP3_INFO_READ are easy to manage. To detect changes in the PCM or MPG format, we compare the header of the new frame, with the *previous_header*, applying a mask to filter out those bits that influence the respective format.

⟨ detect changes $_{184}$ ⟩ ≡   (184)
   if ((*s*→*info*.*header* ⊕ *s*→*previous_header*) & $^\#$FF180CC0)
     s→*info*.*changes* |= MP3_INFO_PCM;
   if ((*s*→*info*.*header* ⊕ *s*→*previous_header*) & $^\#$FF1FF0CF)
     s→*info*.*changes* |= MP3_INFO_MPG;
   s→*previous_header* = *s*→*info*.*header*;   Used in 186.

Note that the masks include part of the syncword. This is a convenient way to make sure a change is signaled at the very beginning of the stream, since the *previous_header* is initialized to zero.

⟨ stream data $_2$ ⟩ +≡   (185)
   unsigned int *previous_header*;

After this preparation, we know about all interesting changes and decide whether to make the call.

⟨ issue *info_callback* $_{186}$ ⟩ ≡   (186)
   ⟨ detect changes $_{184}$ ⟩
   if (*s*→*options*.*flags* & *s*→*info*.*changes*)
   { **int** *result* = *s*→*options*.*info_callback*(&(*s*→*info*));
     s→*info*.*changes* = MP3_INFO_FRAME;
     if (*result* ≠ MP3_CONTINUE) { ⟨ process callback result $_{187}$ ⟩}
   }   Used in 61.

After the call, we have to process the *result*. If negative, we return from *mp3_read* passing the result through.

⟨ process callback result $_{187}$ ⟩ ≡   (187)
   if (*result* < 0) **return** *result*;   Used in 186.

A positive *result* may

- contain an update to the *flags*.

   ⟨ process callback result $_{187}$ ⟩ +≡   (188)
     ⟨ update *flags* $_{181}$ ⟩

- specify an immediate return from *mp3_read*.

  ⟨ process callback result $_{187}$ ⟩ +≡   (189)
  >   **if** (*result* ≡ MP3_BREAK) **return** *s*→*info.samples*;

- or specify a special output mode (see Appendix A.1).

  ⟨ process callback result $_{187}$ ⟩ +≡   (190)
  >   **if** (*result* & MP3_MUTE) *output_mode* = MUTE;
  >   **else if** (*result* & MP3_REPEAT) *output_mode* = REPEAT;
  >   **else if** (*result* & MP3_REPAIR) *output_mode* = REPAIR;
  >   **if** (*result* & MP3_SKIP) *output_mode* = *output_mode* | SKIP;

9 Improving the Bit Packing: Layer II

If we look at an MPEG version 1 layer I bit stream, for example the file `f16.mpg` provided by the standard for compliance checking, we get the following data:

Property	Value
Frequency	44,1 kHz
Bit Rate	384 kbit/s
Mode	stereo
CRC	yes
Frames	49
Bytes	20480

Tab. 10: Properties of layer I file `f16.mpg`

Now let's see how these 20480 bytes are used to encode a total of 37632 Samples from 49 frames · 12 blocks · 2 channels · 32 subbands.

Use		Byte	Bit per Sample	Percentage
Header	$49 \cdot 4 =$	196	0.0052	0.96 %
CRC	$49 \cdot 2 =$	98	0.0025	0.48 %
Bit Allocation	$32 \cdot 2 \cdot 49 \cdot 4/8 =$	1568	0.33	7.66 %
Scalefactor	$32 \cdot 2 \cdot 49 \cdot 6/8 =$	2352	0.50	11.48 %
	Subtotal $=$	4214	0.8377	20.58 %
Samples	$20480 - 4214 =$	16266	3.46	79.42 %

Tab. 11: Statistics for layer I file `f16.mpg`

Bit allocation and scalefactors occupy about 19 % of the bit stream. Hence, it might be a good idea to look into ways of reducing this overhead.

9.1 Bit Allocation Tables

The first observation is that the average number of quantization levels needed to encode a sample varies greatly depending on subband, bit rate, and sample frequency. Therefore, layer II introduces tables, called "layer II bit allocation tables", to tailor the use of bits to the individual needs of the encoding.

⟨ derive further information $_{65}$ ⟩ +≡   (191)
   if $(s{\rightarrow}info.layer \equiv 2)$
   { ⟨ select layer II bit allocation table $_{192}$ ⟩
    ⟨ reduce layer II *bound* $_{194}$ ⟩
   }

There are four different tables: table a, table b, table c, and table d. The complete rules to select the correct table, based on bit rate per channel and sample rate, are as follows:

⟨ select layer II bit allocation table $_{192}$ ⟩ ≡   (192)
   if $(s{\rightarrow}info.version \equiv \texttt{MP3\_V1\_0})$
   { **int** $bit\_rate\_per\_channel = s{\rightarrow}info.bit\_rate/s{\rightarrow}info.channels;$

    if $(bit\_rate\_per\_channel \leq 48000)$
    { **if** $(s{\rightarrow}info.sample\_rate \equiv 32000)$ ⟨ select table d $_{419}$ ⟩
     else ⟨ select table c $_{199}$ ⟩
    }

    else if $(bit\_rate\_per\_channel \leq 80000 \lor s{\rightarrow}info.sample\_rate \equiv 48000)$
     ⟨ select table a $_{417}$ ⟩
    else ⟨ select table b $_{418}$ ⟩
   }   Used in 191.

Lets look at one such table, table c, which is used for sample frequencies of 44.1 kHz or 48 kHz combined with bit rates of 48 kbit/s or less per channel.

Sub-band	bit *nbal*	Index
		0 1 2 3 4 5 6 7 8 9 10 11 12 13 14 15
0	4	– 3 5 9 15 31 63 127 255 511 1023 2047 4095 8191 16383 32767
1	4	– 3 5 9 15 31 63 127 255 511 1023 2047 4095 8191 16383 32767
2	3	– 3 5 9 15 31 63 127
3	3	– 3 5 9 15 31 63 127
4	3	– 3 5 9 15 31 63 127
5	3	– 3 5 9 15 31 63 127
6	3	– 3 5 9 15 31 63 127
7	3	– 3 5 9 15 31 63 127

Tab. 12: Standard layer II bit allocation table B.2c

The first column of the table, gives the number of the subband. It stops after eight subbands, because the bit rate is so low that we can not afford to allocate any bits for all the other subbands. As a consequence, we will have no bit allocation data, no scalefactors, and no sample data either for these subbands. So with each table there is an associated number of subbands for which we have data. When we ⟨select table c 199⟩, we store this number as $sblimit[0]$ ($sblimit[1]$ is used only in layer III).

⟨stream data 2⟩ +≡   (193)
  int $sblimit[\text{CHANNELS}]$;

We have used the variable $bound$ in layer I as an upper bound on the number of subbands for which we might have scalefactors in both channels and have set it to the maximum 32, if joint stereo was not enabled. Now, we can reduce the maximum considerably using the value of $sblimit$.

⟨reduce layer II $bound$ 194⟩ ≡   (194)
  if $(s{\rightarrow}info.mode \neq \text{MP3\_JOINT\_STEREO})$
    $s{\rightarrow}info.bound = s{\rightarrow}sblimit[0]$;   Used in 191.

This setting of $bound$ makes the following code work independent of the actual stereo mode.

⟨read the layer II $bit\_allocation$ 195⟩ ≡   (195)
  { **int** sb, ch;
    for $(sb = 0;\ sb < s{\rightarrow}info.bound;\ sb{+}{+})$
      for $(ch = 0;\ ch < s{\rightarrow}info.channels;\ ch{+}{+})$ ⟨retrieve the $bit\_allocation$ 198⟩
    for $(\ ;\ sb < s{\rightarrow}sblimit[0];\ sb{+}{+})$
    { $ch = 0$;
      ⟨retrieve the $bit\_allocation$ 198⟩
      $side\_info[sb][1].bit\_allocation = side\_info[sb][0].bit\_allocation$;
    }
  }   Used in 210.

The second column of the table, called $nbal$, gives for each subband the number of bits needed to encode an index i into the right part of the table, the actual bit allocation. Here, it is four bits for subbands 0 and 1 and three bits for the subbands from 2 to 7. When we ⟨select table c 199⟩, we point the variable $nbal$ to this column of the table.

⟨stream data 2⟩ +≡   (196)
  const char $*nbal$;

In the right part of the table, we find for each index and subband the number of quantization steps, which is directly related to the number of bits needed to store the samples. We can therefore derive from it a table, called $nbit$, that gives for each subband sb and column index i, the number of bits used to encode one sample. When we ⟨select table c 199⟩, we make $nbit$ point to this table.

⟨stream data 2⟩ +≡   (197)
  const char $(*nbit)[16]$;

We summarize: To ⟨retrieve the *bit_allocation* $_{198}$⟩ for a certain subband *sb* <
bound ≤ *sblimit*[0], we take *nbal* from the table. If *nbal* is not zero, we read that
many bits from the stream, and use it as index *i* into the *nbit* table. Here, we finally
find the correct *bit_allocation*.

⟨retrieve the *bit_allocation* $_{198}$⟩ ≡   (198)
   { **int** *n*, *nbal* = *s*→*nbal*[*sb*];

     if (*nbal* > 0)
     { **int** *i*;

       i = *getbit*(*s*, *nbal*);
       n = *s*→*nbit*[*sb*][*i*];
     }

     else *n* = 0;
     side_info[*sb*][*ch*].*bit_allocation* = *n*;
   }   Used in 195.

    To have a complete example, this is how we

⟨select table c $_{199}$⟩ ≡   (199)
   { **static const char** *nbal*[32] = { 4, 4, 3, 3, 3, 3, 3, 3 };
    static const char *nbit*[8][16] = {
      { 0, −5, −7, −10, 4, 5, 6, 7, 8, 9, 10, 11, 12, 13, 14, 15 },
      { 0, −5, −7, −10, 4, 5, 6, 7, 8, 9, 10, 11, 12, 13, 14, 15 },
      { 0, −5, −7, −10, 4, 5, 6, 7 },
      { 0, −5, −7, −10, 4, 5, 6, 7 },
      { 0, −5, −7, −10, 4, 5, 6, 7 },
      { 0, −5, −7, −10, 4, 5, 6, 7 },
      { 0, −5, −7, −10, 4, 5, 6, 7 },
      { 0, −5, −7, −10, 4, 5, 6, 7 }
    };

    s→*sblimit*[0] = 8;
    s→*nbal* = *nbal*;
    s→*nbit* = *nbit*;
   }   Used in 192.

The other tables are given in Appendix A.8.

    The process of repeated table lookup is very complicated, and we conclude this
section with a complete example computation using table c. Table c indicates in the
nbal column that for subband 5, we need to read 3 bits. Assume, we read the three
bits "100", then these bits are interpreted as the number 4, and we find under index
i = 4 in the right part of the table that subband 5 is encoded with 15 quantization
levels. Four bits are just enough to encode that many levels and indeed, looking into
the *nbit* table above, we find for *i* = 4 and *sb* = 5 the number 4. This is the required
bit_allocation.

But things get even more complex. Assume we read the three bits "011", then these bits are interpreted as the number 3, and we find under index $i = 3$ in the right part of the table that subband 5 is encoded with 9 quantization levels.

Nine levels? How many bits are needed to encode nine levels? Three bits can encode 7 different levels and four bits encodes 15 different levels. So, 3 is not enough and 4 is too much. The *nbit* table displayed above gives a value of -10 which won't help us either. Here, an other bit saving technique is used: grouping.

9.2 Grouping

Grouping together three sample values, of nine levels each, we can store the whole group with only 10 bits. That is $10/3 = 3.33$ bit per value—just about what is needed for nine levels. Grouping is needed for 3, 5, and 9 levels. All the other levels have the form $2^n - 1$ and can be efficiently encoded with n bits without grouping.

3 values with 3 levels each make $3 \cdot 3 \cdot 3 = 27$ combinations and can be encoded with 5 bits; 3 values with 5 levels each make $5 \cdot 5 \cdot 5 = 125$ combinations and can be encoded with 7 bits; and 3 values with 9 levels each make $9 \cdot 9 \cdot 9 = 729$ combinations and can easily be encoded with 10 bits.

The trick is simply to encode the three values as a three digit number in a number system which uses the number of levels as base. Then, if *nlevels* is the number of levels and c is the code for the whole group, we obtain the three "digits" *s0*, *s1*, and *s2* by

$\langle$ degrouping c $_{200}$ $\rangle \equiv$ (200)
    { **int** *tmp*;

      s0 = *c* % *nlevels*;
      tmp = *c*/*nlevels*;
      s1 = *tmp* % *nlevels*;
      tmp = *tmp*/*nlevels*;
      s2 = *tmp* % *nlevels*;

    }
                                                           Used in 422.

To be able to tell samples that are encoded as a group from samples encoded without grouping, we use negative values for the *bit_allocation* to indicate grouping.

It is faster to precompute the degrouped and scaled samples and put them into an array, from where we can $\langle$ read three grouped samples $_{424}$ $\rangle$. The tables are generated in Appendix A.9.

Using this information, we can

$\langle$ read a scaled sample group $_{201}$ $\rangle \equiv$ (201)
    { **int** *sample*;

      if $(n > 0)$
        { $\langle$ read the *sample* $_{125}$ $\rangle$
        $\boldsymbol{y}[i][ch][sb] = sample * f$;
        $\langle$ read the *sample* $_{125}$ $\rangle$
        $\boldsymbol{y}[i+1][ch][sb] = sample * f$;

⟨ read the *sample* ₁₂₅ ⟩

$y[i+2][ch][sb] = sample * f;$

}

else if $(n < 0)$ ⟨ read three grouped samples ₄₂₄ ⟩

else $y[i][ch][sb] = y[i+1][ch][sb] = y[i+2][ch][sb] = 0.0;$

}

Used in 218.

The above code is simple. If the number n of bits to read is positive, we have no grouping. Hence, we perform the same reading procedure as in layer I, but three times and we get three consecutive samples for the same subband. A negative value of n indicates grouping. In this case, we ⟨ read three grouped samples ₄₂₄ ⟩. If n is zero, no bits are allocated, and the sample value is zero.

9.3 Scalefactors

Scalefactors offer a separate opportunity to save some extra bits. Musical signals often exhibit some stationary behavior if observed in the frequency domain. If this is the case, information for one block of samples, for instance the scalefactors, can be reused for a second or third block of data. To facilitate the reuse of scalefactors, layer II packs three groups of 12 blocks of samples into one frame. In layer I, 12 subband samples shared the same scalefactors; as an improvement, in layer II the same scalefactor can be shared by up to three groups.

⟨ private declarations ₁ ⟩ +≡   (202)

#**define** GROUPS 3

The scalefactor selection information is stored in the stream right after the bit allocation information.

⟨ read the scalefactor selection information ₂₀₃ ⟩ ≡   (203)

   { **int** sb, ch;

     for $(sb = 0; \ sb < s{\rightarrow}sblimit[0]; \ sb{+}{+})$

       for $(ch = 0; \ ch < s{\rightarrow}info.channels; \ ch{+}{+})$

         if $(side\_info[sb][ch].bit\_allocation \neq 0) \ side\_info[sb][ch].scfi = getbit(s, 2);$

   }

Used in 210.

For each subband below the *sblimit* and for each channel, as long as there is some sample data at all, two bits give the necessary sharing information, which we store as part of the

⟨ side information ₁₀₅ ⟩ +≡   (204)

   char *scfi*;

We will use them below to ⟨ read shared scalefactors ₂₀₅ ⟩.

The sharing information of these two bits is given by the following table:

Bit	$scfi$	Scalefactor sharing information
00	0	three separate scalefactors for group 0, 1, and 2
01	1	two scalefactors; group 0 and 1 share the same scalefactor
10	2	one scalefactors; group 0, 1, and 2 share the same scalefactor
11	3	two scalefactors; group 1 and 2 share the same scalefactor

Tab. 13: Scalefactor sharing information

As in layer I, we get the scalefactors from the global *mfactors* table and store them as part of the ⟨ side information $_{105}$ ⟩. Here it comes in handy that for each subband, we have allocated not only a single *mfactor* but one for each group (see page 52).

Using the information of Table 13, we can

⟨ read shared scalefactors $_{205}$ ⟩ ≡   (205)
```
{ int i;
   if (scfi ≡ 0)
   { ⟨read scalefactor index i 113⟩
     si→mfactor[0] = mfactors[n][i];
     ⟨read scalefactor index i 113⟩
     si→mfactor[1] = mfactors[n][i];
     ⟨read scalefactor index i 113⟩
     si→mfactor[2] = mfactors[n][i];
   }
   else if (scfi ≡ 1)
   { ⟨read scalefactor index i 113⟩
     si→mfactor[1] = si→mfactor[0] = mfactors[n][i];
     ⟨read scalefactor index i 113⟩
     si→mfactor[2] = mfactors[n][i];
   }
   else if (scfi ≡ 2)
   { ⟨read scalefactor index i 113⟩
     si→mfactor[0] = si→mfactor[1] = si→mfactor[2] = mfactors[n][i];
   }
   else
   { ⟨read scalefactor index i 113⟩
     si→mfactor[0] = mfactors[n][i];
     ⟨read scalefactor index i 113⟩
     si→mfactor[2] = si→mfactor[1] = mfactors[n][i];
   }
}
```
Used in 206.

In the bit stream, layer II scalefactors come right after the scalefactor sharing information. Scalefactors are read for all subbands below $sblimit[0]$ that have a nonzero
$bit\_allocation$. As a difference to layer I (see page 52), we observe sharing and—not
unexpected—some special handling of negative n values, indicating grouping.

$\langle$ read the layer II scalefactors $_{206}\,\rangle \equiv$ (206)
```
{ int sb, ch;
  for (sb = 0; sb < s→sblimit[0]; sb++)
    for (ch = 0; ch < s→info.channels; ch++)
    { side_information *si = &(side_info[sb][ch]);
      int n = si→bit_allocation;
      int scfi = si→scfi;
      if (n ≠ 0)
      { if (n < 0) ⟨handle negative n for grouped values 207⟩
        ⟨read shared scalefactors 205⟩
      }
      else  si→mfactor[0] = si→mfactor[1] = si→mfactor[2] = 1.0;
    }
}
```
                                                                            Used in 210.

The processing of modified factor has to be adapted for grouped values ($n = -5$,
-7, and -10). In the layer I table, we find the right values only if the number of
quantization levels has the form $2^n - 1$. In the case of grouped values this is not
always the case. For $n = -5$, we have 3 steps. Since $3 = 2^2 - 1$, we are lucky and can
use $n = 2$ instead. Not so for $n = -7$ and $n = -10$.

Fortunately, the table we use to store the $mfactors$ for layer I did not use the
columns for $n = 0$ and $n = 1$. We can now use column 0 to store the $mfactors$ that
belong to $n = -10$ and column 1 to store the $mfactors$ for $n = -7$.

This is how we

$\langle$ handle negative n for grouped values $_{207}\,\rangle \equiv$ (207)
```
{ if (n ≡ -5) n = 2;
  else if (n ≡ -7) n = 1;
  else if (n ≡ -10) n = 0;
}
```
                                                                            Used in 206.

Next, we consider how to get the right values into the global $mfactors$ table. For
$n = -7$, we have 5 steps and the correct value to scale the raw sample value is
according to the standard (Table B4) 8/5. Similar, for $n = -10$, that is 9 steps, we
should scale with the factor 16/9. The following code is very similar to the layer I
code for the $\langle$ modified factor $_{127}\,\rangle$ (see page 58).

$\langle$ layer II modified factor for $n = -10$ $_{208}\,\rangle \equiv$ (208)
```
-1 * ⟨output scalefactor 136⟩ *
⟨fi 126⟩/
(9 * (((int) 1) ≪ ((sizeof(int) * 8) - 1 - 4)))
```
                                                                            Used in 132.

Observe that the 16 of 16/9 is hidden in the 4 that is subtracted from the amount of shifting applied to 1. Remember, $1 \ll n-1-4$ is 2^{n-1-4}, and $\cdots/9*2^{n-1-4} = \cdots 2^4/9*2^{n-1} = \cdots 16/9*2^{n-1}$. The equation for the factor 8/5 is similar.

⟨ layer II modified factor for $n = -7$ ₂₀₉ ⟩ ≡   (209)
   $-1 * $⟨ output scalefactor ₁₃₆ ⟩ $*$
   ⟨ f_i ₁₂₆ ⟩/
   $(5 * (((\mathbf{int})\ 1) \ll ((\mathbf{sizeof}\,(\mathbf{int}) * 8) - 1 - 3)))$ Used in 133.

This concludes the bit saving measures taken by layer II. We summarize this by giving the layer II specific code to

⟨ decode layer II side information ₂₁₀ ⟩ ≡   (210)
   { ⟨ read the layer II *bit_allocation* ₁₉₅ ⟩
    ⟨ read the scalefactor selection information ₂₀₃ ⟩
    ⟨ read the layer II scalefactors ₂₀₆ ⟩
   }   Used in 216.

9.4 Computing the CRC

The protected bits in layer II include the bit allocation information and the scalefactors. Due to the complicated procedure just described, the number of scalefactors transmitted depends on the bit allocation data. Hence, the number of protected bits can not be derived from the header, but depends on the actual data in the side information.

To compute the CRC for n *bits*, we use the function

⟨ private declarations ₁ ⟩ +≡   (211)
   static unsigned short int
     bitcrc(**unsigned short int** *crc*, **unsigned short int** *bits*, **int** *n*);

To accomplish the reading of bits and the computation of the CRC simultaneously, we use a variation of the the the code to ⟨ get n bits ₁₄₂ ⟩.

⟨ get n CRC bits ₂₁₂ ⟩ ≡   (212)
   ⟨ get n bits ₁₄₂ ⟩
   $bits = (bits \gg (\mathbf{sizeof}\ (bits) * 8 - n));$
   $crc = bitcrc(crc, (\mathbf{unsigned\ short\ int})\ bits, n);$ Used in 213 and 214.

With this code, we can read and check the layer II bit allocation data (see page 79) and, at the same time, calculate the number *nsf* of transmitted scalefactors.

⟨ read and check layer II *bit_allocation* ₂₁₃ ⟩ ≡   (213)
   $nsf = 0;$
   for $(sb = 0;\ sb < s{\rightarrow}info.bound;\ sb\text{++})$
    for $(ch = 0;\ ch < s{\rightarrow}info.channels;\ ch\text{++})$
    { $n = s{\rightarrow}nbal[sb];$
     if $(n > 0)$
     { ⟨ get n CRC bits ₂₁₂ ⟩
      if $(bits \neq 0)$ $nsf\text{++};$

```
          }
        }
  for ( ;  sb < s→sblimit [0];  sb++)
  {  n = s→nbal [sb];
     if (n > 0)
     {  ⟨get n CRC bits ₂₁₂⟩
        if (bits ≠ 0)  nsf = nsf + s→info.channels;
     }
  }
}
```
Used in 215.

A scalefactor is transmitted for each channel where the bit allocation is not zero.
For each scalefactor, the frame then contains two protected bits. To ⟨check the
scalefactors ₂₁₄⟩, we read the remaining bits in the current byte, then check bytewise,
and conclude with checking the remaining bits in the last byte.

⟨check the scalefactors ₂₁₄⟩ ≡   (214)
```
  {  int sfbit = nsf * 2;

     if (bit_offset > 0)
     {  n = min(8 − bit_offset, sfbit);
        ⟨get n CRC bits ₂₁₂⟩
        sfbit = sfbit − n;
     }
     while (sfbit ≥ 8)
     {  ⟨compute the CRC for one byte ₄₄₁⟩;
        sfbit = sfbit − 8;
     }
     if (sfbit > 0)
     {  n = sfbit;
        ⟨get n CRC bits ₂₁₂⟩
     }
  }
```
Used in 215.

This concludes evaluating the CRC for layer II.

⟨compute the CRC for layer II ₂₁₅⟩ ≡   (215)
```
  {  char bit_offset = 0;
     unsigned int bits;
     int sb, ch, nsf;

     ⟨read and check layer II bit_allocation ₂₁₃⟩
     ⟨check the scalefactors ₂₁₄⟩
  }
```
Used in 101.

9.5 Reading Layer II Subband Samples

Necessarily, the new format of layer II frames, the grouping of samples into triplets, and the extension to three groups each containing 12 blocks, is reflected in how we

⟨generate output data ₆₆⟩ +≡   (216)
case LAYER_II:
  ⟨decode layer II side information ₂₁₀⟩
  { **int** g;
    for $(g = 0;\ g < \text{GROUPS};\ g{+}{+})$
    { *layer_II_decode_samples*(s, g);
      output_blocks$(s, \textit{buffer} + s{\to}\textit{info}.\textit{samples}, 12)$;
    }
  }
  $s{\to}\textit{frame} = \textit{next\_frame}(s)$;
  break;

The most prominent difference to layer I is the loop over the three groups after the decoding of the side information. Inside the loop, we encounter the same ingredients that we used in layer I: a function to read 12 blocks of subband samples followed by the function to *output_blocks*.

The function to read the subband samples has an additional parameter for the group. Otherwise, the structure is similar to the *layer_I_decode_samples* function: localization of the bit stream, reading loop, and globalization.

⟨auxiliary functions ₆₉⟩ +≡   (217)
  static void *layer_II_decode_samples*(**stream** $*s$, **int** g)
  { ⟨localize the bit stream ₁₄₆⟩
    ⟨layer II subband samples loop ₂₁₈⟩
    ⟨globalize the bit stream ₁₄₇⟩
  }

The reading loop reads 12 blocks of subband samples. Within each block, we distinguish

- the subbands from 0 to *bound* − 1, where we read stereo samples,
- from the subbands from *bound* to *sblimit*, where one sample is shared among both channels,
- and the rest, where we use a sample value of zero.

⟨layer II subband samples loop ₂₁₈⟩ ≡   (218)
  { **int** i;
    for $(i = 0;\ i < 12;\ i = i + 3)$
    { **int** $sb,\ ch$;
      for $(sb = 0;\ sb < s{\to}\textit{info}.\textit{bound};\ sb{+}{+})$
        for $(ch = 0;\ ch < s{\to}\textit{info}.\textit{channels};\ ch{+}{+})$

```
    { double f = side_info[sb][ch].mfactor[g];
      int n = side_info[sb][ch].bit_allocation;
      ⟨ read a scaled sample group ₂₀₁ ⟩
    }
  for (sb = s→info.bound; sb < s→sblimit[0]; sb++)
  { const double f = side_info[sb][0].mfactor[g];
    const double r = side_info[sb][1].mfactor[g]/f;
    int n = side_info[sb][0].bit_allocation;
    ch = 0;
    ⟨ read a scaled sample group ₂₀₁ ⟩
    if (s→info.channels > 1)
    { y[i][1][sb] = y[i][0][sb] * r;
      y[i+1][1][sb] = y[i+1][0][sb] * r;
      y[i+2][1][sb] = y[i+2][0][sb] * r;
    }
  }
  for (sb = s→sblimit[0]; sb < SUBBANDS; sb++)
  { y[i][0][sb] = y[i+1][0][sb] = y[i+2][0][sb] = 0.0;
    if (s→info.channels > 1) y[i][1][sb] = y[i+1][1][sb] = y[i+2][1][sb] = 0.0;
  }
  }
}
```

Used in 217.

10 The Mathematics of Analyzing Components

Mathematics is the art of reducing complicated systems to simple models, which can be understood, while preserving enough structure to allow a meaningful interpretation of results. This is the key to understanding mathematics. To illustrate this point, consider a simple example: numbers.

Numbers do not exist like apples or pears do exist, they are abstractions. If there are five apples in a basket and two apples are added, mathematics can be used to figure out that there are now seven apples in the basket. But what if two pears are added instead of the two apples? 5+2 is still 7. But 7 of what? To be able to apply the mathematical operation of addition, we replace the apples by an abstract model, the number 5. This takes away the smell and color of the apples as unimportant features and leaves behind an abstract mathematical object. The same can be applied to the two pears. Abstraction has simplified reality to a mathematical model, the two numbers 5 and 2. Any two numbers can be added. Here the result is 7. But is there a meaningful interpretation of the result? May be yes. But more likely, there was just too much simplification and we need a better model to cope with this type of problem. The "better" mathematical model for this situation uses vectors.

10.1 Vectors

Vectors are used to model all kinds of things that have components. One can even say, a vector is nothing but an abstract thing with numbers as components. Given the basket with five apples and two pears, it can be modeled by the vector $(5, 2)$. Adding two apples and one pear to the basket can be modeled by the addition of vectors $(5, 2) + (2, 1) = (7, 3)$, since the addition of vectors is defined as componentwise addition (with the provision that both vectors must have the same number of components). If three baskets with five apples and two pears each are joined, the computation $3 \cdot (5, 2) = (15, 6)$ reveals that there are now 15 apples and 6 pears. Multiplication of a vector with a number is done componentwise again. And that is about all that one needs to know about vectors; the rest comes as consequences of these simple rules.

Vectors are very useful abstractions in many applications. Dealing with audio coding, an input signal is sampled and thereby split into components: a vector of PCM samples. From PCM samples frequencies are derived: a vector of frequencies. The core of this computation, and why we can interpret the result as frequencies, can be understood easily with a little more theory on vectors.

But wait, is'nt a vector something like an arrow? With length, direction, and a pointed head? No, not really. Points and directed line segments are part of geometry, and for a long time, geometry and algebra were two separate disciplines. Geometry was done with ruler and compass, Algebra with numbers and equations, until Descartes made a revolutionary discovery: the coordinate system. It enabled him to split the position of a point into an x and a y component and hence model points by vectors. Lines, that is sets of points, where modeled by linear equations, that is the set of vectors satisfying the equation, and so on. He was able to translate, or model, geometric objects by algebraic objects and solve geometric problems with algebraic methods. Later, the famous problem to construct, with ruler and compass alone, from a circle a square with the same area—a problem of geometry—was finally solved, or better proven to be impossible to solve, by algebraic means.

So directed line segments are not vectors—in much the same way as audio signals are not vectors—but they can be modeled by vectors.

To distinguish vectors from other mathematical objects, we use lower case bold letters for them like t, u, v, w, x, y, or z. Components of vectors are written with a subscript and, if the components are numbers, not with bold letters. For example, the 5th component of v is v_5. If we have an enumeration of vectors, we write $v_1, v_2, \ldots$ instead.

10.2 Linear Combinations

So far, we have defined only two operations on vectors: addition and multiplication with a number. Combining both operations, we can take a couple of vectors $v_1, v_2, \ldots, v_n$ and some numbers $y_1, y_2, \ldots, y_n$ and make a new vector

$$x = y_1 v_1 + y_2 v_2 + \cdots + y_n v_n.$$

The vector x is then called a linear combination of the vectors $v_1, v_2, \ldots, v_n$. In a way, the equation tells us that x is composed from ingredients v_i according to the proportions given by the y_i (just think of fruit baskets).

We will illustrate the power of this principle using another example. Consider the function $f : t \mapsto (t/2)^2$ in the range $t \in [0, 2\pi]$ (Fig. 20). Sampling f at 5 points, equally spaced, the vector $x = (0, 0.61, 2.46, 5.55, 9.87)$ is obtained. This vector represents a very simplified model of the function f.

Now we obtain five other vectors v_i, for i from 1 to 5, using the same principle from the functions $g_i : t \mapsto \cos(ti/4)$ (Fig. 20).

Solving the equation

$$x = y_1 v_1 + y_2 v_2 + y_3 v_3 + y_4 v_4 + y_5 v_5$$

yields:
$$x = 7.36 v_1 - 12.19 v_2 + 6.76 v_3 - 2.32 v_4 + 0.39 v_5$$

This is a representation of the vector x, derived from a simple polynom, as a linear combination of vectors v_i, derived from cosine waves. Can we interpret this result?

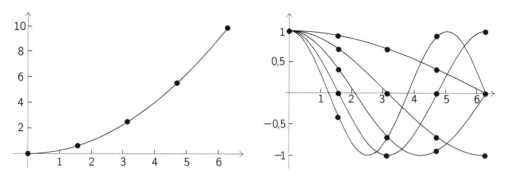

Fig. 20: Sampling $f : t \mapsto (t/2)^2$ and $g_i : t \mapsto \cos(ti/4)$, $i = 1, \ldots, 5$

Does it mean, that the polynom $(t/2)^2$ has $\cos(ti/4)$ waves as components? What about the function $\tilde{f}$ defined from the functions g_i reusing the proportions y_i?

$$\tilde{f} = 7.36g_1 - 12.19g_2 + 6.76g_3 - 2.32g_4 + 0.39g_5$$

Do we have $f \approx \tilde{f}$? Does it mean that y_i is the frequency content of f for the frequency $i/4$?

Yes and No! The vectors are only a simplified model. Only a few points of the function are taken into the model and the sample points are taken from a limited stretch of the function f.

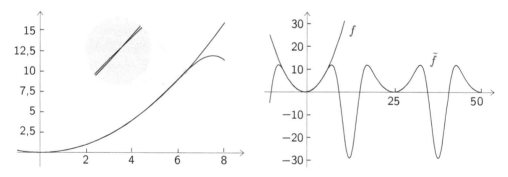

Fig. 21: Comparing f and $\tilde{f}$

While $\tilde{f}$ is pretty close to f in the interval $[0, 2\pi]$, it even matches f in the five sample points exactly, the two functions are quite different, as can be seen from Figure 21. Both functions exhibit a completely different global behavior. $\tilde{f}$ is an approximation to the parable f between 0 and 2π, but otherwise its a periodic function. f is not periodic at all. Whether one can associate a frequency content with f or even with vector $\boldsymbol{x}$ is more than questionable.

What is to be learned from this example? That computing with vectors is a powerful tool, to analyze and extract components of objects; that new objects can be synthesized, once their components are known; and that the interpretation of results need critical judgment because the method will not fail, even if the model is only a poor representation of the objects in question. Thus warned about possible mis- and over-interpretation of results, the next section investigates the existence and uniqueness of such results and reaches fundamental conclusions about vector spaces.

10.3 The Basis

From a given set of vectors, other vectors can be constructed as linear combinations. Two properties of such sets of vectors are of interest:

- If the set is large enough that each and every vector (with the same number of components of course) can be represented, the set is called a **system of generators**. When a vector is analyzed in regard to its components relative to a given set of vectors, using a system of generators ensures that the analysis is possible. A solution will exist.

- If the set is too large, one (or more) of its vectors is already a linear combination of the other vectors, and any linear combination involving this vector can equally well be written without it. Such a set is called **linear dependent**. Sets that are not linear dependent are called **linear independent**.

The optimal situation for analysis as well as for synthesis is a linear independent system of generators. Such a set is called a **basis**.

A basis has the following properties:

- A basis is a minimal system of generators.
    That is, if any vector is removed from a basis, it is no longer a system of generators.

- A basis is a maximal linear independent set.
    That is, if any vector is added to a basis, it is no longer linear independent.

- Every vector space has a basis.
    This is a very strong theorem. No proof is given here, but it is easy to find one in a good book on linear algebra, for example the classic book by Greub[13].

- If a vector space has a finite basis, any basis of it will have the same number of vectors. This number of vectors is called its **dimension**. Again, this claim requires a proof, but this book will not give one (Sorry!).

Back to the above example. The vectors in this example, for example the vector x, have five components and it is immediately visible that the five vectors $(1, 0, 0, 0, 0)$, $(0, 1, 0, 0, 0)$, $(0, 0, 1, 0, 0)$, $(0, 0, 0, 1, 0)$, and $(0, 0, 0, 0, 1)$ constitute a basis of the vector space. Just try to write any of them as a linear combination of the others and it quickly becomes apparent that they are linear independent. Still easier to solve is the problem of representing an arbitrary vector $(x_1, x_2, x_3, x_4, x_5)$ as a linear combination of them. Hence, it is a system of generators. The dimension of this vector space therefore is 5, and it is not accidental that we choose five different frequencies for analysis. The five vectors derived from the five cosine functions will constitute a basis, provided they are linear independent.

The common criteria to check a set of vectors $v_1, v_2, \ldots, v_n$ for linear independence is the following: The vectors $v_1, v_2, \ldots, v_n$ are linear independent if and only if the equation

$$y_1 v_1 + y_2 v_2 + \cdots + y_n v_n = 0$$

has exactly one solution $y_1 = y_2 = \cdots = y_n = 0$.

Clearly, setting all factors y_1 to y_n to zero is a solution of the above equation, and if there would be any other solution, with let's say $y_i \neq 0$, we could solve the equation for v_i and get a representation of v_i as a linear combination of the other vectors. This contradicts the linear independence of the vectors.

Checking the five example vectors reveals that they are indeed linear independent and, as a maximal linear independent set, also a basis or a system of generators. In conclusion, any vector with five components can be written as a linear combination of these vectors (whether it was derived from a periodic function or not).

Were we extraordinarily lucky in obtaining linear independent vectors from the frequencies chosen? No, not really. Just consider the two-dimensional case. Two vectors in a two-dimensional space (we call this a plane) are linear dependent, exactly if one of them is a multiple of the other, that is, they have the same direction, like two parallel line segments. How likely is it that two line segments, picked at random, are parallel? Very unlikely! As a general rule, linear independence is the "normal" case, linear dependency is the result of precise planing. Just try to draw two, exactly parallel line segments with a ruler. Even if one of them is only a tiny little bit out of axis, the directions are no longer "linear dependent"—in strict mathematical terms. We would like to say, they are almost linear dependent. This would require a notion of more or less linear dependency, and we will see such a notion in the next section.

10.4 Scalar Product

It is tempting to define the product of two vectors componentwise as the vector of the products. While possible, a much more useful definition of the product is the following:

$$v \cdot x = v_1 x_1 + v_2 x_2 + \cdots + v_n x_n \,.$$

This formula yields as the product of two vectors a plain number. In geometry, entities like numbers that do not have a "direction" were called "scalar", and therefore, this product is called, until today, the scalar product, because it yields a number. The two most important applications of the scalar products are the definitions of length and angle as we will see now.

The geometric measure of how similar the directions of two line segments are is the angle between the two lines. Because we are interested in vectors with 32 or even 512 components, we need a general notion of an angle between two vectors. This general notion is, however, inspired by the geometric interpretation of vectors.

In Figure 22, the vectors $v = (v_1, v_2)$ and $x = (x_1, x_2)$ are shown as directed line segments. Using the Pythagorean law, we can compute the length of vector v, written

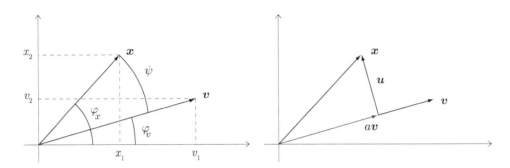

Fig. 22: Angle between vectors   Fig. 23: Orthogonal projection

as $|\boldsymbol{v}|$, with the formula

$$|\boldsymbol{v}| = \sqrt{v_1^2 + v_2^2}.$$

The angle φ_v between the "vector" $\boldsymbol{v}$ and the horizontal axis of the coordinate system is given by:

$$\cos \varphi_v = v_1/|\boldsymbol{v}| \qquad \text{or} \qquad \sin \varphi_v = v_2/|\boldsymbol{v}|.$$

Similar equations hold for $\boldsymbol{x}$ and the angle φ_x between $\boldsymbol{x}$ and the horizontal axis. Using these equations, the cosine of the angle ψ between $\boldsymbol{v}$ and $\boldsymbol{x}$ can be computed as

$$\cos \psi = \cos(\varphi_x - \varphi_v) = \cos \varphi_x \cos \varphi_v + \sin \varphi_x \sin \varphi_v = \frac{v_1 x_1 + v_2 x_2}{|\boldsymbol{v}|\,|\boldsymbol{x}|}.$$

For the three dimensional case, where $\boldsymbol{v} = (v_1, v_2, v_3)$ and $\boldsymbol{x} = (x_1, x_2, x_3)$, we can find, with some more geometric intuition, along the same lines the formulas:

$$|\boldsymbol{v}| = \sqrt{v_1^2 + v_2^2 + v_3^2} \qquad \text{and} \qquad \cos \psi = \frac{v_1 x_1 + v_2 x_2 + v_3 x_3}{|\boldsymbol{v}|\,|\boldsymbol{x}|}.$$

In the general n-dimensional case, we find again along the same lines—but with substantially more intuition—for $\boldsymbol{v} = (v_1, v_2, \ldots, v_n)$ and $\boldsymbol{x} = (x_1, x_2, \ldots, x_n)$:

$$|\boldsymbol{v}| = \sqrt{v_1^2 + v_2^2 + \cdots + v_n^2} \qquad \text{and} \qquad \cos \psi = \frac{v_1 x_1 + v_2 x_2 + \cdots + v_n x_n}{|\boldsymbol{v}|\,|\boldsymbol{x}|}.$$

Using the scalar product, as defined above, we write this:

$$|\boldsymbol{v}| = \sqrt{\boldsymbol{v} \cdot \boldsymbol{v}} \qquad \text{and} \qquad \cos \psi = \frac{\boldsymbol{v} \cdot \boldsymbol{x}}{|\boldsymbol{v}|\,|\boldsymbol{x}|}.$$

10.5 Orthogonal Projections

A 90° angle is an important special case. Because $\cos 90° = 0$, two vectors v and x that enclose a 90° angle have a scalar product of zero. This is easy to see. If we have $v \cdot x / |v| \, |x| = \cos 90° = 0$ then this can be the case if and only if $v \cdot x = 0$. The vectors v and x are then called orthogonal and we write $v \bot x$.

Using this simple observation, we can obtain a very powerful tool: orthogonal projection. In the easiest case (Fig. 23), we have two vectors v and x and we want to split x into two components: one in direction of v and a remainder u that is orthogonal to v. Hence, we have the equation

$$x = yv + u \qquad \text{with} \qquad u \bot v.$$

The trick to solve this equation is, to multiply both sides with the vector v. We obtain $x \cdot v = yv \cdot v + u \cdot v$ and because $u \bot v$ implies $u \cdot v = 0$, we conclude $x \cdot v = yv \cdot v$. This gives the solution

$$y = \frac{x \cdot v}{v \cdot v} \qquad \text{and} \qquad u = x - yv.$$

As a matter of fact, the vector yv is the best approximation that is possible as a multiple of v to the vector x. Or in other words, the vector $u = x - yv$ is the vector with minimal length $|u|$ that spans the distance between x and any multiple of v.

With two or three vectors v_1, v_2, and v_3 the procedure is similar. With $x = y_1 v_1 + y_2 v_2 + y_3 v_3 + u$ and $u \bot v_i$, we obtain the equations

$$x \cdot v_1 = y_1 v_1 \cdot v_1 + y_2 v_2 \cdot v_1 + y_3 v_3 \cdot v_1$$
$$x \cdot v_2 = y_1 v_1 \cdot v_2 + y_2 v_2 \cdot v_2 + y_3 v_3 \cdot v_2 \qquad (Eq.\ 2)$$
$$x \cdot v_3 = y_1 v_1 \cdot v_3 + y_2 v_2 \cdot v_3 + y_3 v_3 \cdot v_3 \,.$$

Solving these three equations for y_1, y_2, and y_3 is straight forward, and we obtain the best possible approximation for x as a linear combination of v_1, v_2, and v_3.

As an illustration, we use an earlier example: approximation of $f : t \mapsto (t/2)^2$ by $g_i : t \mapsto \cos(ti/4)$ (see page 90). This time, however, we use only three functions g_1, g_2, and g_3. From these, we compute only three vectors v_1, v_2, and v_3, and these are not sufficient to represent the vector x derived from function f as a linear combination. For all numbers y_1, y_2, and y_3, we have

$$x \neq y_1 v_1 + y_2 v_2 + y_3 v_3 \,.$$

What we can do is solve the equations (2) for an optimal approximation. We obtain $y_1 = 6.41$, $y_2 = -9.64$, and $y_3 = 3.48$. The result is shown in Figure 24. It shows a successful approximation of a vector with five components using only three vectors.

In effect, we have now a much more robust method to separate a given vector into given components. We are no longer bound to a full basis of the vector space but can pick a number of interesting components. The result of our analysis will then

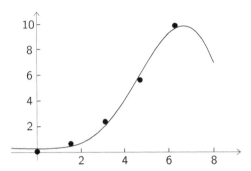

Fig. 24: Approximation of f at five points, but using only three functions g_1, g_2, and g_3. The distances of the dots, representing the sample vector $\boldsymbol{x}$, to the line, representing

$$y_1 g_1 + y_2 g_2 + y_3 g_3,$$

visualize the difference vector $\boldsymbol{u}$, which obviously has become quite small.

reflect the similarity of the given vector to the predefined components. If there is no similarity, it will just return a large difference vector $\boldsymbol{u}$.

Solving the equations (2) becomes even simpler, if the vectors $\boldsymbol{v}_i$ are orthogonal to each other. That is, if $\boldsymbol{v}_i \perp \boldsymbol{v}_j$ for $i \neq j$. In this case, we have $\boldsymbol{v}_i \cdot \boldsymbol{v}_j = 0$ for $i \neq j$ and equations (2) reduce to

$$\boldsymbol{x} \cdot \boldsymbol{v}_1 = y_1 \boldsymbol{v}_1 \cdot \boldsymbol{v}_1$$
$$\boldsymbol{x} \cdot \boldsymbol{v}_2 = y_2 \boldsymbol{v}_2 \cdot \boldsymbol{v}_2 \qquad\qquad (Eq.\ 3)$$
$$\boldsymbol{x} \cdot \boldsymbol{v}_3 = y_3 \boldsymbol{v}_3 \cdot \boldsymbol{v}_3 .$$

A good example of this is the layer I encoder specification, which we will study in the next section.

10.6 Layer I Frequency Analysis

Consider the problem of splitting a PCM coded sound sample into 32 frequency components. To solve the problem, we could just take (almost any) 32 Cosine waves, sample them into vectors, and use these wave-vectors to represent any sequence of 32 PCM samples as a linear combination. After what we have learned so far, we should not do it this way. While the mathematics would work, we will get some values that sometimes can, and sometimes should not be interpreted as the frequencies of our input. A better approach is to take a longer stretch $\boldsymbol{x}$ of PCM samples, let say 512 samples, and still use only 32 frequencies for analysis. Further, we should choose the frequencies in such a way that the sampled waves are orthogonal. We take a look at the standard and choose the following cosine waves: $g_i : k \mapsto \cos((k-16)(2i+1)2\pi/128)$ for i from 0 to 31. We sample these functions for k from 0 to 511 to get 32 vectors $\boldsymbol{v}_i$ with 512 components each. It is pretty easy to check, using a computer algebra tool, that these vectors are indeed orthogonal to each other and even have the same length, $|\boldsymbol{v}_i| = 256$. Using equations similar to (3), we solve the problem of frequency analysis by computing $y_i = \boldsymbol{x} \cdot \boldsymbol{v}_i/32$ for i from 0 to 31 and have the desired vector of 32 frequencies $\boldsymbol{y} = (y_0, y_1, \ldots, y_{31})$. Well, that's almost it—but the use of a bit signal processing theory can improve the result of this primitive frequency analysis considerably. The trick to improve the quality is "windowing".

Recall Chapter 2, where we analyzed digital filters. A digital filter was just a formula like $y = 0.5x_{j-1} + x_j + 0.5x_{j+1}$, which we can now write as a scalar product:

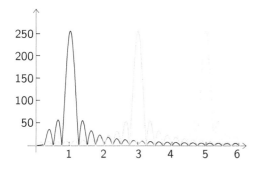

Fig. 25: The frequency response of three digital filters as defined by the vectors v_0, v_1, and v_2 with

$$v_i = \big(\cos((k-16)(2i+1)2\pi/128)\big)$$

for $k = 0,\ldots,511$.

These filters are derived from cosine waves $g_i : k \mapsto \cos((k-16)f_i 2\pi)$ with frequencies $f_i = (2i+1)/128$.

$y = (x_{j-1}, x_j, x_{j+1}) \cdot (0.5, 1, 0.5)$. Further, we can interpret the result y as the component of the input vector (x_{j-1}, x_j, x_{j+1}) in direction of $(0.5, 1, 0.5)$. While the vector $(0.5, 1, 0.5)$ has no special meaning, the vectors v_i with components $\cos((k-16)(2i+1)2\pi/128)$ for k from 0 to 511, have a meaning. They represent pure tones of frequency $(2i+1)/128$. (To simplify the discussion, we do these calculations assuming a sample rate of 1Hz.) If we use this interpretation of v_i, we have a good idea of what it means that a stretch of input samples x has a component y_i in direction of v_i.

The notion of "frequency" always implies a certain time interval. There is nothing like the frequency of a signal at a single point in time. If we have only a single time sample of our signal, there is no way of extracting any frequency from it. To know the periodic qualities of a signal 100 % exactly, one needs to know its values from the beginning of time to the end of time. (It might behave very different in the future!) In summary, the more precise we know the frequency, the less precise we know the time, and vice versa.

A similar effect is known from quantum mechanics: the uncertainty principle. It states that one can not know precisely the energy of a particle at a precise point in time. Knowing that in quantum mechanics particles are waves, and the energy of a particle is directly proportional to its frequency, explains the similarity.

This consideration leads to the same conclusion, we made before. Trying to extract 32 frequencies, we should not use just 32 input samples but a larger input vector. Using 512 PCM samples for analysis, we get a sufficient frequency resolution.

To judge the quality of the frequency resolution, we developed in Chapter 2 the notion of "frequency response". The frequency response of the primitive set of 32 filters v_i, just defined, is shown in Figure 25. It shows the frequency response of the first three filters. These filters have a sharp peek at the center frequency and many additional small peaks on both sides. As a consequence, even signals with frequencies far from the center frequency of v_i will have a slight component in direction of v_i. On the other hand, a strong signals that differs only slightly from the center frequency will have already a significantly smaller component in direction of v_i.

This is far from the desired frequency response of the perfect filter (Fig. 7), which we discussed in Chapter 2. Its frequency response is 0 outside the filter's frequency range and 1 inside. Ignoring completely frequencies that do not belong to the filter's frequency band and treating as equal all frequencies that do belong to the filter's band. But we know, such a filter is not possible—at least not with vectors of finite length. We can, however, improve the situation by using a "windowing" function.

A windowing function determines, so to speak, the volume level of the input signal. We start with zero volume at the beginning, fade the sample in, reach full volume in the middle, and fade the signal out again. With this windowing, the samples at the beginning and at the end of the input vector enter the computation of the scalar product with a reduced weight, and the samples in the middle of the vector mainly determine the value of the scalar product. Instead of computing the average frequency for the whole sequence, this will focus the frequency analysis more on the middle of the input vector.

With a suitable windowing function, we can also find a good compromise between time and frequency resolution. For instance, we can trade some of the frequency resolution inside the frequency band for better frequency resolution at the borders of the frequency band. Doing this, the center peek of the frequency response will be flattened, but the suppression of frequencies outside the filter will improve.

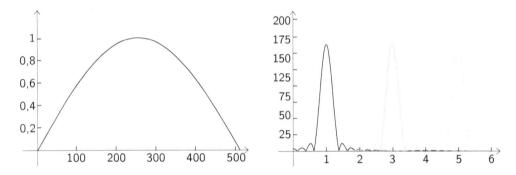

Fig. 26: Sin window and its effect on the frequency response

A simple window—used in layer III as we see in Section 11.2—is the sin window. Combining this window with the plain frequency analysis done so far has a positive effect on the frequency response. The window and the frequency response are shown in Figure 26. The frequency response has now a much lower and broader center peak, and all but two small secondary peaks to the left and to the right seem to have disappeared.

The ultimate idea is: To combine a windowing function with the coefficients of the perfect filter (Eq. 1 on page 6). This will give a filter that

- has only finitely many coefficients, because the windowing function is zero outside a finite interval, and therefore, only finitely many coefficients of the perfect filter do matter.

- has a frequency response close to the perfect filter, if the windowing function is properly chosen.

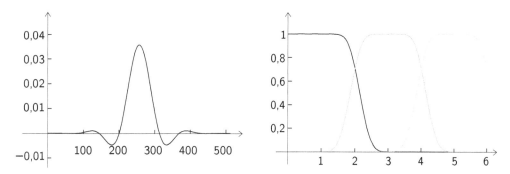

Fig. 27: Window used by layer I encoder and its frequency response

The window used by the MPEG encoder, shown in Figure 27 with its frequency response, does a pretty good job in this respect. It was obtained by applying numerical optimization to filters constructed using theoretical concepts as we have discussed them here. For more on signal theory, consult the excellent book by Hartmann[14].

Our next aim is to get a complete understanding of the encoding and decoding algorithm of layer I.

10.7 Layer I Encoding

Using our current understanding, a first and simple attempt at encoding could be this (Fig. 29):

1. **Copy**: *Copy the first 512 input samples into vector x, then advance the input by 32 samples.*

2. **Windowing**: *Apply the layer I windowing function to x to yield vector z.*

3. **Scalar Products**: *Calculate 32 subband frequencies $y_i = v_i \cdot z$, as scalar products using the vectors $v_i = \big(\cos((k-16)(2i+1)2\pi/128)\big)$ for $k = 0,\ldots,511$ and $i = 0,\ldots,31$.*

Let's compare this with the following (informal) specification of the encoding procedure as presented by the standard in Section C.1.3 and the associated flow diagram figure C.4.

1. **Shifting**: *Move the contents of the vector x 32 places to the right. That is, for i=511 down to 32 do $x_i = x_{i-64}$. The vector x is to be initialized with zeros during startup.*

2. **Input Samples**: *Input the next 32 PCM samples into $x_{31}, x_{30}, \ldots$ to x_0.*

3. **Windowing**: *Next the elements of vector x are scaled by the elements of vector c (given by a large table C.1 in the standard) yielding a vector z with $z_j = x_j \cdot c_j$ for $j = 0,\ldots,511$.*

4. **Partial Calculation** *Compute vector $\boldsymbol{u}$ with 64 components as*

$$u_i = \sum_{j=0}^{7} z_{i+64j} \quad for \quad i = 0, \ldots, 63.$$

5. **Matrixing**: *Calculate 32 subband samples*

$$y_i = \sum_{k=0}^{63} m_{ik} u_k \quad with \quad i = 0, \ldots 32 \text{ and } m_{ik} = \cos\big((2i+1)(k-16)\pi/64\big).$$

A closer look reveals that both algorithms are the same, except for a few optimizations implemented by the standard.

The first obvious optimization is the removal of the copy operation of step 1. Instead, the standard keeps the vector $\boldsymbol{x}$, shifts it to make room for the next 32 input samples, and places the next 32 samples into $\boldsymbol{x}$. This process also keeps the samples in $\boldsymbol{x}$ in chronological order from left to right.

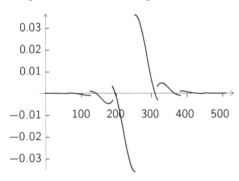

Fig. 28: The window function of the layer I encoder is combined with scaling to compensate for the scaling in the matrixing step and it incorporates a sign change every 64 elements, which is needed to shorten the computation of the scalar product.

The windowing is the same in both algorithms, except for a strangely different windowing function (Fig. 28), which we explain in a moment.

The two steps for Partial Calculation and Matrixing, are just a clever way to compute the scalar products $\boldsymbol{v}_i \cdot \boldsymbol{z}$. The coefficients of $\boldsymbol{v}_i$ are taken from the periodic cosine function. The cosine wave repeats itself after the wavelength 2π and within the interval from 0 to 2π the second half of the wave is identical to the first half of the wave except for a reversed sign.

Consequently, the first 128 components of $\boldsymbol{v}_i = \big(\cos((k-16)(2i+1)2\pi/128)\big)$ will be the same as the next 128 components and so on... Even better, the first 64 components of $\boldsymbol{v}_i$ will equal the next 64 components, except for a reversed sign, and the next 64 components will again equal the first 64 components with the correct sign, and so on... This discovery can be used to speed up the computation of the scalar product. Let $\boldsymbol{v}$ be one of the $\boldsymbol{v}_i$, then we have

$$
\begin{aligned}
\boldsymbol{v} \cdot \boldsymbol{z} &= v_0 z_0 + v_1 z_1 + \cdots + v_{64} z_{64} + v_{65} z_{65} + \cdots + v_{128} z_{128} + \cdots + v_{511} z_{511} \\
&= v_0 z_0 + v_1 z_1 + \cdots - v_0 z_{64} - v_1 z_{65} - \cdots + v_0 z_{128} + \cdots - v_{63} z_{511} \\
&= v_0(z_0 - z_{64} + z_{128} - \cdots) + v_1(z_1 - z_{65} + \cdots) + \cdots + v_{63}(\cdots - z_{511}) \\
&= \boldsymbol{v}' \cdot \boldsymbol{u}'.
\end{aligned}
$$

Here, v' contains just the first 64 components of v and u' is almost the vector computed in the Partial Calculation step. Almost, except for the alternating signs. The alternating signs explain the difference between the windowing function we have used in the unoptimized algorithm (Fig. 27) and the windowing function of the optimized algorithm (Fig. 28). The designers of the standard algorithm have merged the sign changes into the windowing function.

By rearranging the computation, we obtained a scalar product with only 64 coefficients instead of 512, which reduces the number of required multiplications by 87.5 %.

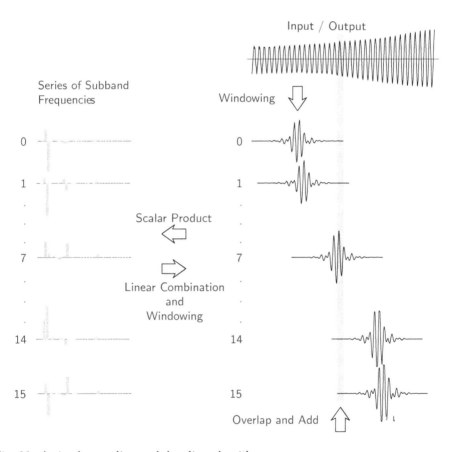

Fig. 29: A simple encoding and decoding algorithm

10.8 Layer I Decoding

The decoding algorithm reverses the computations from the encoding algorithm. Let us start with an attempt at inverting the simple algorithm:

1. **Linear Combination**: *Take the next vector $\boldsymbol{y} = (y_0, \ldots, y_{31})$ of 32 subband frequencies and compute the linear combination $\boldsymbol{z} = y_0 \boldsymbol{v}_0 + y_1 \boldsymbol{v}_1 + \cdots + y_{31} \boldsymbol{v}_{31}$, using the vectors $\boldsymbol{v}_i = \big(\cos((k-16)(2i+1)2\pi/128) \big)$ for $k = 0, \ldots, 511$ and $i = 0, \ldots, 31$.*

2. **Windowing**: *Apply the layer I windowing function to $\boldsymbol{z}$ to yield vector $\boldsymbol{w}$.*

3. **Overlap and Add**: *Perform the previous two steps 16 times and compute 16 consecutive vectors $\boldsymbol{w}_j$, with $j = 0, \ldots, 15$. Shift each vector $\boldsymbol{w}_j$ exactly $j \cdot 32$ places to the right, add them all together, and take the segment of 32 values where all the $\boldsymbol{w}_j$ overlap as 32 new output values.*

The algorithm can be understood, if we consider the intention of the windowing function: slowly fading in and out of the signal. Computing the linear combination $\boldsymbol{z}$ gives a signal with a constant amplitude and a constant frequency content over all 512 samples. The frequency composition of $\boldsymbol{z}$ will match more or less only those few samples that were in the middle of the window when the frequency composition was computed. To reconstruct the original signal, we should play from the vector $\boldsymbol{z}$ only 32 samples exactly when we need to reproduce those original 32 samples that are best represented by $\boldsymbol{z}$. Cutting out short pieces of consecutive $\boldsymbol{z}$ vectors and pasting them together to regain the original signal will not work very well, because the individual pieces would not join nicely at their borders. Instead, we imitate a disk-jockey, fade in one piece slowly, and while fading it out already fade in the next, to make the transition inaudible—only that we manage to fade in 8 pieces, and fade out 8 pieces, at the same time (Fig. 29). To fade in and out the $\boldsymbol{z}$ vectors, we reuse the windowing function. It is part of the art and science of window function design to compute window functions that can be inverted that way.

Now we compare the simple decoder to the decoder specification of the standard, which this book quotes on page 9. Disguised by a slightly different notation, we can recognize the computation of vector $\boldsymbol{z}$ as a linear combination with coefficients y_k in step 3 of the standard, called "Matrixing". Instead of computing all 512 components of $\boldsymbol{z}$, the matrixing step computes only the first 64. This is the same optimization, we have seen in the encoding algorithm: since the vector $\boldsymbol{z}$ is periodic, we compute only the first 64 components. The rest is just repetition with alternating signs.

Instead of recomputing 16 vectors in each iteration, the standard stores the shortened $\boldsymbol{z}$ vectors in the vector $\boldsymbol{v}$. So in each iteration, only one new vector $\boldsymbol{z}$ needs to be computed from the next $\boldsymbol{y}$ vector.

The biggest waste of the simple algorithm is the windowing, shifting, and adding of 16 long $\boldsymbol{z}$ vectors, only to throw away almost all of the result and to retain only 32 output samples. Indeed, it is better to take from each $\boldsymbol{z}$ vector just the 32 components needed for the final result, apply to them just the right segment of the windowing vector, and add only those pieces. As can be easily seen from Figure 29, this process will use each segment of the windowing function exactly once. This observation is used by the standard decoder. In step 4, called reduction, it copies the necessary segments of the different $\boldsymbol{z}$ vectors stored in $\boldsymbol{v}$ into a vector $\boldsymbol{u}$ just in the right order, so that when windowing vector $\boldsymbol{u}$ in step 5, each $\boldsymbol{z}$ segment meets its corresponding windowing segment. What remains in step 6, is to calculate the 32 output samples by adding up the 16 windowed segments.

The reduction of the computational complexity, in terms of multiplications and additions, to 1/16 of the simple algorithm is quite considerable. Still, this was only the starting point for the optimizations we applied in Chapter 3. To be able to manage these optimizations properly and to cope with the even more complex code transformations that we will need in the implementation of layer III, we need some more useful mathematics: linear mappings and matrices.

10.9 Linear Mappings and Matrices

The standard uses a special name for the encoding step, where it computes the scalar product, and for the decoding step, where it computes a linear combination of wave-vectors. Both times, it calls this step "Matrixing". To explain the concept of a Matrix, which unites the concepts of scalar product and linear combination, we first need the notion of a linear mapping.

A **linear mapping** is a mapping f that obeys the following two equations:

$$f(\boldsymbol{v} + \boldsymbol{w}) = f(\boldsymbol{v}) + f(\boldsymbol{w})$$
$$f(y\boldsymbol{v}) = y f(\boldsymbol{v}) \,. \qquad\qquad (Eq.\ 4)$$

In short, a mapping is linear if it is compatible with decomposition into components and synthesis from components, as we have studied these operations so far. If we decompose an object into components, we can either apply f to the composition $y_1\boldsymbol{v} + y_2\boldsymbol{v}_2 + \cdots + y_n\boldsymbol{v}_n$, or apply f to each component $\boldsymbol{v}_i$ separately, and compose the results. Because of this, linear mappings play an important role in the theory of vectors.

Not that most mappings that we encounter in physics, finance, and daily housekeeping were linear—but linear mappings are important anyway, because they are easy to deal with, and if we are not too pedantic, most mappings are at least approximately linear.

Using the compatibility of function application and decomposition, we discover quickly that a linear mapping can be computed entirely from the values it has on a basis of the vector space. That is, if $\boldsymbol{v}_1, \boldsymbol{v}_2, \ldots, \boldsymbol{v}_n$ is a basis and we know $f(\boldsymbol{v}_1), f(\boldsymbol{v}_2), \ldots, f(\boldsymbol{v}_n)$, we can compute $f(\boldsymbol{w})$ for an arbitrary vector $\boldsymbol{w}$ as follows:

$$f(\boldsymbol{w}) = f(y_1\boldsymbol{v}_1 + y_2\boldsymbol{v}_2 + \cdots + y_n\boldsymbol{v}_n)$$
$$= y_1 f(\boldsymbol{v}_1) + y_2 f(\boldsymbol{v}_2) + \cdots + y_n f(\boldsymbol{v}_n) \,.$$

We write $\boldsymbol{w}$ as a linear combination of vectors from the basis and use that f is a linear function. The same equation tells us, that we can extend any value assignment on the basis to a linear function on the whole vector space.

Our next observation comes from a closer look at linear mappings from vectors to numbers. Assume, as an example, a mapping f that assigns the following values to the standard basis:

$$(1,0,0) \mapsto 5, \quad (0,1,0) \mapsto 9, \quad \text{and} \quad (0,0,1) \mapsto 6.$$

What is the value of f on the vector $(1, 3, 4)$? Using the formula above, we compute:

$$f((1, 3, 4)) = f(1 \cdot (1, 0, 0) + 3 \cdot (0, 1, 0) + 4 \cdot (0, 0, 1))$$
$$= 1 \cdot f((1, 0, 0)) + 3 \cdot f((0, 1, 0)) + 4 \cdot f((0, 0, 1))$$
$$= 1 \cdot 5 + 3 \cdot 9 + 4 \cdot 6$$

Does this look familiar? It is a scalar product: $(1, 3, 4) \cdot (5, 9, 6)$. The values of f on the vectors of the standard basis form a vector $(5, 9, 6)$ and the value of f on any vector $\boldsymbol{w}$ can be computed as $\boldsymbol{w} \cdot (5, 9, 6)$. So linear mappings from vectors to numbers are again vectors. They have as components their values on the standard basis, and the natural way to compute these linear mappings is the scalar product.

Here again, we see the power of the theory of vector spaces. Representing linear mappings as vectors, makes all the tools developed so far immediately available for linear mappings: we can decompose a linear mapping into components, find a basis of linear mappings and write any such mapping as a linear combination of the basis, find the length of a linear mapping $|f|$ and, yes, the angle between two linear mappings. We can even find the best approximation to one linear mapping as a linear combination of some other linear mappings.

There is, however, a confusing element to all this. The vectors $(1, 3, 4)$ and $(5, 9, 6)$ look pretty much alike. How do we know that $(5, 9, 6)$ is the mapping and $(1, 3, 4)$ is the vector. It could be very well the other way round: Using the scalar product $(1, 3, 4) \cdot (5, 9, 6)$ the vector $(1, 3, 4)$ maps the linear mapping $(5, 9, 6)$ to a number, and is a linear mapping itself. (Think about it!)

We could also add the two vectors $(1, 3, 4) + (5, 9, 6) = (6, 12, 10)$. But what would be the meaning of the result? Probably none! Remember the fruit baskets? We model objects using mathematical abstractions. That two objects have the same abstract form does not mean that we can mix them at will. While many operations are possible, not all operations, and hence not all results, do have a sensible interpretation.

As a next step, we study linear mappings from vectors to vectors. An other example will help. Again, we define a linear mapping f by the values it gives to the vectors of the standard basis:

$$(1, 0, 0) \mapsto \begin{pmatrix} 1 \\ 5 \end{pmatrix}, \quad (0, 1, 0) \mapsto \begin{pmatrix} 6 \\ 9 \end{pmatrix}, \quad \text{and} \quad (0, 0, 1) \mapsto \begin{pmatrix} 2 \\ 6 \end{pmatrix}.$$

The value of $f((1, 3, 4))$ can be computed like this:

$$f((1, 3, 4)) = f(1 \cdot (1, 0, 0) + 3 \cdot (0, 1, 0) + 4 \cdot (0, 0, 1))$$
$$= 1 \cdot f((1, 0, 0)) + 3 \cdot f((0, 1, 0)) + 4 \cdot f((0, 0, 1))$$
$$= 1 \cdot \begin{pmatrix} 1 \\ 5 \end{pmatrix} + 3 \cdot \begin{pmatrix} 6 \\ 9 \end{pmatrix} + 4 \cdot \begin{pmatrix} 2 \\ 6 \end{pmatrix}$$
$$= \begin{pmatrix} 1 \cdot 1 + 3 \cdot 6 + 4 \cdot 2 \\ 1 \cdot 5 + 3 \cdot 9 + 4 \cdot 6 \end{pmatrix}$$
$$= \begin{pmatrix} (1, 6, 2) \cdot (1, 3, 4) \\ (5, 9, 6) \cdot (1, 3, 4) \end{pmatrix}$$

Looking at equations (4) that define linear mappings, we observe that all the operations, equality, addition, and multiplication, are defined componentwise. Therefore, a linear mapping of vectors to vectors will be linear in each component, and can be written, as shown in the above example as a sequence of scalar products, one for each component. This gives a compact notation for linear mappings: we write them as a rectangular schema of numbers, where each line, or row, contains the linear mapping for the corresponding component written as a vector. For the above example, we write the mapping f as

$$A = \begin{pmatrix} 1 & 6 & 2 \\ 5 & 9 & 6 \end{pmatrix}$$

We call such a rectangular schema of numbers a "matrix" and use upper case bold letters like A, B, P, or Q for them. If we want to be more precise, we call A an $n \times m$ matrix if it has n rows and m columns. The above matrix A is an example of a 2×3 matrix. An $n \times m$ matrix describes a linear mapping from vectors with m components to vectors with n components. The result of applying the linear mapping f to the vector v can be obtained componentwise by computing the scalar product of v with each row of the matrix A. We write this Av and have $Av = f(v)$.

There is a second possible interpretation of a matrix, not only are the lines componentwise descriptions of the linear mapping, the columns of the matrix have a good interpretation, too. A look at the above example reveals that the columns are exactly the values that the linear mapping gives to the vectors of the standard basis. Further, the value of any vector (y_1, y_2, y_3) under the linear mapping will just be the obvious linear combination of these vectors:

$$y_1 \cdot \begin{pmatrix} 1 \\ 5 \end{pmatrix} + y_2 \cdot \begin{pmatrix} 6 \\ 9 \end{pmatrix} + y_3 \cdot \begin{pmatrix} 2 \\ 6 \end{pmatrix}$$

This is no coincidence, but is true in general for all matrices and vectors. The application of a matrix to a vector can be interpreted equally well as scalar products with the rows of the matrix or as linear combination of the columns of the matrix.

Corresponding to this change in perspective, we have a simple but important operation on matrices, the transposition. Given any matrix A, we obtain a new matrix $A^\top$, the transposed matrix, by exchanging the role of rows and columns. The rows of A are the columns of $A^\top$ and vice versa. For example, we have

$$\begin{pmatrix} 1 & 6 & 2 \\ 5 & 9 & 6 \end{pmatrix}^\top = \begin{pmatrix} 1 & 5 \\ 6 & 9 \\ 2 & 6 \end{pmatrix}.$$

Applying transposition twice, will result in the same matrix again: $\left(A^\top\right)^\top = A$.

10.10 Matrix Multiplication

It should come as no surprise, that matrices are vectors. After all, it is immediately visible that an $n \times m$ matrix has $n \cdot m$ components. The interpretation of componentwise addition and multiplication by a number are simple: they correspond to the natural operations on the corresponding linear mappings. Given two linear mappings f and g, and a number y, we define

$$(f + g)(\boldsymbol{v}) = f(\boldsymbol{v}) + g(\boldsymbol{v})$$
$$(yf)(\boldsymbol{v}) = yf(\boldsymbol{v})$$

It is easy to verify, using the properties of the scalar product, that if f is described by the matrix $\boldsymbol{P}$ and g by $\boldsymbol{Q}$ then $f + g$ is described by $\boldsymbol{P} + \boldsymbol{Q}$ and yf by $y\boldsymbol{P}$.

A pleasant surprise, however, is that there is a natural multiplication on matrices that corresponds to the composition of two linear mappings. The composition of two mappings f and g is defined by

$$f \circ g(\boldsymbol{v}) = f(g(\boldsymbol{v})),$$

that is by successive application of g and then f.

Assume again, that f is represented by the matrix $\boldsymbol{P}$ and g is represented by $\boldsymbol{Q}$. We use two different interpretations of these matrices. We view the matrix $\boldsymbol{Q}$, as the matrix that has the images of the standard basis as columns and we view $\boldsymbol{P}$ as the matrix that has the componentwise linear mappings as lines.

$$\boldsymbol{P} = \begin{pmatrix} \boldsymbol{p}_1 \\ \boldsymbol{p}_2 \\ \vdots \\ \boldsymbol{p}_n \end{pmatrix} \qquad \boldsymbol{Q} = \begin{pmatrix} \boldsymbol{q}_1 & \boldsymbol{q}_2 & \cdots & \boldsymbol{q}_m \end{pmatrix}$$

given a vector $\boldsymbol{v} = (v_1, \ldots, v_m)$, we compute $f \circ g(\boldsymbol{v})$ as follows

$$f \circ g(\boldsymbol{v}) = f(g(\boldsymbol{v}))$$
$$= f(v_1 \boldsymbol{q}_1 + v_2 \boldsymbol{q}_2 + \cdots + v_m \boldsymbol{q}_m)$$
$$= v_1 f(\boldsymbol{q}_1) + v_2 f(\boldsymbol{q}_2) + \cdots + v_n f(\boldsymbol{q}_n)$$
$$= v_1 \begin{pmatrix} \boldsymbol{p}_1 \cdot \boldsymbol{q}_1 \\ \boldsymbol{p}_2 \cdot \boldsymbol{q}_1 \\ \vdots \\ \boldsymbol{p}_n \cdot \boldsymbol{q}_1 \end{pmatrix} + v_2 \begin{pmatrix} \boldsymbol{p}_1 \cdot \boldsymbol{q}_2 \\ \boldsymbol{p}_2 \cdot \boldsymbol{q}_2 \\ \vdots \\ \boldsymbol{p}_n \cdot \boldsymbol{q}_2 \end{pmatrix} + \cdots + v_m \begin{pmatrix} \boldsymbol{p}_1 \cdot \boldsymbol{q}_n \\ \boldsymbol{p}_2 \cdot \boldsymbol{q}_n \\ \vdots \\ \boldsymbol{p}_n \cdot \boldsymbol{q}_m \end{pmatrix}$$

From the last expression, we can read off the images of the standard basis under the mapping $f \circ g$ and hence the representation of $f \circ g$ as a matrix:

$$\begin{pmatrix} \boldsymbol{p}_1 \cdot \boldsymbol{q}_1 & \boldsymbol{p}_1 \cdot \boldsymbol{q}_2 & \cdots & \boldsymbol{p}_1 \cdot \boldsymbol{q}_m \\ \boldsymbol{p}_2 \cdot \boldsymbol{q}_1 & \boldsymbol{p}_2 \cdot \boldsymbol{q}_2 & \cdots & \boldsymbol{p}_2 \cdot \boldsymbol{q}_m \\ \vdots & \vdots & \ddots & \vdots \\ \boldsymbol{p}_n \cdot \boldsymbol{q}_1 & \boldsymbol{p}_n \cdot \boldsymbol{q}_2 & \cdots & \boldsymbol{p}_n \cdot \boldsymbol{q}_m \end{pmatrix} = \boldsymbol{P}\boldsymbol{Q}$$

We define this to be the matrix product PQ and have $f \circ g(v) = PQv$. To be explicit, the product of an $n \times r$ matrix P with elements p_{ik}, $i = 1, \ldots, n$ and $k = 1, \ldots, r$ and a $r \times m$ matrix Q with elements q_{ik}, $i = 1, \ldots, r$ and $k = 1, \ldots, m$ is an $n \times m$ matrix PQ, with elements $p_i \cdot q_k$ for $i = 1, \ldots, n$ and $k = 1, \ldots, m$.

$$PQ = \left(\sum_{j=1}^{r} p_{ij} q_{jk} \right) \quad \text{with } i = 1, \ldots, n \text{ and } k = 1, \ldots, m.$$

Once we can multiply matrices, we can of course also compute powers of matrices. We write A^2 for AA and A^3 for AAA and so on. But be aware, we have defined a product PQ only if the number of columns of P matches the number of rows in Q. Therefore, AA is defined only for matrices where the number of columns is equal to the number of rows. Such matrices are called square matrices, and we restrict the exponent notation to these square matrices.

With numbers, we are used to the extended notation where the exponent can be an arbitrary whole number. With matrices, we can easily write A^1 for A, but what about A^0 and A^{-1} ?

For a number x, we have $x^0 = 1$, the unit element, and we would like to define A^0 as the unit matrix. The characteristic property of the unit element is usually $1 \cdot x = x \cdot 1 = x$. It is neutral in regard to multiplication. Does such a matrix exist? Yes it does. It is called the identity matrix (defined below) and we write it $\mathcal{I}_n$. We define then $A^0 = \mathcal{I}_n$.

The characteristic property of x^{-1} for numbers is $x^{-1} \cdot x = 1 = x \cdot x^{-1}$. It is the inverse element of x in regard to multiplication. For the inverse matrix, we should require $AA^{-1} = \mathcal{I}_n = A^{-1}A$. It is easy to see that not every square matrix has an inverse matrix, but some do have, as we will see. To be precise, the set of square matrices of size $n \times n$ form a Ring (see Appendix B.1).

So if the inverse matrix of A exists, we can write it as A^{-1} and we can extend the exponent notation to all whole numbers. We have then, for instance, $A^{-1}A^{-1} = A^{-2}$ or $A^{-7}A^3 = A^{-4}$.

We will not cover here the topic of how to compute A^{-1}. Anyway, computing the inverse of a matrix is not very common. It is computationally expensive and often numerically not very stable (i.e. the precision of numerical results is not very good). In practice, usually more sophisticated methods are used.

There are however special cases, where the inverse matrix is easy to obtain. Recall equations (2) on page 95. Knowing about matrices, we can recognize the right hand sides of the equations as a product of matrices: If we have $A = (v_1 \, v_2 \, v_3)$, the matrix that has the vectors v_i as columns, the right hand side is just $AA^\top$ times the vector (y_1, y_2, y_3).

The equations (2) could be simplified significantly to equations (3) if the vectors v_i were orthogonal. In this case, the matrix $AA^\top$ is almost the identity matrix (except for the factors $|v_i|^2$). And indeed, after scaling the rows, the matrix $A^\top$ is, in this case, the inverse of A. Here, we have an important example where the inverse is easy to compute and useful.

10.11 Working with Matrices

A matrix is the Swiss-Army-Knife of the mathematician. There are often more elegant
ways to open the can, but if you have no specialized tool at hand, try a matrix. Just
to get the necessary preparation for the following chapters, here are some standard
can-openers:

- The zero matrix $\mathcal{Z}_n$.
  This matrix maps any vector to the zero vector. Especially it
  maps any vector of the standard basis to a zero vector. Since
  the columns of a matrix contain the images of the standard
  basis, its columns are just zero vectors. So all its elements
  are zero. This matrix is the neutral element in respect to
  matrix addition.

$$\begin{pmatrix} 0 & 0 & 0 & 0 & 0 \\ 0 & 0 & 0 & 0 & 0 \\ 0 & 0 & 0 & 0 & 0 \\ 0 & 0 & 0 & 0 & 0 \\ 0 & 0 & 0 & 0 & 0 \end{pmatrix}$$

- The identity matrix $\mathcal{I}_n$.
  This matrix maps any vector $\boldsymbol{x}$ to itself. Especially it maps
  any vector of the standard basis onto itself. That is, its
  columns are just the vectors of the standard basis, so its
  elements will be all zero except the elements in the diagonal.
  From the top left to the bottom right, the elements in the
  diagonal are all 1. This matrix is the neutral element in
  respect to matrix multiplication.

$$\begin{pmatrix} 1 & 0 & 0 & 0 & 0 \\ 0 & 1 & 0 & 0 & 0 \\ 0 & 0 & 1 & 0 & 0 \\ 0 & 0 & 0 & 1 & 0 \\ 0 & 0 & 0 & 0 & 1 \end{pmatrix}$$

- The diagonal matrix $\mathcal{D}(a_i)$.
  This matrix is a variation of the identity matrix. Instead
  of 1s in the diagonal, it has the values a_i in the diagonal. It maps a vector $\boldsymbol{x} = (x_0, x_1, \ldots, x_n)$ to the vector
  $(a_0 x_0, a_1 x_1, \ldots, a_n x_n)$.
    The zero matrix and the identity matrix are just special
  cases of a diagonal matrix, but also the application of a
  windowing function to a vector of samples can be described
  as the application of a diagonal matrix.

$$\begin{pmatrix} 1 & 0 & 0 & 0 & 0 \\ 0 & 2 & 0 & 0 & 0 \\ 0 & 0 & 3 & 0 & 0 \\ 0 & 0 & 0 & 2 & 0 \\ 0 & 0 & 0 & 0 & 1 \end{pmatrix}$$

- The reverse diagonal matrix $\mathcal{R}_n$.
  This matrix looks like the identity matrix, but the 1's are
  not in the diagonal from top-left to bottom-right, but in
  the diagonal from bottom-left to top-right. Applied to the
  standard basis, it will just reverse the order of the vectors.
  Similarly, applied to any vector $\boldsymbol{x} = (x_0, x_1, \ldots, x_n)$, it will
  reverse the order of its elements to yield $(x_n, \ldots, x_1, x_0)$.

$$\begin{pmatrix} 0 & 0 & 0 & 0 & 1 \\ 0 & 0 & 0 & 1 & 0 \\ 0 & 0 & 1 & 0 & 0 \\ 0 & 1 & 0 & 0 & 0 \\ 1 & 0 & 0 & 0 & 0 \end{pmatrix}$$

- The permutation matrix $\mathcal{P}(\sigma)$.
  If σ is any permutation, that is a reordering of the components of a vector, this reordering can be achieved by applying
  the matrix $\mathcal{P}(\sigma)$. How does it look like? Apply the reordering σ to the vectors of the standard basis and you have the
  rows of $\mathcal{P}(\sigma)$.

$$\begin{pmatrix} 0 & 1 & 0 & 0 & 0 \\ 1 & 0 & 0 & 0 & 0 \\ 0 & 0 & 0 & 1 & 0 \\ 0 & 0 & 0 & 0 & 1 \\ 0 & 0 & 1 & 0 & 0 \end{pmatrix}$$

If σ reorders the vector to put the first component in position i, then the first vector of the standard basis will end up in row i. Applying the matrix, the scalar product with row i will extract the first component of the vector and make it component i.

- The projection matrix $\mathcal{F}_k$ and $\mathcal{L}_k$

  Taking from the identity matrix only the first k rows yields the matrix $\mathcal{F}_k$. Taking the last k rows yields $\mathcal{L}_k$. Row i of the identity matrix is the i'th vector of the standard basis. The scalar product with this vector extracts just the i'th component. Applying the matrix $\mathcal{F}_k$ will therefore give a shorter vector, containing just the first k components. Similarly, applying $\mathcal{L}_k$ will give the last k components.

  $$\begin{pmatrix} 1 & 0 & 0 & 0 & 0 \\ 0 & 1 & 0 & 0 & 0 \\ 0 & 0 & 1 & 0 & 0 \end{pmatrix}$$

  $$\begin{pmatrix} 0 & 0 & 1 & 0 & 0 \\ 0 & 0 & 0 & 1 & 0 \\ 0 & 0 & 0 & 0 & 1 \end{pmatrix}$$

- The injection matrix $\mathcal{F}_k^\top$ and $\mathcal{L}_k^\top$

  The transposed projection matrix is almost the inverse of it. It does not reduce the dimension, it injects a vector into a vector space with higher dimension. It takes a shorter vector and makes it longer by either appending zeros at the end ($\mathcal{F}_k^\top$) or at the beginning ($\mathcal{L}_k^\top$).

  We have $\mathcal{F}_k \mathcal{F}_k^\top v = v$, because the application of $\mathcal{F}_k$ just removes the zeros that were added by $\mathcal{F}_k^\top$. We have $\mathcal{F}_k^\top \mathcal{F}_k v = v$ only if the last components of v were zero anyway. Similar equations hold for $\mathcal{L}_k^\top$.

  $$\begin{pmatrix} 1 & 0 & 0 \\ 0 & 1 & 0 \\ 0 & 0 & 1 \\ 0 & 0 & 0 \\ 0 & 0 & 0 \end{pmatrix}$$

- Block matrix.

  It is often convenient, to construct a matrix using other matrices as building blocks. For instance, a matrix that leaves the first half of a vector unchanged and reverses the second half can be defined using the matrix $\mathcal{I}_{n/2}$ and $\mathcal{R}_{n/2}$. To operate on the first part of the vector, the matrix $\mathcal{I}_{n/2}$ must be in the first columns, to impact the first part of the output, the matrix $\mathcal{I}_{n/2}$ must be in the first rows. So $\mathcal{I}_{n/2}$ makes up the top left of the block matrix, and $\mathcal{R}_{n/2}$ will make up the bottom right. The rest is filled with zeros. We write such a matrix as

  $$\begin{pmatrix} 1 & 0 & 0 & 0 & 0 & 0 \\ 0 & 1 & 0 & 0 & 0 & 0 \\ 0 & 0 & 1 & 0 & 0 & 0 \\ 0 & 0 & 0 & 0 & 0 & 1 \\ 0 & 0 & 0 & 0 & 1 & 0 \\ 0 & 0 & 0 & 1 & 0 & 0 \end{pmatrix}$$

$$\begin{pmatrix} \mathcal{I}_{n/2} & 0 \\ 0 & \mathcal{R}_{n/2} \end{pmatrix}.$$

10.12 Fast Discrete Cosine Transform

Applying a matrix to a vector, to analyze the vectors components or to synthesize a new vector as linear combination, is an elegant mathematical method. Unfortunately, it can be a very costly operation. Clever use of the matrix calculus can, however, simplify the calculations enormously. The best known example for such a reduction in computational complexity is the Fast Fourier Transformation[7].

Here, we will demonstrate the principle using a simple but still useful special case: The fast, discrete, type III, cosine transform. This transform is defined as

$$\mathrm{DCT}_n^{\mathrm{III}} = \left(\cos(\frac{\pi}{n}(i + \frac{1}{2})k) \right) \quad \text{for i=0 to n-1 and k=0 to n-1.} \qquad (Eq.\ 5)$$

It is used in Section 11.3 for $n = 18$ and in Section 11.4 for $n = 6$ to synthesize sequences of subband samples.

In this section, we keep the exposition as simple and short as possible and discuss only the small matrix $\mathrm{DCT}_6^{\mathrm{III}}$. For this matrix, we derive a matrix decomposition and use it, in Appendix A.5, to generate efficient C code.

The matrix $\mathrm{DCT}_6^{\mathrm{III}}$ looks like this:

$$\mathrm{DCT}_6^{\mathrm{III}} = \begin{pmatrix} \cos(0) & \cos(\frac{\pi}{12}) & \cos(\frac{\pi}{6}) & \cos(\frac{\pi}{4}) & \cos(\frac{\pi}{3}) & \cos(\frac{5\pi}{12}) \\ \cos(0) & \cos(\frac{\pi}{4}) & \cos(\frac{\pi}{2}) & \cos(\frac{3\pi}{4}) & \cos(\pi) & \cos(\frac{5\pi}{4}) \\ \cos(0) & \cos(\frac{5\pi}{12}) & \cos(\frac{5\pi}{6}) & \cos(\frac{5\pi}{4}) & \cos(\frac{5\pi}{3}) & \cos(\frac{25\pi}{12}) \\ \cos(0) & \cos(\frac{7\pi}{12}) & \cos(\frac{7\pi}{6}) & \cos(\frac{7\pi}{4}) & \cos(\frac{7\pi}{3}) & \cos(\frac{35\pi}{12}) \\ \cos(0) & \cos(\frac{3\pi}{4}) & \cos(\frac{3\pi}{2}) & \cos(\frac{9\pi}{4}) & \cos(3\pi) & \cos(\frac{15\pi}{4}) \\ \cos(0) & \cos(\frac{11\pi}{12}) & \cos(\frac{11\pi}{6}) & \cos(\frac{11\pi}{4}) & \cos(\frac{11\pi}{3}) & \cos(\frac{55\pi}{12}) \end{pmatrix}$$

To apply an $n \times n$ matrix to a vector, in general n^2 multiplications and $n(n-1)$ additions are required. In this special case, because $\cos(0) = 1$, $\cos(\pi/2) = 0$ and $\cos(\pi) = -1$), we have only 26 multiplications and 28 additions. Still far too much.

The key to an efficient algorithm is the observation that the rows (and columns) of the matrix have a periodic structure. To make this structure visible, we show the same matrix again using graphs.

$$\mathrm{DCT}_6^{\mathrm{III}} = \left(\begin{matrix} \end{matrix} \right)$$

Here, we discover for example that the first row v_1 and the last row v_6 have the same entries except for the sign, which is always positive in the first row, and alternates in the last row. The sum of the first and the last row has therefore only three non zero elements, because elements with opposite sign cancel each other. Similarly the difference of both rows as only three non zero elements, because elements with the same sign cancel each other.

$$v_1 + v_6 = \qquad\qquad\qquad v_1 - v_6 =$$

Because of these zeros, the scalar product with $v_1 + v_6$ and $v_1 - v_6$ can be computed twice as fast as the scalar product with v_1 and v_6. On the other hand, we can obtain

$v_1 z$ and $v_6 z$ easily from $\frac{1}{2}(v_1 + v_6)z$ and $\frac{1}{2}(v_1 - v_6)z$ using one addition and one subtraction.

Closer inspection of $\mathrm{DCT}_6^{\mathrm{III}}$ reveals that the same trick works also for rows 2 and 5, and rows 3 and 4. We package the addition and subtraction operation for each pair of rows in the following matrix:

$$Q_1 = \begin{pmatrix} 1 & 0 & 0 & 0 & 0 & 1 \\ 0 & 1 & 0 & 0 & 1 & 0 \\ 0 & 0 & 1 & 1 & 0 & 0 \\ 0 & 0 & -1 & 1 & 0 & 0 \\ 0 & -1 & 0 & 0 & 1 & 0 \\ -1 & 0 & 0 & 0 & 0 & 1 \end{pmatrix}$$

and have $\mathrm{DCT}_6^{\mathrm{III}} = Q_1 Q_1^{-1} \mathrm{DCT}_6^{\mathrm{III}}$ with

$$Q_1^{-1}\mathrm{DCT}_6^{\mathrm{III}} = \begin{pmatrix} 0 & \frac{1+\sqrt{3}}{2\sqrt{2}} & 0 & \frac{1}{\sqrt{2}} & 0 & \frac{-1+\sqrt{3}}{2\sqrt{2}} \\ 0 & \frac{1}{\sqrt{2}} & 0 & -\frac{1}{\sqrt{2}} & 0 & -\frac{1}{\sqrt{2}} \\ 0 & \frac{-1+\sqrt{3}}{2\sqrt{2}} & 0 & -\frac{1}{\sqrt{2}} & 0 & \frac{1+\sqrt{3}}{2\sqrt{2}} \\ 1 & 0 & -\frac{\sqrt{3}}{2} & 0 & \frac{1}{2} & 0 \\ 1 & 0 & 0 & 0 & -1 & 0 \\ 1 & 0 & \frac{\sqrt{3}}{2} & 0 & \frac{1}{2} & 0 \end{pmatrix} = \begin{pmatrix} \text{[waveform plots]} \end{pmatrix}$$

We rearrange the columns by applying a permutation matrix

$$P_1 = \begin{pmatrix} 0 & 1 & 0 & 0 & 0 & 0 \\ 0 & 0 & 0 & 1 & 0 & 0 \\ 0 & 0 & 0 & 0 & 0 & 1 \\ 1 & 0 & 0 & 0 & 0 & 0 \\ 0 & 0 & 1 & 0 & 0 & 0 \\ 0 & 0 & 0 & 0 & 1 & 0 \end{pmatrix}$$

to get $\mathrm{DCT}_6^{\mathrm{III}} = Q_1\big(Q_1^{-1}\mathrm{DCT}_6^{\mathrm{III}} P_1^{-1}\big)P_1$ with

$$Q_1^{-1}\mathrm{DCT}_6^{\mathrm{III}} P_1^{-1} = \begin{pmatrix} \frac{1+\sqrt{3}}{2\sqrt{2}} & \frac{1}{\sqrt{2}} & \frac{-1+\sqrt{3}}{2\sqrt{2}} & 0 & 0 & 0 \\ \frac{1}{\sqrt{2}} & -\frac{1}{\sqrt{2}} & -\frac{1}{\sqrt{2}} & 0 & 0 & 0 \\ \frac{-1+\sqrt{3}}{2\sqrt{2}} & -\frac{1}{\sqrt{2}} & \frac{1+\sqrt{3}}{2\sqrt{2}} & 0 & 0 & 0 \\ 0 & 0 & 0 & 1 & -\frac{\sqrt{3}}{2} & \frac{1}{2} \\ 0 & 0 & 0 & 1 & 0 & -1 \\ 0 & 0 & 0 & 1 & \frac{\sqrt{3}}{2} & \frac{1}{2} \end{pmatrix}$$

In summary: We have reduced the computational cost of a matrix multiplication from n^2 to $2*(n/2)^2 + n$ by replacing the multiplication with an $n \times n$ matrix by a permutation P_1 (no computational cost), two matrix multiplications of size $(n/2) \times$

$(n/2)$ and a multiplication with a simple add and subtract matrix Q_1 (computational cost $n/2$ additions and $n/2$ subtractions).

For our special case, where $n = 6$ and some of the entries are 0, 1, or -1, we are down from 26 multiplications and 28 additions to 13 multiplications and 16 additions. But the best thing is, the two new, smaller matrices have a similar periodic structure as the big matrix we started with. So we can use the same idea again and reduce these matrices further. The total computational complexity is then $n \log_2 n$ instead of n^2.

The process gets slightly more complex if n is not a multiple of 2. Fortunately, the two remaining matrices of size 3×3 are already pretty small, and we can cope with that.

We repeat the add and subtract trick with row 1 and row 3 for the upper left block and row 4 and row 6 for the lower right block using matrix Q_2 with

$$
Q_2 = \begin{pmatrix}
1 & 0 & 1 & 0 & 0 & 0 \\
0 & 1 & 0 & 0 & 0 & 0 \\
-1 & 0 & 1 & 0 & 0 & 0 \\
0 & 0 & 0 & 1 & 0 & 1 \\
0 & 0 & 0 & 0 & 1 & 0 \\
0 & 0 & 0 & -1 & 0 & 1
\end{pmatrix}
$$

We arrive at $\mathrm{DCT}_6^{\mathrm{III}} = Q_1 Q_2 \big(Q_2^{-1} Q_1^{-1} \mathrm{DCT}_6^{\mathrm{III}} P_1^{-1} \big) P_1$ with

$$
Q_2^{-1} Q_1^{-1} \mathrm{DCT}_6^{\mathrm{III}} P_1^{-1} = \begin{pmatrix}
\frac{1}{2\sqrt{2}} & \frac{1}{\sqrt{2}} & -\frac{1}{2\sqrt{2}} & 0 & 0 & 0 \\
\frac{1}{\sqrt{2}} & -\frac{1}{\sqrt{2}} & -\frac{1}{\sqrt{2}} & 0 & 0 & 0 \\
\frac{\sqrt{\frac{3}{2}}}{2} & 0 & \frac{\sqrt{\frac{3}{2}}}{2} & 0 & 0 & 0 \\
0 & 0 & 0 & 0 & -\frac{\sqrt{3}}{2} & 0 \\
0 & 0 & 0 & 1 & 0 & -1 \\
0 & 0 & 0 & 1 & 0 & \frac{1}{2}
\end{pmatrix}
$$

While the lower right block is already quite satisfactory, for the upper right block we need another add and subtract operation, this time on column 1 and column 3. We do this with the matrix

$$
P_2 = \begin{pmatrix}
1 & 0 & 1 & 0 & 0 & 0 \\
0 & 1 & 0 & 0 & 0 & 0 \\
-1 & 0 & 1 & 0 & 0 & 0 \\
0 & 0 & 0 & 1 & 0 & 0 \\
0 & 0 & 0 & 0 & 1 & 0 \\
0 & 0 & 0 & 0 & 0 & 1
\end{pmatrix}
$$

We have now $\mathrm{DCT}_6^{\mathrm{III}} = Q_1 Q_2 \big(Q_2^{-1} Q_1^{-1} \mathrm{DCT}_6^{\mathrm{III}} P_1^{-1} P_2^{-1} \big) P_2 P_1$ with

$$Q_2^{-1}Q_1^{-1}\mathrm{DCT}_6^{\mathrm{III}}P_1^{-1}P_2^{-1} = \begin{pmatrix} 0 & \frac{1}{\sqrt{2}} & -\frac{1}{2\sqrt{2}} & 0 & 0 & 0 \\ 0 & -\frac{1}{\sqrt{2}} & -\frac{1}{\sqrt{2}} & 0 & 0 & 0 \\ \frac{\sqrt{\frac{3}{2}}}{2} & 0 & 0 & 0 & 0 & 0 \\ 0 & 0 & 0 & 0 & -\frac{\sqrt{3}}{2} & 0 \\ 0 & 0 & 0 & 1 & 0 & -1 \\ 0 & 0 & 0 & 1 & 0 & \frac{1}{2} \end{pmatrix}$$

As a last step, we use the diagonal matrix

$$Q_3 = \mathcal{D}\left(\frac{1}{2\sqrt{2}}, \frac{-1}{\sqrt{2}}, \frac{\sqrt{3/2}}{2}, \frac{-\sqrt{3}}{2}, 1, 1\right)$$

to scale the remaining rows. The final result is

$$\mathrm{DCT}_6^{\mathrm{III}} = Q_1 Q_2 Q_3 (Q_3^{-1}Q_2^{-1}Q_1^{-1}\mathrm{DCT}_6^{\mathrm{III}}P_1^{-1}P_2^{-1})P_2 P_1, \qquad (Eq.\ 6)$$

with

$$Q_3^{-1}Q_2^{-1}Q_1^{-1}\mathrm{DCT}_6^{\mathrm{III}}P_1^{-1}P_2^{-1} = \begin{pmatrix} 0 & 1+1 & -1 & 0 & 0 & 0 \\ 0 & 1 & 1 & 0 & 0 & 0 \\ 1 & 0 & 0 & 0 & 0 & 0 \\ 0 & 0 & 0 & 0 & 1 & 0 \\ 0 & 0 & 0 & 1 & 0 & -1 \\ 0 & 0 & 0 & 1 & 0 & \frac{1}{2} \end{pmatrix}.$$

The application of this matrix can be done with 1 multiplication by 0.5, 3 additions, and 2 subtractions. Using equation (6), we can compute the application of $\mathrm{DCT}_6^{\mathrm{III}}$ using 4 more multiplications (for Q_3), and 12 more additions/subtractions (for Q_1, Q_2, and P_2). We arrive at a total of 5 multiplications and 17 additions/subtractions. The algorithm generated from this decomposition is used in Appendix A.5.

11 New Ideas: Layer III

At the very basis of MPEG audio compression is the general observation that typical audio signals are better described by their frequency content than by the changes in air-pressure levels which transport audible sound. While the air-pressure levels exhibit rapid changes, the frequency content is very much a stationary signal. Therefore MPEG audio compression transforms the signal description from the time domain to the frequency domain. This idea is taken one step further in layer III.

Recall the data flow from layer I and layer II (Fig. 8). The audio signal was stored in the bit stream as a series of subband samples for 32 subbands. Each subband represents a certain frequency roughly resembling one critical band of human hearing. Through Matrixing, combined with Shifting, Storing, and a final Windowing step, the frequency representation was transformed back to the PCM representation.

In layer III, the subband samples are not stored directly in the bit stream. Instead from each subband, the encoder takes a series of 18 consecutive subband samples and transforms it, using an MDCT, into 18 sub frequencies. This leads to $32 \cdot 18 = 576$ frequency values. In the decoder, these frequencies are transformed back to the subband representation, which finally yields 576 PCM values. The reconstruction process (Fig. 30) involves some more steps than just applying an inverse MDCT, and we will discuss these in great detail in the Sections 11.1, 11.2, 11.3, and 11.11 below.

The finer frequency resolution of layer III offers more choices for the encoder to separate audible from inaudible information and ultimately leads to better compression. It comes, however, at a price. The procedure will work as expected only if the underlying assumption of an audio signal with a more or less stationary frequency content holds. We will discuss this problem further in Section 11.4 on "Short Blocks".

Stereo signals offer an other opportunity for saving precious bits. Since both channels are not independent but carry very similar signals, a joint representation of both channels can be more compact. This phenomenon is studied in Section 11.10 on "Joint Stereo".

A further refinement of layer III is the use of Huffman coding to store the 576 frequency lines as compact as possible. Huffman Coding is the technique of choice for lossless data compression and is the basis for all the well known data compression programs (like Winzip, Pkzip, Stuffit, or Gzip). We will discuss Huffman coding in Chapter 12.

As a consequence of Huffman Coding, the size of the compressed frame is less predictable than before. This necessitates a more sophisticated layout of layer III

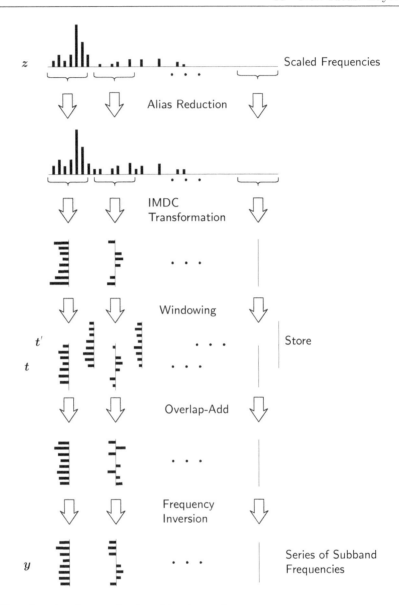

Fig. 30: Transforming frequencies to subband samples

frames, which we discuss in Chapter 13. For now, it will suffice to know that one frame contains two so called granules, which can share data between them.

11.1 Simple Encoding with the Discrete Cosine Transform

In layer III, each granule contains $576 = 32 \cdot 18$ different frequency values. Groups of 18 values each, called a block, are used to compute 18 time consecutive values for one subband each. Subbands are then processed in the same way as in layers I and II. The enhanced frequency resolution provides more opportunities for compact encoding.

Converting time consecutive values into frequencies (encoding) and back (decoding) can be done with the Discrete Cosine Transform. There are several variants of this transformation, and we start by using DCT^{IV}.

$$DCT_n^{IV} = \left(\cos(\frac{\pi}{n}(i + \frac{1}{2})(k + \frac{1}{2})) \right) \quad \text{for i=0 to n-1 and k=0 to n-1}$$

This matrix is symmetric,

$$DCT_n^{IV}{}^{\top} = DCT_n^{IV},$$

and its own inverse (at least almost),

$$DCT_n^{IV} \cdot DCT_n^{IV} = \frac{n}{2}\mathcal{I}_n,$$

and we can use it for both encoding and decoding. If needed, we add a factor of $\sqrt{n/2}$ to obtain an exact inverse.

To simplify the discussion, we will restrict our attention now to a single subband, and a single example: suddenly switching on the frequency in this subband from zero to one. Since the transition from one granule to the next granule is one of the problems we have to solve, we consider two granules, the first will switch on the signal in the middle of the granule (12 zeros followed by 6 ones), the second granule keeps the signal constant (18 ones). To encode the two time vectors y_0 and y_1, we compute two frequency vectors

$$z_0 = 1/3 \cdot DCT_{18}^{IV}y_0 \quad \text{and} \quad z_1 = 1/3 \cdot DCT_{18}^{IV}y_1.$$

To decode z_0 and z_1, we multiply again by $1/3 \cdot DCT_{18}^{IV}$ and obtain again

$$y_0 = 1/3 \cdot DCT_{18}^{IV}z_0 \quad \text{and} \quad y_1 = 1/3 \cdot DCT_{18}^{IV}z_1.$$

In order not to create confusion, a word on notation: So far, the symbol y was used for a vector of frequencies and x was used for a vector of PCM samples. Now suddenly the z vector is used for frequencies and decoded to a vector of time consecutive values y. What remains constant is the use of y for subband frequencies. The change in perspective is this: We used to consider y as a vector that spans 32 different subbands for the same point in time, hence as a frequency vector. Now we consider only a single subband and its values at 18 or 36 consecutive points in time; using this view of y, as a series of values over time, we can decompose it into a frequency vector z.

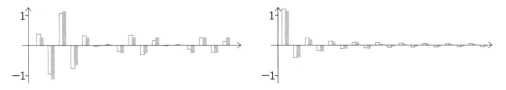

Fig. 31: Comparison of z_0 (white) versus $\bar{z}_0$ (gray) and z_1 versus $\bar{z}_1$

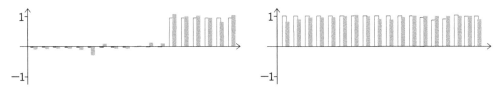

Fig. 32: Comparison of $\boldsymbol{y}_0$ (white) versus $\bar{\boldsymbol{y}}_0$ (gray) and $\boldsymbol{y}_1$ versus $\bar{\boldsymbol{y}}_1$

The white bars of Figure 31 and Figure 32 show the vectors $\boldsymbol{y}_0$ and $\boldsymbol{z}_0$, respectively $\boldsymbol{y}_1$ and $\boldsymbol{z}_1$. The subband values can be recovered exactly from the frequency values. At the heart of MPEG audio compression is, however, data reduction by ignoring "inaudible" details. So, we replace the exact frequency values $\boldsymbol{z}_0$ and $\boldsymbol{z}_1$ by simplified versions $\bar{\boldsymbol{z}}_0$ and $\bar{\boldsymbol{z}}_1$.

The simplified frequency values have the form $\text{sign}(u)|u|^{4/3}2^{k/4}$, where u and k are integer values (see Section 11.6 Quantization). The k is determined by the global gain and the scalefactor and the u is produced by the Huffman decoder. For our example, we choose $k = -6$ to quantize $\boldsymbol{z}_0$ and $k = -11$ to quantize $\boldsymbol{z}_1$. The encoder obtains the vectors $\boldsymbol{u}_0$ and $\boldsymbol{u}_1$ by solving the equation

$$z = \text{sign}(u)|u|^{4/3}2^{k/4}$$

for each component. These values are then rounded to the nearest integer to obtain the quantized vectors $\bar{\boldsymbol{u}}_0$ and $\bar{\boldsymbol{u}}_1$. After transmission to the decoder, it then computes $\bar{\boldsymbol{z}}_i$ from $\bar{\boldsymbol{u}}_i$, using the same equation, and obtains $\bar{\boldsymbol{y}}_i = 1/3\text{DCT}^{\text{IV}}\bar{\boldsymbol{z}}_i$. The vectors $\bar{\boldsymbol{z}}_0$, $\bar{\boldsymbol{z}}_1$, $\bar{\boldsymbol{y}}_0$, and $\bar{\boldsymbol{y}}_1$ are shown in Figure 31 and Figure 32 in gray. The next table gives numerical results for encoding of $\boldsymbol{y}_0$ to $\bar{\boldsymbol{u}}_0$ and its decoding to $\bar{\boldsymbol{y}}_0$.

$\boldsymbol{y}_0$	=	0	0	0	0	0	0	0	0	0	0	0	0	1	1	1	1	1	1
$\boldsymbol{z}_0$	=	0.51	−1.28	1.44	−1.03	0.44	−0.05	0.04	−0.27	0.46	−0.42	0.21	−0.03	0.03	−0.18	0.33	−0.32	0.17	−0.02
$\boldsymbol{u}_0$	=	1.32	−2.62	2.86	−2.24	1.17	−0.22	0.2	−0.83	1.22	−1.14	0.68	−0.14	0.14	−0.6	0.94	−0.92	0.57	−0.13
$\bar{\boldsymbol{u}}_0$	=	1	−3	3	−2	1	0	0	−1	1	−1	1	0	0	−1	1	−1	1	0
$\bar{\boldsymbol{z}}_0$	=	0.35	−1.53	1.53	−0.89	0.35	0	0	−0.35	0.35	−0.35	0.35	0	0	−0.35	0.35	−0.35	0.35	0
$\bar{\boldsymbol{y}}_0$	=	−0.1	−0.09	−0.07	−0.07	−0.12	−0.3	0.1	−0.07	−0.07	0.01	0.14	0.11	1.13	1.06	1.08	1.01	0.87	1.1

Tab. 14: Simple encoding with $\text{DCT}^{\text{IV}}_{18}$

Fig. 33: Signal reconstructed from $\overline{u}_0$ and $\overline{u}_1$

It is obvious that the value of $k = -6$ was not chosen to provide perfect reconstruction, but to produce some visible distortion. Look at the values of $\overline{u}_0$. Using Huffman Code Table 6, we need only $5 + 6 + 3 + 3 + 2 + 3 + 3 + 2 + 3 = 30$ bits plus 6 sign bits, a total of 36 bits or 2 bits per value, to code the entire vector. Figure 33 gives an idea of the signal reconstructed from $\overline{u}_0$ and $\overline{u}_1$. It illustrates two problems:

- There is a sudden change in signal level going from the first granule to the second. While the exact signal goes smoothly from one granule to the next, the different errors introduced by the compression for both granules cause the signal to jump at the border. Such a discontinuity, if periodically repeated at the end of each and every granule, will cause a quite audible tonal noise.

  Windowing is the solution to this problem.

- The signal distortion introduced in a granule is spread out over the entire granule. While it might be hidden behind the strong signal, once it is switched on, the distortion is completely exposed in the silence before the signal sets in. An effect known as pre-echo. Ordinarily, echos are muted (and often distorted) copies of the original signal, caused by reflections on nearby walls, that arrive slightly later than the main signal. An echo that arrives earlier is an unnatural sensation.

  Short Blocks provide a solution to this problem.

11.2 Windowing

We have seen the use of windowing before, now we look at the very details. The standard doubles the size of a block to contain 36 values and two adjacent blocks have an overlap of 18 values. For the fade-in and fade-out, a sin curve is prescribed. To illustrate the new schema and demonstrate the improvements, we redo the previous example.

We consider a new vector y by extending the old y_0 with 18 zeros to the left, and a second vector y', by extending y_1 with y_0 to the left.

$$y = (0, y_0)$$
$$y' = (y_0, y_1)$$

As required, the two new vectors overlap by 18 values, which just contain the jump in signal level under study (Fig. 34).

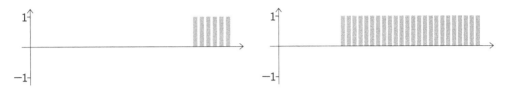

Fig. 34: Input vectors $\boldsymbol{y}$ and $\boldsymbol{y}'$

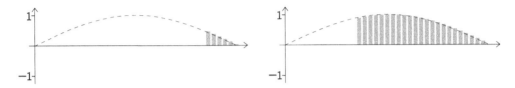

Fig. 35: Windowed vectors $\boldsymbol{W}_{36}\boldsymbol{y}$ and $\boldsymbol{W}_{36}\boldsymbol{y}'$

The windowing can be described by the diagonal matrix $\boldsymbol{W}_{36}$, defined by:

$$\boldsymbol{W}_n = \mathcal{D}\big(\sin(\frac{\pi}{n}(i + \frac{1}{2}))\big) \quad \text{for i=0 to n-1.}$$

Figure 35 illustrates the effect of applying $\boldsymbol{W}_{36}$ to our sample vectors $\boldsymbol{y}$ and $\boldsymbol{y}'$. The windowing with $\boldsymbol{W}_{36}$ is actually done twice: The vector $\boldsymbol{y}$ is multiplied by $\boldsymbol{W}_{36}$ before the encoding, with a positive effect on the frequency response, and again after decoding, for a smooth transition between blocks. In effect, every component y_i of $\boldsymbol{y}$ is multiplied twice by $\sin(\frac{\pi}{36}(i + \frac{1}{2}))$ to yield $y_i \cdot \sin^2(\frac{\pi}{36}(i + \frac{1}{2}))$.

For a precise and convenient notation to describe the overlap add process, we use the two matrices $\mathcal{F}_{18}$ and $\mathcal{L}_{18}$. The result of adding the second half of $\boldsymbol{W}_{36}{}^2\boldsymbol{y}$ to the first half of $\boldsymbol{W}_{36}{}^2\boldsymbol{y}'$ is then just $\mathcal{L}_{18}\boldsymbol{W}_{36}{}^2\boldsymbol{y} + \mathcal{F}_{18}\boldsymbol{W}_{36}{}^2\boldsymbol{y}'$. Using that $\mathcal{F}_{18}\boldsymbol{y}' = \mathcal{L}_{18}\boldsymbol{y} = \boldsymbol{y}_0$, that is $y_i' = y_{i+18}$ for $i = 0$ to 17, we can calculate an element of this sum as

$$y_i' \cdot \sin^2(\frac{\pi}{36}(i + \frac{1}{2})) + y_{i+18} \cdot \sin^2(\frac{\pi}{36}(i + 18 + \frac{1}{2})) =$$

$$y_{i+18} \cdot (\sin^2(\frac{\pi}{36}(i + \frac{1}{2})) + \sin^2(\frac{\pi}{36}(i + 18 + \frac{1}{2}))) =$$

$$y_{i+18} \cdot (\sin^2(\frac{\pi}{36}(i + \frac{1}{2})) + \sin^2(\frac{\pi}{2} + \frac{\pi}{36}(i + \frac{1}{2}))) =$$

$$y_{i+18} \cdot (\sin^2(\frac{\pi}{36}(i + \frac{1}{2})) + \cos^2(\frac{\pi}{36}(i + \frac{1}{2}))) = y_{i+18} \cdot 1$$

In total, $\mathcal{F}_{18}\boldsymbol{W}_{36}{}^2\boldsymbol{y}' + \mathcal{L}_{18}\boldsymbol{W}_{36}{}^2\boldsymbol{y} = \mathcal{F}_{18}\boldsymbol{y}' = \boldsymbol{y}_0$. The overlap, the double windowing, and the adding will exactly reproduce the original input values as illustrated by Figure 36 and 37.

Having solved the problem of smoothly joining two blocks together, we have created a new problem: Instead of encoding 18 values per block, we now encode 36 values

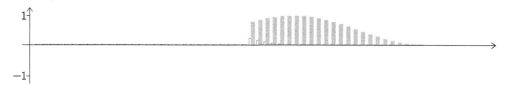

Fig. 36: Vectors $\boldsymbol{y}$ (white) and $\boldsymbol{y}'$ (gray) windowed twice and overlaid

Fig. 37: Vectors $\boldsymbol{y}$ and $\boldsymbol{y}'$ windowed twice, overlaid and added

per block. This doubling of the data rate seems unnecessary. For theoretical reasons, the decoder should be able to produce 18 decoded values from only 18 input values, and common sense tells us that when adding together two windowed signals, that differ only by fixed windowing, one of the windowed signals is redundant and can be computed from the other. MPEG audio coding solves this problem by using a Modified Discrete Cosine Transform, which we study next.

11.3 The Modified Discrete Cosine Transform

The standard specifies that for each subband, 18 time consecutive values of vector $\boldsymbol{y}$ are computed from 18 sub-frequency values of vector $\boldsymbol{z}$ and the previous 18 sub-frequency values $\boldsymbol{z}'$ by applying an Inverse Modified Discrete Cosine Transform (IMDCT), windowing, overlapping, and adding. To be precise:

$$y = \mathcal{L}_{18}\boldsymbol{W}_{36}\mathrm{IMDCT}_{36}z' + \mathcal{F}_{18}\boldsymbol{W}_{36}\mathrm{IMDCT}_{36}z.$$

The Modified Discrete Cosine Transform, used for encoding, is defined by the matrix:

$$\mathrm{MDCT}_n = \left(\cos(\frac{\pi}{2n}(2k + 1 + \frac{n}{2})(2i + 1)) \right) \quad \text{for } i = 0 \text{ to } \frac{n}{2} - 1 \text{ and } k = 0 \text{ to } n - 1.$$

For the decoding, the Inverse Modified Discrete Cosine Transform is used.

$$\mathrm{IMDCT}_n = \left(\cos(\frac{\pi}{2n}(2i + 1 + \frac{n}{2})(2k + 1)) \right) \quad \text{for } k = 0 \text{ to } \frac{n}{2} - 1 \text{ and } i = 0 \text{ to } n - 1.$$

The MDCT_n matrix has n input values and $n/2$ output values, and the IMDCT_n matrix has $n/2$ input values and n output values, exactly as required.

The definition of IMDCT looks suspiciously similar to the definition of $\mathrm{DCT}^{\mathrm{IV}}$, and indeed, there is a very simple matrix $\boldsymbol{T}_n$ that rearranges the matrix $\mathrm{DCT}_n^{\mathrm{IV}}$ to yield IMDCT_{2n}. We have

$$\mathrm{IMDCT}_{2n} = \boldsymbol{T}_n \cdot \mathrm{DCT}_n^{\mathrm{IV}}.$$

A similar equation can be derived for MDCT_n. We use that MDCT_n is just the transposed of IMDCT_n (just look at the definition) and that DCT^{IV} is symmetric to conclude:

$$\text{MDCT}_{2n} = \text{IMDCT}_{2n}^\top = (\boldsymbol{T}_n \cdot \text{DCT}_n^{\text{IV}})^\top = \text{DCT}_n^{\text{IV}\top} \cdot \boldsymbol{T}_n^\top = \text{DCT}_n^{\text{IV}} \cdot \boldsymbol{T}_n^\top.$$

According to the above formulas, encoding as well as decoding can be done with $\text{DCT}_{18}^{\text{IV}}$. Encoding with MDCT_{36} means first applying $\boldsymbol{T}_{18}^\top$ and then encoding with $\text{DCT}_{18}^{\text{IV}}$ while decoding with IMDCT_{36} can be done by decoding with $\text{DCT}_{18}^{\text{IV}}$ and then applying $\boldsymbol{T}_{18}$.

We will understand the effect of $\boldsymbol{T}_n$ better after we have seen the effect of the transposed matrix:

$$\boldsymbol{T}_n^\top = \begin{pmatrix} 0 & 0 & -\mathcal{R}_{\frac{n}{2}} & -\mathcal{I}_{\frac{n}{2}} \\ \mathcal{I}_{\frac{n}{2}} & -\mathcal{R}_{\frac{n}{2}} & 0 & 0 \end{pmatrix}$$

When the matrix $\boldsymbol{T}_{18}^\top$ is applied to a vector $\boldsymbol{w} = \boldsymbol{W}_{36}\boldsymbol{y}$, the top right block of $\boldsymbol{T}_{18}^\top$, that is $(-\mathcal{R}_9, -\mathcal{I}_9)$ will operate on the second half $\boldsymbol{w}_1 = \mathcal{L}_{18}\boldsymbol{w}$ of $\boldsymbol{w}$ and the lower left block, that is $(\mathcal{I}_9, -\mathcal{R}_9)$ will operate on the first half $\boldsymbol{w}_0 = \mathcal{F}_{18}\boldsymbol{w}$ of $\boldsymbol{w}$; the rest of the matrix is zero.

Note that the matrix $(\mathcal{I}_{\frac{n}{2}}, -\mathcal{R}_{\frac{n}{2}})$ is just the upper half of the difference $\mathcal{I}_n - \mathcal{R}_n$. As a formula:

$$\left(\mathcal{I}_9, -\mathcal{R}_9 \right) \boldsymbol{w}_0 = \mathcal{F}_9(\mathcal{I}_{18} - \mathcal{R}_{18})\boldsymbol{w}_0.$$

The effect of $\mathcal{I}_{18} - \mathcal{R}_{18}$ on $\boldsymbol{w}_0$ is just subtracting the reverse of $\boldsymbol{w}_0$ from itself. Subtracting from a vector $\overrightarrow{\boldsymbol{w}}_0$ the reverse of the same vector $\overleftarrow{\boldsymbol{w}}_0$ yields a symmetric vector. Its right half is the negative reverse of the left half. This symmetry is called odd-symmetry, since it is the same symmetry exhibited by the graphs of polynomial functions with odd exponents like x^1 or x^3. There is no need to retain both sides of a symmetric vector, one of them is enough. Therefore the matrix $(\mathcal{I}_9, -\mathcal{R}_9)$ will pass only the first half of it on to the $\text{DCT}_{18}^{\text{IV}}$ matrix.

Now to the processing of $\boldsymbol{w}_1$. Adding a vector $\overrightarrow{\boldsymbol{w}}_1$ with the reverse of the same vector $\overleftarrow{\boldsymbol{w}}_1$ yields again a symmetric vector. The right half is the reversed left side. This is called even-symmetric, since it is the same symmetry exhibited by the graphs of polynomial functions with even exponents like x^2 or x^4. The matrix $(-\mathcal{R}_9, -\mathcal{I}_9)$ computes the second half of the (negated) even symmetric content of $\boldsymbol{w}_1$ and passes it on to the $\text{DCT}_{18}^{\text{IV}}$ matrix.

Figures 38 to 42 illustrate the effect of applying $\boldsymbol{T}_{18}^\top$ to the vector $\boldsymbol{W}_{36}\boldsymbol{y}'$. Both, even as well as odd symmetric vectors, can be easily reproduced from either half of it. After all, they are symmetric. The reproduction is done by $\boldsymbol{T}_n$:

$$\boldsymbol{T}_n = \begin{pmatrix} 0 & \mathcal{I}_{n/2} \\ 0 & -\mathcal{R}_{n/2} \\ -\mathcal{R}_{n/2} & 0 \\ -\mathcal{I}_{n/2} & 0 \end{pmatrix}$$

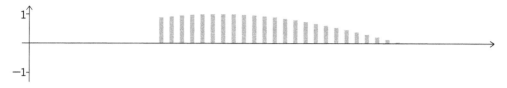

Fig. 38: Windowed vector $\boldsymbol{W}_{36}\boldsymbol{y}'$

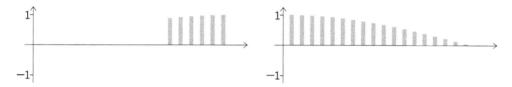

Fig. 39: $\mathcal{F}_{18}\boldsymbol{W}_{36}\boldsymbol{y}'$ and $\mathcal{L}_{18}\boldsymbol{W}_{36}\boldsymbol{y}'$, the left and right half of $\boldsymbol{W}_{36}\boldsymbol{y}'$

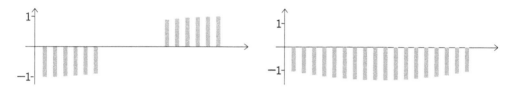

Fig. 40: Odd and negated even symmetric part of left and right half of $\boldsymbol{W}_{36}\boldsymbol{y}'$

Fig. 41: Joining the negated even and the odd half of $\boldsymbol{W}_{36}\boldsymbol{y}'$

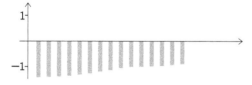

Fig. 42: The vector $\boldsymbol{T}_{18}^{\top}\boldsymbol{W}_{36}\boldsymbol{y}'$

Adding the even symmetric part, contained in one granule, to the odd symmetric part, stored in the next granule, will recombine the necessary information to reconstruct 18 complete output values. This process is captured in Figures 43 to 45. The reconstruction of the intersection of $\boldsymbol{y}$ and $\boldsymbol{y}'$ is shown on Figure 45. It compares favorably with our previous result from Figure 33. The following diagram, in Figure 46, showing the decoded section in the context of an earlier and a later granule, however, demonstrates that the problem of pre-echos still remains.

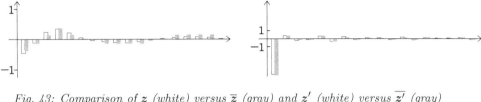

Fig. 43: Comparison of z (white) versus $\overline{z}$ (gray) and z' (white) versus $\overline{z'}$ (gray)

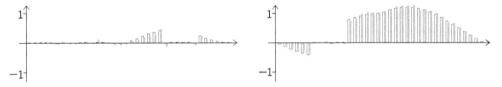

Fig. 44: Comparison of y (white) versus $\overline{y}$ (gray) and y' (white) versus $\overline{y'}$ (gray)

Fig. 45: Overlapping and adding $\mathcal{L}_{18}\overline{y}$ and $\mathcal{F}_{18}\overline{y'}$

Fig. 46: Overlapping and adding $\overline{y}$ and $\overline{y'}$ in context

Enlarging the vectors to 36 values has even aggravated this problem. Now, errors introduced by quantized frequencys are spread over 36 values for one subband. Since 32 subbands together yield 32 PCM samples, the pre echo can precede its "cause" by up to $32*36 = 1152$ samples. At a sample rate of 44.1 kHz this translates into 26 ms— a real problem. To solve this problem, MPEG audio coding introduces the concept of short blocks, which we will discuss in Section 11.4. To conclude this section, we present the implementation of the decoding process for long blocks.

The most complex and computationally demanding procedure is the $\mathrm{DCT}_{18}^{\mathrm{IV}}$ transformation, which we have used instead of IMDCT_{36}. Indeed, there is another variation of the Discrete Cosine Transformation, called $\mathrm{DCT^{III}}$, that can be computed even faster, and of course, we will use this transformation instead. The $\mathrm{DCT}_n^{\mathrm{III}}$ transformation, defined by Equation (5), was studied in detail in Section 10.12. The following equation shows how to obtain from it the matrix $\mathrm{DCT}_n^{\mathrm{IV}}$:

$$
\begin{aligned}
\mathrm{DCT}_n^{\mathrm{IV}} &= \boldsymbol{R}_n \mathrm{DCT}_n^{\mathrm{III}} \boldsymbol{S}_n \qquad \text{where} \\
\boldsymbol{R}_n &= \mathcal{D}\bigl(1/(2*\cos(\pi(i+1/2)/2n)]\bigr) \\
\boldsymbol{S}_n &= \bigl(\delta_{i,k} + \delta_{i,k+1}\bigr) \qquad \text{with} \\
\delta_{i,j} &= 1 \text{ for } i = j \quad \text{and} \quad \delta_{i,j} = 0 \text{ otherwise.}
\end{aligned}
\qquad (Eq.\ 7)
$$

As we will see, the multiplication with $\boldsymbol{R}_n$ can be combined with the windowing operation at no extra computational cost. For the $\mathrm{DCT}_{18}^{\mathrm{III}}$, an automatic tool, called fftw[10], was used to generate the code. The code produced by fftw computes, for internal reasons, $2 \cdot \mathrm{DCT}_{18}^{\mathrm{III}}$. To compensate for the extra factor of 2, we add a factor of $1/2$ when we use the matrix $\boldsymbol{R}_{18}$ in the computations below. The generated code was further modified to include the multiplication with $\boldsymbol{S}_{18}$. The computation $\boldsymbol{t} = 2 \cdot \mathrm{DCT}_{18}^{\mathrm{III}} \boldsymbol{S}_{18} \boldsymbol{z}$ is packaged into the function $dct18$.

$\langle$ private declarations $_1 \rangle +\equiv$ ⟨⟩(219)
    extern void $dct18$ (**const double** $*z$, **double** $*t$);

A full description of this function can be found in Appendix A.4.

For the overlap and add operation, we need $\mathcal{F}_{18} \boldsymbol{W}_{36} \mathrm{IMDCT}_{36} \boldsymbol{z}$ and the result from the previous granule, $\mathcal{L}_{18} \boldsymbol{W}_{36} \mathrm{IMDCT}_{36} \boldsymbol{z}'$. Of course, we need not bother to store all 36 values of the vector $\mathrm{IMDCT}_{36} \boldsymbol{z}'$, we need only the second half of it. But we can do even better. We split the computation of $\mathcal{L}_{18} \boldsymbol{W}_{36} \mathrm{IMDCT}_{36} \boldsymbol{z}' = \mathcal{L}_{18} \boldsymbol{W}_{36} \boldsymbol{T}_{18} \boldsymbol{R}_{18} \mathrm{DCT}_{18}^{\mathrm{III}} \boldsymbol{S}_{18} \boldsymbol{z}'$ in two parts: First we compute $\boldsymbol{t}' = 2 \cdot \mathrm{DCT}_{18}^{\mathrm{III}} \boldsymbol{S}_{18} \boldsymbol{z}'$ using $dct18$ and then $\mathcal{L}_{18} \boldsymbol{W}_{36} \boldsymbol{T}_{18} (1/2) \boldsymbol{R}_{18} \boldsymbol{t}'$.

Since $\boldsymbol{T}_{18}$ is a block matrix, that uses exclusively the first half of $\boldsymbol{R}_{18} \boldsymbol{t}'$ to compute the second half of its output, all we need to store is the nine element vector $\mathcal{F}_9 \boldsymbol{t}'$ and we can use $\mathcal{F}_9^\top$ to reconstruct the required vector. Hence, we store in the stream only 9 values and postpone the multiplication with $\mathcal{L}_{18} \boldsymbol{W}_{36} \boldsymbol{T}_{18} (1/2) \boldsymbol{R}_{18} \mathcal{F}_9^\top$ until we actually need the values.

$\langle$ stream data $_2 \rangle +\equiv$ ⟨⟩(220)
    double t'[CHANNELS][SUBBANDS][SUBFREQUENCIES/2];

$\langle$ store a long block for subband sb $_{221} \rangle \equiv$ ⟨⟩(221)
    { **double** $*t' = s{\to}t'[ch][sb]$;
      $t'[0] = t[0]$; $t'[1] = t[1]$; $t'[2] = t[2]$; $t'[3] = t[3]$; $t'[4] = t[4]$; $t'[5] = t[5]$;
      $t'[6] = t[6]$; $t'[7] = t[7]$; $t'[8] = t[8]$;
    }
                                                                    Used in 223 and 234.

To obtain 18 new subband samples, we process the stored vector $\boldsymbol{t}'$ appropriately and add it to $\mathcal{F}_{18} \boldsymbol{W}_{36} \boldsymbol{T}_{18} (1/2) \boldsymbol{R}_{18} \boldsymbol{t}$. We can formulate this operation, using plenty of mathematics, as:

$$
\boldsymbol{y} = \mathcal{L}_{18} \boldsymbol{W}_{36} \boldsymbol{T}_{18} (1/2) \boldsymbol{R}_{18} \mathcal{F}_9^\top \boldsymbol{t}' + \mathcal{F}_{18} \boldsymbol{W}_{36} \boldsymbol{T}_{18} (1/2) \boldsymbol{R}_{18} \boldsymbol{t}
\qquad (Eq.\ 8)
$$

Now a confession is overdue: All the formulas presented so far—and there are more
to come—are not the product of computations using paper and pencil. The formulas
and the illustrating diagrams were developed with a symbolic algebra tool (here
Mathematica[28]). This is far less error prone, faster, and even fun. We are now also
at the point where we can reap the main benefit of this approach: from equation (8),
we can automatically generate the following code:

$\langle$ window, overlap, and add a long block for subband sb $_{222}$ $\rangle$ $\equiv$ (222)

```
 { double *t′ = s→t′[ch][sb];

   double(*ỹ)[CHANNELS][SUBBANDS];
   ỹ = (double(*)[CHANNELS][SUBBANDS]) & y[0][ch][sb];
   ỹ[0][0][0]  = 0.016141215071515232 * t[9] − 0.33876269203672448 * t′[8];
   ỹ[1][0][0]  = 0.053603179340958942 * t[10] − 0.3124222244434797 * t′[7];
   ỹ[2][0][0]  = 0.10070713368098732 * t[11] − 0.28939587067395209 * t′[6];
   ỹ[3][0][0]  = 0.16280817683323032 * t[12] − 0.2688008181734919 * t′[5];
   ỹ[4][0][0]  = 0.25 * t[13] − 0.25 * t′[4];
   ỹ[5][0][0]  = 0.38388735268512201 * t[14] − 0.23251417322569559 * t′[3];
   ỹ[6][0][0]  = 0.62061144742717948 * t[15] − 0.21596714512355858 * t′[2];
   ỹ[7][0][0]  = 1.1659756150367535 * t[16] − 0.20004978874768518 * t′[1];
   ỹ[8][0][0]  = 3.8720752882039943 * t[17] − 0.18449493249753878 * t′[0];
   ỹ[9][0][0]  = −4.2256286787972681 * t[17] − 0.16905845809573499 * t′[0];
   ỹ[10][0][0] = −1.5195290056300272 * t[16] − 0.15350360184558858 * t′[1];
   ỹ[11][0][0] = −0.97416483802045324 * t[15] − 0.13758624546971519 * t′[2];
   ỹ[12][0][0] = −0.73744074327839577 * t[14] − 0.12103921736757817 * t′[3];
   ỹ[13][0][0] = −0.60355339059327376 * t[13] − 0.10355339059327376 * t′[4];
   ỹ[14][0][0] = −0.51636156742650409 * t[12] − 0.084752572419781859 * t′[5];
   ỹ[15][0][0] = −0.45426052427426109 * t[11] − 0.064157519919321673 * t′[6];
   ỹ[16][0][0] = −0.4071565699342327 * t[10] − 0.041131166149794058 * t′[7];
   ỹ[17][0][0] = −0.36969460566478899 * t[9] − 0.014790698556549281 * t′[8];
 }
```
                                                                    Used in 223 and 234.

The constants in this code are just the result of matrix operations.

   One complication of the above code arises from the different organization of the
vector y and the vector z. Unlike the vector z, the vector y is not stored in order
of increasing frequencies, but it is ordered by blocks, subbands, and channels. As
an optimization, inserted manually, we use a pointer $ỹ$ and initialize it to the right
address for the first value of the subband in question, and then just change the block
number.

   What remains is to put the two operations together. We simply iterate over all
SUBBANDS, taking for each subband a stretch of 18 values from vector z, pass it to
the $dct18$ function, use the output and the stored vector $t′$ to produce 18 values for
vector y and store the other half away for the next granule.

$\langle$ IMDCT a long block $_{223}$ $\rangle$ $\equiv$ (223)

```
 { int sb;
```

```
   for (sb = 0; sb < SUBBANDS; sb++)
   { double t[18];

      if (sb < s→sblimit[ch]) dct18(z[ch] + sb * SUBFREQUENCIES, t);
      else ⟨ zero t  224 ⟩
      ⟨ window, overlap, and add a long block for subband sb  222 ⟩
      ⟨ store a long block for subband sb  221 ⟩
   }

}
```
Used in 234.

Subbands that are empty for the current granule may not be empty for the next granule, therefore it is necessary to

⟨ zero t 224 ⟩ ≡   (224)
```
   { int i;

      for (i = 0; i < 18; i++) t[i] = 0.0;
   }
```
Used in 223, 230, and 234.

11.4 Short Blocks

The disadvantage of the finer frequency resolution is the loss in temporal resolution. This is not a problem as long as the transformation and the reverse transformation are without errors. The very essence of MPEG audio compression, however, is nothing but introducing the right "errors". As a consequence, the output signal will differ from the input signal, by a certain amount that we estimate is below the threshold of audible distortion. When generating a whole stretch of output samples from the same slightly changed frequency lines the same threshold level applies for the whole output sequence. This can be a problem if the overall level of the signal changes dramatically during this period. Then, noise that is inaudible during loud parts of the signal might become audible during the softer parts of the signal. The phenomenon is known as "pre-echo", a slight audible noise that precedes a sharp signal attack (Fig. 46).

Frequency resolution and time resolution are closely coupled. Increasing one of them will invariably diminish the other. Hence, if we need increased time resolution, we have to reduce the frequency resolution. For this purpose, layer III will subdivide one "long" block, with 36 values, into three short blocks, with 12 values each. These shorter blocks are then windowed with W_{12}, encoded with $MDCT_{12}$, decoded with $IMDCT_{12}$ and windowed again with W_{12}. Whatever we have said about this process in the previous section holds in analogy for short blocks. Using short blocks, the spread of noise is reduced to a shorter time span, where it is subject to temporal masking. Further, we can spend some additional bits precisely to encode the sudden transition, as we will see below.

What deserves some further consideration is the mixing of different block types. Recall that windowing corresponds to fade in and fade out of overlapping blocks. Now this crossfade is three times faster for short blocks than it is for long blocks. Slowly fading out a long block and at the same time quickly fading in a short block does not work. The overall sound level will change whenever the fade-out and the fade-in are not synchronized. Therefore we need two additional block types:

- A "start" block that fades in slowly and, in preparation of the expected short block, fades out quickly.
- A "stop" block that fades in quickly and fades out slowly to switch back to the long blocks.

In summary, there are four *block_type*s.

⟨ private declarations $_1$ ⟩ +≡   (225)
#**define** LONG_BLOCK   0
#**define** START_BLOCK   1
#**define** SHORT_BLOCK   2
#**define** STOP_BLOCK   3

Layer III allows to switch the stream from the usual long blocks to short blocks. Switching is possible on a per granule and per channel basis. The *block_type* is stored in the stream data.

⟨ stream data $_2$ ⟩ +≡   (226)
   int *block_type*[GRANULES][CHANNELS];

A granule can contain either one long block—in regard to most aspects, except for the windowing, start and stop blocks are like long blocks— or is subdivided into three short blocks. To switch from a short block to a long block, a start block is necessary, and a stop block manages the transition back to long blocks. Figure 47 shows the windowing applied to two granules with long blocks, followed by a start block, then a granule with three short blocks, then one stop block, and again two long blocks.

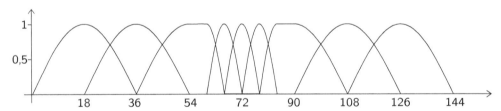

Fig. 47: Overlap of different windows

The windowing function for a start block is in its first half identical to the windowing function of a long block, then it stays constant at 1 for six samples, then it fades out with the second half of the windowing function of a short block, and finally it is zero for six more values. The windowing function of the stop block is just the reverse. We define:

$$
\boldsymbol{W}_{\text{start}} = \begin{pmatrix} \mathcal{F}_{18}\boldsymbol{W}_{36} & 0 & 0 & 0 \\ 0 & \mathcal{I}_6 & 0 & 0 \\ 0 & 0 & \mathcal{L}_6\boldsymbol{W}_{12} & 0 \\ 0 & 0 & 0 & \mathcal{Z}_6 \end{pmatrix}
$$

$$
\boldsymbol{W}_{\text{stop}} = \mathcal{R}_{36}\boldsymbol{W}_{\text{start}}
$$

To see the new concepts in action, we return to our example. We use a start block for y, which turns out to be very simple, since after windowing it is entirely zero. We use a short block for y' followed by a stop block encoding a constant sequence of 1. The result is shown in Figures 48 to 50.

Fig. 48: Values of z' (white) and $\overline{z'}$ (gray) for three short blocks

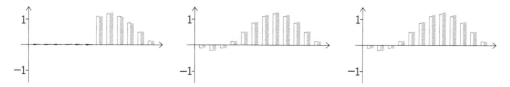

Fig. 49: Values of y' (white) and $\overline{y'}$ (gray) for three short blocks

Fig. 50: Overlapping and adding of y' together with a start and a stop block

A comparison of Figure 50 with Figure 46 reveals the reduction of pre-echos as a consequence of using short blocks. Table 15 complements Figures 48 to 50 with numerical data. It shows the encoding process leading from original values y', to encoded values z', to quantized values u'. The values of u' are derived using the formula $z' = \text{sign}(u')|u'|^{4/3}2^{k/4}$ (see Section 11.6 on Quantization), with $k = -15$ for the first short block and $k = 0$ for the other two. We use a finer quantization for the first of the three short blocks and spend more bits for its encoding because the 12 values that are encoded in this short block contain the jump in signal level. We use fewer bits for the two other short blocks. The values of u' are then rounded to whole integers $\overline{u}'$, which are Huffman coded (see Chapter 12) and transmitted. The decoding process starts with the values of $\overline{u}'$, uses quantization to get $\overline{z}'$, decodes each short block with IMDCT_{12}, applies windowing with W_{12}, and with overlapping and adding obtains $\overline{y}'$. The result is shown in the context of an appropriate start and stop block in Figure 50.

$\boldsymbol{y}'$ =	0	0	0	0	0	0	1	1	1	1	1	1	1	1	1	1	1	1
$\boldsymbol{z}'$ =	−2.01	−0.79	0.29	0.29	−0.21	−0.21	−2.45	0	0	0	0	0	−2.45	0	0	0	0	0
$\boldsymbol{u}'$ =	−11.87	−5.88	2.77	2.77	−2.19	−2.19	−1.96	0	0	0	0	0	−1.96	0	0	0	0	0
$\overline{\boldsymbol{u}}'$ =	−12	−6	3	3	−2	−2	−2	0	0	0	0	0	−2	0	0	0	0	0
$\overline{\boldsymbol{z}}'$ =	−2.04	−0.81	0.32	0.32	−0.19	−0.19	−2.52	0	0	0	0	0	−2.52	0	0	0	0	0
$\overline{\boldsymbol{y}}'$ =	0	0.01	0	0	−0.02	0	1.01	1.05	0.99	1	1.04	1.03	1.03	1.03	1.03	1.03	1.03	1.03

Tab. 15: Encoding with short blocks

Huffman coding of $\overline{\boldsymbol{u}}'$ with Table 13 needs $12 + 9 + 7 + 6 + 1 + 1 + 6 + 1 + 1 = 44$ bits plus 6 sign bits $= 50$ bits or 2.8 bit per value. Using a combination of two tables, table 24 for the first pair $(10 + 7$ bits$)$ and table 2 for the rest $6 + 5 + 1 + 1 + 5 + 1 + 1$, results in a total of 37 bits plus 6 sign bits $= 43$ bits or 2.4 bits per value.

To obtain working code for short blocks, we repeat the method proven successful for long blocks: precise mathematical formulation.

For each of the 32 subbands, the standards requirements for short blocks are:

- Compute $\boldsymbol{W}_{12}\text{IMDCT}_{12}$ separately on the three short blocks in a granule.

- Overlap and add the three result vectors, in the same way as long blocks, except for a shorter overlap of only 6 elements. This yields a 24 value vector.

- Extend the 24 values by 6 zeros on the front and 6 zeros on the end to obtain a 36 value vector $\boldsymbol{t}$.

- Add the first half of $\boldsymbol{t}$ to the last half of the $\boldsymbol{t}'$ vector from the previous granule to get 18 values of $\boldsymbol{y}$.

- Store the last half of $\boldsymbol{t}$ as $\boldsymbol{t}'$ to be used with the next granule.

The overlap/add/extend operation for the three short blocks can be accomplished with the following matrix:

$$
\boldsymbol{A} = \begin{pmatrix}
\mathcal{Z}_6 & 0 & 0 & 0 & 0 & 0 \\
\mathcal{I}_6 & 0 & 0 & 0 & 0 & 0 \\
0 & \mathcal{I}_6 & \mathcal{I}_6 & 0 & 0 & 0 \\
0 & 0 & 0 & \mathcal{I}_6 & \mathcal{I}_6 & 0 \\
0 & 0 & 0 & 0 & 0 & \mathcal{I}_6 \\
0 & 0 & 0 & 0 & 0 & \mathcal{Z}_6
\end{pmatrix}.
$$

As before, we replace IMDCT_{12} by $\boldsymbol{T}_6\boldsymbol{R}_6\text{DCT}_6^{\text{III}}\boldsymbol{S}_6$. We will fuse together the matrix $\boldsymbol{T}_6\boldsymbol{R}_6$ with the windowing and package $\text{DCT}_6^{\text{III}}\boldsymbol{S}_6$ into the function *dct6*.

⟨ private declarations $_1$ ⟩ +≡   (227)
  extern void *dct6* (**const double** *∗z*, **double** *∗t*);

The implementation of *dct6* is in Appendix A.5.

We collect together the three results of *dct6* in a vector t of 18 elements. The matrix B can be used to reconstruct from t the original output of the $W_{12}\mathrm{IMDCT}_{12}$ transformation. The block matrix B is given by

$$B = \begin{pmatrix} W_{12}T_6R_6 & 0 & 0 \\ 0 & W_{12}T_6R_6 & 0 \\ 0 & 0 & W_{12}T_6R_6 \end{pmatrix}$$

Using A after B, we get the input to the overlap-add operation and have

$$y = \mathcal{F}_{18}ABt + \mathcal{L}_{18}ABt'$$

Optimizing the required amount of storage for t', we observe that $\mathcal{L}_{18}ABt'$ can be computed from elements 6, 7, 8, and 12 to 17 of t' only. Therefore, we use the matrix

$$C = \begin{pmatrix} \mathcal{Z}_3 & \mathcal{I}_3 & \mathcal{Z}_3 & \mathcal{Z}_3 \\ & \mathcal{Z}_6 & & \mathcal{I}_6 \end{pmatrix}$$

to extract these elements from t and store them in t'. From the equation $t' = Ct$ we generate the following code:

⟨store a short block for subband *sb* ₂₂₈⟩ ≡   (228)

```
{ double *t′ = s→t′[ch][sb];
  t′[0] = t[6]; t′[1] = t[7]; t′[2] = t[8]; t′[3] = t[12]; t′[4] = t[13]; t′[5] = t[14];
  t′[6] = t[15]; t′[7] = t[16]; t′[8] = t[17];
}
```
                                                                Used in 230.

We use $C^\top$ to convert t' back into an 18 value vector, with all the values at the right place. This gives the equation:

$$y = \mathcal{F}_{18}ABt + \mathcal{L}_{18}ABC^\top t'$$

from which we generate the following code:

⟨window, overlap, and add a short block for subband *sb* ₂₂₉⟩ ≡   (229)

```
{ double(*ỹ)[CHANNELS][SUBBANDS];
  double *t′ = s→t′[ch][sb];
  ỹ = (double(*)[CHANNELS][SUBBANDS]) & y[0][ch][sb];
  ỹ[0][0][0] = −0.62484444888695941 * t′[2] + 0.10720635868191788 * t′[6];
  ỹ[1][0][0] = −0.5 * t′[1] + 0.5 * t′[7];
  ỹ[2][0][0] = −0.40009957749537036 * t′[0] + 2.3319512300735069 * t′[8];
  ỹ[3][0][0] = −0.30700720369117716 * t′[0] − 3.0390580112600545 * t′[8];
  ỹ[4][0][0] = −0.2071067811865475 * t′[1] − 1.2071067811865475 * t′[7];
  ỹ[5][0][0] = −0.082262332299588115 * t′[2] − 0.81431313986846541 * t′[6];
  ỹ[6][0][0] = 0.107206358681917884 * t′[3] − 0.62484444888695941 * t′[5];
  ỹ[7][0][0] = 0.5 * t[4] − 0.5 * t′[4];
```

$$\tilde{y}[8][0][0] = 2.33195123007350693 * t[5] - 0.40009957749537036 * t'[3];$$
$$\tilde{y}[9][0][0] = -3.03905801126005446 * t[5] - 0.30700720369117716 * t'[3];$$
$$\tilde{y}[10][0][0] = -1.20710678118654752 * t[4] - 0.20710678118654752 * t'[4];$$
$$\tilde{y}[11][0][0] = -0.81431313986846541 * t[3] - 0.082262332299588115 * t'[5];$$
$$\tilde{y}[12][0][0] = -0.62484444888695941 * t[2] + 0.10720635868191788 * t[9];$$
$$\tilde{y}[13][0][0] = -0.5 * t[1] + 0.5 * t[10];$$
$$\tilde{y}[14][0][0] = -0.40009957749537036 * t[0] + 2.3319512300735069 * t[11];$$
$$\tilde{y}[15][0][0] = -0.307007203691177164 * t[0] - 3.0390580112600545 * t[11];$$
$$\tilde{y}[16][0][0] = -0.207106781186547524 * t[1] - 1.2071067811865475 * t[10];$$
$$\tilde{y}[17][0][0] = -0.082262332299588115 * t[2] - 0.81431313986846541 * t[9];$$
}

Used in 230.

The code actually uses only 6 pairs of constants, so reordering it might improve performance on some machines. The code above relies on a good compiler to optimize the load instructions.

Now we can put all three steps together: To process a short block we apply the function *dct6* three times and collect the function output in the vector t. From t, we compute for each subband the vector y and t'.

⟨ IMDCT a short block ₂₃₀ ⟩ ≡   (230)
```
  for ( ; sb < SUBBANDS; sb++)
  { double t[18];

    if (sb < s→sblimit[ch])
    { dct6 (z[ch] + sb * 18, t);
      dct6 (z[ch] + sb * 18 + 1, t + 6);
      dct6 (z[ch] + sb * 18 + 2, t + 12);
    }

    else ⟨ zero t ₂₂₄ ⟩
    ⟨ window, overlap, and add a short block for subband sb ₂₂₉ ⟩
    ⟨ store a short block for subband sb ₂₂₈ ⟩
  }
```
Used in 234.

The above code does not initialize sb because of a further complication, a "mixed" block, discussed below. Further one should note that the three parts of the short block are stored interleaved with one another in the vector z.

11.5 Start and Stop Blocks

The code derived in the previous sections assumes that long blocks are preceded by long blocks and short blocks are preceded by short blocks. This assumption was used in the processing of t' before the overlap-add operation. Now we consider what should happen if start and stop blocks occur in the stream.

A start block is always preceded by a long block. Therefore we can use the processing of t' that we developed for long blocks. Further, the windowing function that is applied to the first half of a start block, is the same as for a long block and hence, the computation of y is done exactly the same way as for a long block.

The second half of the start block is different. In preparing t', it has to simulate a short block so that the following short block can use t'.

The standard requires storing $\mathcal{L}_{18}W_{\text{start}}\text{IMDCT}_{36}z$. We know already from the discussion of long blocks (see page 125), that this vector can be reproduced from $\mathcal{F}_9 \cdot 2 \cdot \text{DCT}_{18}^{\text{III}} S_{18}z$ by applying $\mathcal{L}_{18}W_{\text{start}}T_{18}(1/2)R_{18}\mathcal{F}_9^\top$. The difficulty is, however, that the following short block will use the matrix $\mathcal{L}_{18}ABC^\top$ on t', assuming it was preceded by an other short block. To cancel the effect of $\mathcal{L}_{18}ABC^\top$, we could use the inverse matrix—if it existed. But this matrix is not even a square matrix. We note, however, that the matrix A will supply a stretch of zeros at the beginning and the end of its result. While the first zeros are cut away by applying $\mathcal{L}_{18}$, the last six zeros remain. They are equal for both a short block and a start block. Fortunately, the next three elements, windowed with the downslope of the short window, are equally the same for both blocks and the real difference between both blocks is only the computation of the remaining 9 values. Checking $\mathcal{F}_9\mathcal{L}_{18}ABC^\top$, we realize that this matrix is indeed invertible and we can use the equation

$$t' = (\mathcal{F}_9\mathcal{L}_{18}ABC^\top)^{-1}\mathcal{F}_9 W_{\text{start}}T_{18}(1/2)R_{18}\mathcal{F}_9^\top t$$

to compute t' in such a way, that

$$\mathcal{L}_{18}W_{\text{start}}\text{IMDCT}_{36}z' = \mathcal{L}_{18}ABC^\top t'.$$

We use the first equation, to generate the code to

⟨ store a start block for subband sb 231 ⟩ ≡   (231)
  { **double** $*t' = s{\rightarrow}t'[ch][sb]$;

    $t'[0] = 0.34021759826241347 * t[5] + 0.46631140047156712 * t[6]$;
    $t'[1] = 0.19134171618254489 * t[4] + 0.53794025136387497 * t[7]$;
    $t'[2] = 0.054289373022064996 * t[3] + 0.53342619745279293 * t[8]$;
    $t'[3] = 0.49619469809174553 * t[0]$;
    $t'[4] = 0.46592582628906829 * t[1]$;
    $t'[5] = 0.40630778703664996 * t[2]$;
    $t'[6] = 0.31642165430726767 * t[3] - 0.053886988879063598 * t[8]$;
    $t'[7] = 0.19134171618254489 * t[4] - 0.092295955641257263 * t[7]$;
    $t'[8] = 0.058372111545827878 * t[5] - 0.047107017561910602 * t[6]$;
  }
                                                 Used in 234.

It would hardly be possible to derive this code without an appropriate tool.

Last, the stop block. This time, the computation of t' is easy, it is obviously the same as for long blocks (same transformation, same windowing for the second half of both blocks). The computation of y may assume that t' was prepared by a short block. Hence, we can compute y as

$$y = \mathcal{F}_{18}W_{\text{stop}}T_{18}(1/2)R_{18}t + \mathcal{L}_{18}ABC^\top t'$$

With this equation, we generate the code to

⟨ window, overlap, and add a stop block for subband sb $_{232}$ ⟩ ≡   (232)
  { **double** $*t' = s{\rightarrow}t'[ch][sb]$;

    double$(*\tilde{y})$[CHANNELS][SUBBANDS];
    $\tilde{y} = ($**double**$(*)$[CHANNELS][SUBBANDS]$)$ & $y[0][ch][sb]$;
    $\tilde{y}[0][0][0] = -0.62484444888695941 * t'[2] + 0.10720635868191788 * t'[6]$;
    $\tilde{y}[1][0][0] = -0.5 * t'[1] + 0.5 * t'[7]$;
    $\tilde{y}[2][0][0] = -0.40009957749537036 * t'[0] + 2.3319512300735069 * t'[8]$;
    $\tilde{y}[3][0][0] = -0.30700720369117716 * t'[0] - 3.0390580112600545 * t'[8]$;
    $\tilde{y}[4][0][0] = -0.20710678118654752 * t'[1] - 1.2071067811865475 * t'[7]$;
    $\tilde{y}[5][0][0] = -0.082262332299588115 * t'[2] - 0.81431313986846541 * t'[6]$;
    $\tilde{y}[6][0][0] = 0.15076513703422529 * t[15] - 0.62484444888695941 * t'[5]$;
    $\tilde{y}[7][0][0] = 0.73296291314453414 * t[16] - 0.5 * t'[4]$;
    $\tilde{y}[8][0][0] = 3.4890530666445053 * t[17] - 0.40009957749537036 * t'[3]$;
    $\tilde{y}[9][0][0] = -4.5470224836405378 * t[17] - 0.30700720369117716 * t'[3]$;
    $\tilde{y}[10][0][0] = -1.7695290056300272 * t[16] - 0.20710678118654752 * t'[4]$;
    $\tilde{y}[11][0][0] = -1.1451749096832876 * t[15] - 0.082262332299588115 * t'[5]$;
    $\tilde{y}[12][0][0] = -0.83137738085576039 * t[14]$;
    $\tilde{y}[13][0][0] = -0.65328148243818826 * t[13]$;
    $\tilde{y}[14][0][0] = -0.54142014255005005 * t[12]$;
    $\tilde{y}[15][0][0] = -0.46528974917589448 * t[11]$;
    $\tilde{y}[16][0][0] = -0.41066990792614539 * t[10]$;
    $\tilde{y}[17][0][0] = -0.37004680823056527 * t[9]$;
  }   Used in 234.

This same code works also when a start block is preceeded by a stop block instead.

Before we can combine the results of the previous sections to write the code to apply the ⟨ IMDCT and overlap add $_{234}$ ⟩, we have to consider one further feature: mixed blocks.

Often, a sharp change in volume level manifests itself mainly in the high frequency part of the spectrum. For this situation, it is a further saving in bits if a long block can be used for some of the lowest subbands and three short blocks are used for the other subbands. Such a block is called a "mixed block". Mixed blocks are indicated by a flag in the stream data.

⟨ stream data $_2$ ⟩ +≡   (233)
  int $mixed\_block$[GRANULES][CHANNELS];

Using this information, we can finally give the code to apply the

⟨ IMDCT and overlap add $_{234}$ ⟩ ≡   (234)
  if $(s{\rightarrow}block\_type[gr][ch] \equiv$ LONG_BLOCK$)$ ⟨ IMDCT a long block $_{223}$ ⟩
  else
  { **int** $sb = 0$;
    double $t[18]$;

    if $(s{\rightarrow}mixed\_block[gr][ch])$
    { **int** $long_subbands = $ ⟨ number of long subbands $_{429}$ ⟩;

```
    for (sb = 0; sb < long_subbands; sb++)
    { if (sb < s→sblimit[ch])  dct18(z[ch] + sb * SUBFREQUENCIES, t);
      else ⟨zero t 224⟩
      ⟨window, overlap, and add a long block for subband sb 222⟩
      ⟨store a long block for subband sb 221⟩
    }
  }
  if (s→block_type[gr][ch] ≡ SHORT_BLOCK) ⟨IMDCT a short block 230⟩
  else if (s→block_type[gr][ch] ≡ START_BLOCK)
  { for ( ; sb < SUBBANDS; sb++)
    { if (sb < s→sblimit[ch])  dct18(z[ch] + sb * SUBFREQUENCIES, t);
      else ⟨zero t 224⟩
      ⟨window, overlap, and add a long block for subband sb 222⟩
      ⟨store a start block for subband sb 231⟩
    }
  }
  else if (s→block_type[gr][ch] ≡ STOP_BLOCK)
  { for ( ; sb < SUBBANDS; sb++)
    { if (sb < s→sblimit[ch])  dct18(z[ch] + sb * SUBFREQUENCIES, t);
      else ⟨zero t 224⟩
      ⟨window, overlap, and add a stop block for subband sb 232⟩
      ⟨store a long block for subband sb 221⟩
    }
  }
}
```
Used in 297.

We continue here with the study of layer III quantization and scaling which leads from integer frequencies, as provided by the Huffman decoding, to the scaled frequencies that are the input to the IMDCT. Quantization and scaling are concepts that we encountered already in layers I and II but are elevated to a new level of sophistication in layer III.

11.6 Quantization

Quantization is the process of converting a real number of (almost) infinite precision, taken from an infinite and continuous set of possible values, into an integer number. This is done during the encoding process. In the decoding process, which concerns us here, the effect of quantization is reversed: From an array, called u, where the process of Huffman decoding has stored raw integer sample values for all 576 frequencies, (well—most of them, starting with *ulimit* they are all zero) we take **short int** values and convert them to **double** values. This requantized value is then, after scaling as discussed in the next section, stored as a scaled frequency.

⟨private declarations 1⟩ +≡   (235)
#**define** FREQUENCIES   576

$\langle$ global variables $_{43}\,\rangle\,+\equiv$ (236)
   static short int u[CHANNELS][FREQUENCIES] = { { 0 } };

Quantization in layer III is not linear, as it is in layer I and layer II, instead the standard prescribes a power-law quantizer: For each raw frequency u the corresponding requantized value is not u itself, but $u^{4/3}$.

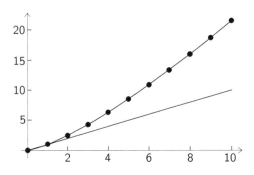

Fig. 51: The comparison of the linear functions $z = u$ (the straight line) and $z = u^{4/3}$ (the dotted line) shows that non linear quantization gives smaller quantization steps for smaller values and larger steps for bigger values. Therefore, it yields a finer resolution for low volume sounds, where it is needed the most.

Figure 51 shows a comparison of linear quantization and power-law quantization. We compute $u^{4/3}$ by looking up the value in a large table $power43$, which is produced by the following code:

$\langle$ print element $_{132}\,\rangle\,+\equiv$ (237)
   static void $power43$ (**int** u)
   { $printf$ ("%.16e", pow (u, 4.0/3.0)); }

$\langle$ print table $_{135}\,\rangle\,+\equiv$ (238)
   $print\_array$ ("static␣const␣double␣power43", POWER43SIZE, $power43$);

Using the $power43$ array, we can compute a quantized value as

$\langle$ private declarations $_1\,\rangle\,+\equiv$ (239)
#**define** sign($u_{ch,i}$) · $|u_{ch,i}|^{4/3}$
   ((u[ch][i] $\geq$ 0) ? $power43$ [u[ch][i]] : $-power43$ [$-u$[ch][i]])

The array lookup is certainly a very fast method, but the cost in memory space is not insubstantial. The array is indexed by the values produced by the Huffman decoder. As we will see there, the largest of these values are 13 bit unsigned integers with an added offset of 15. Hence, the size of the $power43$ array can be defined as:

$\langle$ private declarations $_1\,\rangle\,+\equiv$ (240)
#**define** POWER43SIZE   ((1 $\ll$ 13) + 15)

11.7 Scaling

Scaling follows requantization. A value from the array u is first quantized, then multiplied by a scalefactor f, and finally stored as a scaled frequency in the array z.

$\langle$ global variables $_{43}\,\rangle\,+\equiv$ (241)
   static double z[CHANNELS][FREQUENCIES];

As we have seen earlier, it is not necessary to use an individual factor for each frequency, instead the same factor is shared for a whole group of frequencies, called a *band*. In layer III, the bands do not coincide with the subbands of layers I and II. Normal blocks have 22 bands, but as we will see later, there can be as many as 39 bands.

⟨ private declarations ₁ ⟩ +≡   (242)
#define BANDS   39

One novelty of layer III is that the *width* of a band, that is the range of frequencies it comprises, is not fixed but tailored to the frequency resolution of the human auditory system. The scaling, like the requantization, is not done on a linear scale; scalefactors f are computed from an exponent m as $f = 2^{m/4}$.

Given the *width* of a band, the exponent m, the channel ch, the index i into u, where the band starts, and the index j into z, where the scaled frequencies should go, we can quantize and scale one band with this function:

⟨ auxiliary functions ₆₉ ⟩ +≡   (243)
```
    static void qs_band(const int ch, int i, int j, int width, int m, int step)
    { const double f = 2^{m/4};

      while (width -- > 0)
      { z[ch][j] = sign(u_{ch,i}) · |u_{ch,i}|^{4/3} * f;
        i = i + 1;
        j = j + step;
      }
    }
```

The *step* variable, which is used to increment the target index into z, can have the values 1 or 3. Using 1 will store the scaled frequencies of a band consecutive in z; this is used for normal blocks. For short blocks, the value 3 is used to store the frequency samples of all three short blocks of a granule interleaved in order of increasing frequency. This is necessary, because the IMDCT needs to be applied to blocks of 18 values, belonging to one subband, and the bounds of the 22 bands do not always coincide with the bounds of the 32 subbands.

The *width* and the *start* index of each band is stored in two arrays, indexed by the *band*.

⟨ global variables ₄₃ ⟩ +≡   (244)
```
    static const short int *width[GRANULES][CHANNELS];
    static const short int *start[GRANULES][CHANNELS];
```

The *width* of each band depends on the *sample_rate*. The sample rate, on the other hand, is a one-to-one function of the *frequency_index* and the *version*. These we use to pick the correct table.

⟨ select layer III band *width* ₂₄₅ ⟩ ≡   (245)
```
    width[gr][ch] = width_table[s→info.version][s→info.frequency_index]
        [s→mixed_block[gr][ch]][s→block_type[gr][ch] ≡ SHORT_BLOCK];
```

$$start[gr][ch] = start\_table[s{\rightarrow}info.version][s{\rightarrow}info.frequency\_index]$$
$$[s{\rightarrow}mixed\_block[gr][ch]][s{\rightarrow}block\_type[gr][ch] \equiv \texttt{SHORT\_BLOCK}];$$

Used in 351 and 356.

The computation of suitable tables, as specified by the standard, can be found in Appendix A.12. For each frequency index, the table stores the number of frequencies per band, called the *width* of the band, respectively the frequency where the band starts.

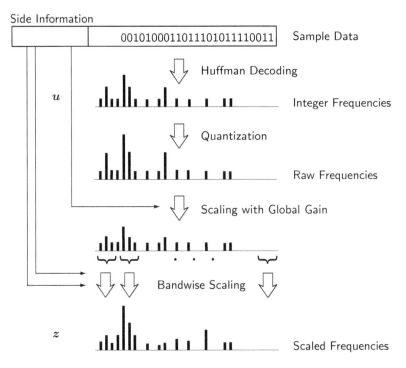

Fig. 52: Transforming Huffman codes to frequencies

We are left with the problem to determine the scalefactor f. As shown in Figure 52, the single precomputed scalefactor f must combine a global gain, used to move the volume level to an average position, with an individual scalefactor for each band, used to color the quantization noise. The standard specifies the formula:

$$f = 2^{\frac{1}{4}(global\_gain\,-210)} \cdot 2^{-(sfi+preemphasis)\cdot multiplier}$$

Let us first turn our attention to the global gain: The layer III bit stream indicates the applicable global gain by an unsigned 8 bit integer. A stereo stream, of course, features separate gain factors for both channels. Finally, layer III frames are subdivided into two so called granules and each of them has its own set of gain factors. After the bit stream has been read (see Chapter 13) the gain factors are stored in the

⟨global variables 43⟩ +≡   (246)
  static unsigned char *global_gain* [GRANULES][CHANNELS];

where

⟨private declarations 1⟩ +≡   (247)
#define GRANULES 2

  To obtain a better spread of gain factors, the value of *global_gain* is requantized as $2^{(global\_gain-210)/4}$. Again, we use a power-law quantizer, as we did before for the scalefactors. The power-of-two operation can be interpreted intuitively through bit shifts. The application of the *global_gain* factor can then be understood as shifting the 16 significant bits of the sample value up to 52.5 bit to the right or 11.25 bit to the left (in one-quarter bit steps!). Note that $0 \leq global\_gain \leq 255$, then the subtraction of 210 moves the range to -210 to $+45$, and the division by four gives -52.5 to $+11.25$. This is the most important use of the *global_gain*: to shift the distribution of the sample values to match the distribution for which the Huffman code tables yield optimal results.

  A fast and simple way to compute the powers of $2^{1/4}$ is a lookup table. The table *power14* is computed as follows:

⟨print element 132⟩ +≡   (248)
  void *power14* (**int** *i*)
  { **int** $m = i -$ POWER14START;
    double $f = pow\,(2.0, 0.25 * m)$;

    printf ("%.16e", $pow\,(2.0, 0.25 * m)$);
  }

⟨print table 135⟩ +≡   (249)
  print_array ("static␣const␣double␣power14", POWER14SIZE, *power14*);

We postpone the determination of POWER14SIZE, the size of this array, and the value of the constant POWER14START. For now, it is enough to note that we will need to compute $2^{m/4}$ for negative m. Arrays in C, however, allow only a non-negative index. Therefore, we will choose POWER14START large enough, to make sure that $m +$ POWER14START ≥ 0. As can be seen from the above definition of *power14* , we can now compute $2^{m/4}$ using a macro.

⟨private declarations 1⟩ +≡   (250)
#define $2^{m/4}$ *power14* [$m +$ POWER14START]

  The correct exponent to use for the given global gain is therefore

⟨exponent for *global_gain* 251⟩ ≡   (251)
  ($global\_gain$ [gr][ch] $- 210$)   Used in 262 and 265.

We do not use this value right away for a table lookup, but we will do a combined table lookup for both, the global gain and the second scaling operation that provides individual scalefactors for each of the 22 frequency bands. The multiplication of both factors is then replaced by an addition of the exponents.

The purpose of the scalefactors is the perfect distribution of quantization noise. As discussed before, quantization noise originates from the rounding of arbitrary precision input values to represent them on a scale with limited precision discrete values. The finer the quantization steps, the lower the quantization noise. By selecting the quantization steps fine enough, the quantization noise should be brought below the threshold of audible distortion. Making the quantization steps finer then necessary, on the other hand, results in a suboptimal compression.

The bit stream basically provides for each channel, each granule, and each band a scalefactor, coded as an **unsigned int** with up to 4 bit. This value is retrieved from the stream and stored in the array *sfi*. From there, we obtain the

⟨ raw scalefactor ₂₅₂ ⟩ ≡   (252)
    $s \rightarrow sfi[ch][band]$ Used in 261 and 265.

Its value m is in the range 0 to 15 and needs to be quantized into the appropriate factor—again on a power-law scale either as 2^{-m} (coarse quantization) or $2^{-m/2}$ (fine quantization). Here we see a chance to reuse the lookup table *power14* which provides us with a fast way to compute powers of $2^{1/4}$. With this table, we can compute the scalefactor as $2^{-4m/4}$ or $2^{-2m/4}$. To switch between both modes of quantization, we need to apply the appropriate *multiplier*, either 4 or 2, or more efficiently, apply a left-shift by either 2 or 1 bit. The appropriate shift is taken from the

⟨ global variables ₄₃ ⟩ +≡   (253)
    static int $scale\_shift[\text{GRANULES}][\text{CHANNELS}]$;

It is enough to set this variable to 1 to

⟨ select fine scalefactor quantization ₂₅₄ ⟩ ≡   (254)
    $scale\_shift[gr][ch] = 1$;   Used in 359.

or to set it to 2 to

⟨ select coarse scalefactor quantization ₂₅₅ ⟩ ≡   (255)
    $scale\_shift[gr][ch] = 2$;   Used in 359.

It is now easy to

⟨ apply the scalefactor multiplier ₂₅₆ ⟩ ≡   (256)
    ≪ $scale\_shift[gr][ch]$ Used in 261 and 265.

As a further sophistication, the bit stream can specify for each granule and channel a "preemphasis". This is an additional boost of high-frequency content. The individual preemphasis values for the different bands are provided by the following table.

⟨ global variables ₄₃ ⟩ +≡   (257)
    static const int $preemphasis\_table[\text{BANDS}] = \{ 0,0,0,0,0,0,0,0,0,0,0,1,1,1,1,2,$
        $2,3,3,3,2,0 \}$;

These values are to be added to the scalefactor of the respective band, in case the header selects this feature. A simple way to switch this feature on and off is a pointer that either points to the *preemphasis_table* or a *zero_table*.

⟨ global variables ₄₃ ⟩ +≡   (258)
    static const int $*preemphasis[\text{GRANULES}][\text{CHANNELS}]$;

 static const int *zero_table* [BANDS] = { 0 };

Now, we can

⟨ switch *preemphasis* on ₂₅₉ ⟩ ≡   (259)
 preemphasis [*gr*][*ch*] = *preemphasis_table*;   Used in 358 and 380.

or

⟨ switch *preemphasis* off ₂₆₀ ⟩ ≡   (260)
 preemphasis [*gr*][*ch*] = *zero_table*;   Used in 358 and 380.

 We put things together and obtain the

⟨ exponent for the scalefactor ₂₆₁ ⟩ ≡   (261)
 (−(((⟨ raw scalefactor ₂₅₂ ⟩ + *preemphasis* [*gr*][*ch*][*band*])
 ⟨ apply the scalefactor multiplier ₂₅₆ ⟩)))   Used in 262.

The scalefactor for a normal block therefore needs the following exponent to the base $2^{1/4}$

⟨ long exponent ₂₆₂ ⟩ ≡   (262)
 (4 ∗ OUTPUT_EXPONENT + ⟨ exponent for *global_gain* ₂₅₁ ⟩ + ⟨ exponent for the
  scalefactor ₂₆₁ ⟩)   Used in 268, 288, and 392.

The 4 ∗ OUTPUT_EXPONENT replaces in layer III the ⟨ output scalefactor ₁₃₆ ⟩ (see the computation of the ⟨ modified factor ₁₂₇ ⟩ in layer I and layer II on page 58).

 Short blocks are slightly different. The preemphasis is not used, but instead, the global gain is modified by a specific *subblock_gain* for each of the three short blocks in a granule.

⟨ global variables ₄₃ ⟩ +≡   (263)
 static char *subblock_gain* [GRANULES][CHANNELS][SUBBLOCKS];

⟨ private declarations ₁ ⟩ +≡   (264)
#**define** SUBBLOCKS 3

 The *subblock_gain* is transmitted using 3 bits; its range is 0 to 7. It is multiplied by 8 and subtracted from the global gain.

⟨ short exponent ₂₆₅ ⟩ ≡   (265)
 (4 ∗ OUTPUT_EXPONENT + ⟨ exponent for *global_gain* ₂₅₁ ⟩ − 8 ∗ *subblock_gain* [*gr*][*ch*][*k*]
 − (((⟨ raw scalefactor ₂₅₂ ⟩)⟨ apply the scalefactor multiplier ₂₅₆ ⟩))
)   Used in 269, 289, and 393.

 The ⟨ long exponent ₂₆₂ ⟩ or the ⟨ short exponent ₂₆₅ ⟩ are used as index m to compute the scalefactor $f = 2^{m/4}$ with a table lookup into *power14*. Now that we have seen the use of this array, we can determine its boundaries.

 From the ranges of the variables $0 \le global\_gain \le 255$, $0 \le$ ⟨ raw scalefactor ₂₅₂ ⟩ $\le$ 15, $0 \le preemphasis \le 3$, $1 \le scale\_shift \le 2$, and $0 \le 8 \cdot subblock\_gain \le 56$, we can tell the range of the lookup table.

The minimum value for long blocks is

 $4 \cdot$ OUTPUT_EXPONENT $+ (0 - 210) - (15 + 3) \cdot 4 = 4 \cdot$ OUTPUT_EXPONENT $- 282$

The minimum value for short blocks is

$4 \cdot \texttt{OUTPUT\_EXPONENT} + (0 - 210 - 8 \cdot 7 - 15 \cdot 4 = 4 \cdot \texttt{OUTPUT\_EXPONENT} - 326$
The maximum value for long blocks
$4 \cdot \texttt{OUTPUT\_EXPONENT} + (255 - 210) - (0 + 0) \cdot 4 = 4 \cdot \texttt{OUTPUT\_EXPONENT} + 45$
The maximum value for short blocks is
$4 \cdot \texttt{OUTPUT\_EXPONENT} + (255 - 210 - 8 \cdot 0 - 0 \cdot 4 = 4 \cdot \texttt{OUTPUT\_EXPONENT} + 45$

Since arrays in C arrays always start with index 0, we have to adjust the index by adding the constant POWER14START before we use the array.

⟨ private declarations $_1$ ⟩ +≡   (266)
#**define** POWER14START $(326 - 4 * \texttt{OUTPUT\_EXPONENT})$

Further, we can now determine the size of the array

⟨ private declarations $_1$ ⟩ +≡   (267)
#**define** POWER14SIZE $(326 + 1 + 45)$

We conclude this subsection with the function qs. The function will perform quantization and scaling for one channel, starting with index i and continuing through all bands as long as $i < limit$. It returns the value of the next $band$ to be quantized and scaled.

⟨ auxiliary functions $_{69}$ ⟩ +≡   (268)
```
    static int qs(stream *s, const int gr, const int ch, int band, int i, const int
            limit)
  { while (i < limit)
    { qs_band(ch, i, i, width[gr][ch][band], ⟨ long exponent 262 ⟩, 1);
      i = i + width[gr][ch][band];
      band ++;
    }
    return band;
  }
```

For short blocks, a very similar function is used. The inner loop of this function iterates over all three short blocks in the band. These blocks share the same width, but do have different scalefactors.

⟨ auxiliary functions $_{69}$ ⟩ +≡   (269)
```
    static int qs_short(stream *s, const int gr, const int ch, int band, int i, const
            int limit)
  { while (i < limit)
    { int k, j = i;
      int size = width[gr][ch][band];
      for (k = 0; k < SUBBLOCKS; k ++, j ++, i = i + size, band ++)
        qs_band(ch, i, j, size, ⟨ short exponent 265 ⟩, 3);
    }
    return band;
  }
```

11.8 Mid/Side Stereo

The two channels of typical stereo signals are not independent, and joint stereo tries to exploit existing similarities. There are two different forms of joint stereo: mid/side stereo and intensity stereo. Mid/side stereo is the simpler concept and we discuss it first.

In mid/side stereo, instead of transmitting the left and right channel separately, a mid signal is derived by adding the left and the right channel and a side signal by subtracting the right from the left channel. We use this method favorably if left and right channel are pretty much equal. In this case, the side signal will be weak, contains relatively little information, and can be encoded much more compact than the signal for a full channel.

For "historic" reasons the standard specifies a formula involving a factor of $1/\sqrt{2}$. It is easy to see why: Assume, we have two signals L and R. We compute $M = L + R$ and $S = L - R$ for a mid and a side signal. Then, we reverse the process and compute $L' = M + S$ and $R' = M - S$. We obtain $L' = M + S = (L + R) + (L - R) = 2L$ and $R' = M - S = (L + R) - (L - R) = 2R$. Effectively, we have doubled the signal level. We could, of course, compensate this effect by dividing by 2 the values of L' and R' or alternatively the values of M and S. Mid/side stereo, however, dates back to the old days of analog sound processing. It was a convenient way to record (using special microphone arrangements) and represent a stereo signal with the option to convert it to a mono signal just by dropping the side signal. If the mid signal is used in its own right as a mono signal, dividing it by two would yield a mono signal with a lower volume than the stereo signal, not dividing it at all would yield a louder signal. The solution is to divide twice by $\sqrt{2}$. Therefore in the old days, the definition of the mid signal was set to be $M = (L + R)/\sqrt{2}$ and correspondingly $S = (L - R)/\sqrt{2}$. Then the formulas, as given by the standard, $L' = (M + S)/\sqrt{2}$ and $R' = (M - S)/\sqrt{2}$ exactly reverse the process: $L' = (M + S)/\sqrt{2} = ((L + R)/\sqrt{2} + (L - R)/\sqrt{2})/\sqrt{2} = 2L/2 = L$ and similar for R.

Instead of computing $M = (L + R)/\sqrt{2}$ and $S = (L - R)/\sqrt{2}$, we compute $M = L/\sqrt{2} + R/\sqrt{2}$ and $S = L/\sqrt{2} - R/\sqrt{2}$ and incorporate the factor $1/\sqrt{2} = 2^{-2/4}$ into the scalefactors f_M and f_S by subtracting 2 from the exponent. Together this results in a function to quantize and scale one band in mid/side stereo mode.

$\langle$ auxiliary functions $_{69}$ $\rangle$ $+\equiv$ (270)

```
static void qs_mid_side_band(int i, int j, int width, int mM, int mS, int step)
{ double fM = 2^{mM−2/4}, fS = 2^{mS−2/4};
    while (width −− > 0)
    { double mid = sign(u0,i) · |u0,i|^{4/3} * fM, side = sign(u1,i) · |u1,i|^{4/3} * fS;
      z[0][j] = mid + side;
      z[1][j] = mid − side;
      i = i + 1;
      j = j + step;
    }
}
```

11.9 Intensity Stereo

In intensity stereo mode, both channels share the same signal, only the loudness in both channels differs. Sounds from the side reach one ear of the listener more easily than the other ear, and therefore the signal will be louder in the ear towards the sound source than in the other ear. In reverse, if a signal is louder in one channel than in the other, the listener will use the difference in sound level as directional information.

In layer I and II, intensity stereo is realized by reusing the same subband frequencies but with different scalefactors for both channels. In layer III, the schema is more sophisticated. The Standard specifies that

$$L' \leftarrow L \cdot \frac{r}{r+1} \quad \text{and} \quad R' \leftarrow L \cdot \frac{1}{r+1}$$

where L' is the signal in channel 0 (left) and R' in channel 1 (right).

This definition has two interesting properties. After splitting L, both components add up to the original value:

$$L' + R' = L \cdot \frac{r}{r+1} + L \cdot \frac{1}{r+1} = L \cdot \left(\frac{r}{r+1} + \frac{1}{r+1}\right) = L \cdot \frac{r+1}{r+1} = L.$$

And the ratio of L' to R' is just r:

$$\frac{L'}{R'} \leftarrow \frac{L \cdot \frac{r}{r+1}}{L \cdot \frac{1}{r+1}} = \frac{r}{1} = r.$$

Consider the range of r. When L' is zero and the signal is entirely in the right channel, the ratio r is zero too. When R' is zero and the signal is entirely in the left channel, the ratio r approaches infinity.

It is not very convenient to compute L' and R' using the original formulas, since $r = \infty$ is impossible to achieve on a computer. Using the equation $L' + R' = L$, we can simply compute R' by multiplication of L with an appropriate factor $p = \frac{1}{r+1}$ ranging from 0 to 1 and then assign to L' the remaining signal. This gives us the simpler formulas $R' \leftarrow p * L$ and $L' \leftarrow L - R'$.

The value L itself, is computed by multiplying $u = \text{sign}(\boldsymbol{u}_{0,i}) \cdot |\boldsymbol{u}_{0,i}|^{4/3}$, with the scalefactor f. Hence, the above method needs two multiplications and one subtraction. We continue by eliminating the subtraction.

To obtain R', we multiply u by f_R, the product of f and p. We can obtain $L' = u \cdot f - u \cdot f \cdot p = u \cdot f \cdot (1 - p)$ by multiplying u with $f_L = f \cdot (1 - p)$. Hence from p, we compute two factors f_L and f_R.

$\langle$ convert p to f_L and f_R 271 $\rangle \equiv$ (271)

```
{ double f = 2^{m/4};

    f_L = f * (1 - p);
    f_R = f * p;
}
```

Used in 273.

Using these two factors, we can

$\langle$ assign intensity stereo values $_{272}\rangle \equiv$ (272)
```
{ double u = sign(u₀,ᵢ) · |u₀,ᵢ|⁴ᐟ³;
```
$$z[0][j] = u * f_L;$$
$$z[1][j] = u * f_R;$$
```
}
```
Used in 273 and 391.

We wrap this code into a function, similar to *qs_mid_side_band*, to quantize and scale a band in intensity stereo.

$\langle$ auxiliary functions $_{69}\rangle +\equiv$ (273)
```
static void qs_intensity_band(int i, int j, int width, int m, int sp, int step)
{ double f_L, f_R;
```
$\quad\langle$ compute p $_{277}\rangle$
$\quad\langle$ convert p to f_L and f_R $_{271}\rangle$
```
  while (width-- > 0)
```
$\quad\{$ $\langle$ assign intensity stereo values $_{272}\rangle$
$\quad\quad i = i + 1;$
$\quad\quad j = j + step;$
```
  }
}
```

In order to $\langle$ compute p $_{277}\rangle$, we still have to determine how to obtain the right value of the ratio r. The ratio r is chosen according to an intensity stereo position sp, which is a value between 0 and 6, where 0 indicates $r = 0$ and 6 indicates $r = \infty$. Basically any reasonable function that ranges from 0 to ∞ could be used to compute r, (or p) from sp. The standard prescribes

$$r = \tan(sp * \frac{\pi}{12}).$$

Recall that $\tan \phi = \sin \phi / \cos \phi$ is the ratio of the length of the two sides a and b of a rectangular triangle as illustrated in Figure 53.

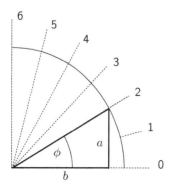

Fig. 53: Intensity stereo positions sp range from 0 to 6, defining the ratio of left to right channel as the ratio of the sides a and b of a rectangular triangle. With an angle

$$\phi = sp \cdot 15°,$$

the sides and the ratio are

$$a = \sin \phi, \quad b = \cos \phi, \quad and \quad \frac{a}{b} = \tan \phi.$$

When the angle ϕ changes from 0 to 15, 30, 45, 60, 75, and 90 degree, the ratio of the two sides changes from 0 to ∞ exactly as the ratio of left and right channel is supposed to do. The stereo position simply selects an angle in increments of $\pi/12$ which is 15 degrees.

To avoid complications with infinity (or division by zero) we use the formula

$$p = \frac{1}{r+1} = \frac{1}{\tan\phi + 1} = \frac{1}{\sin\phi/\cos\phi + 1} = \frac{\cos\phi}{\sin\phi + \cos\phi}.$$

⟨ compute intensity stereo factor p 274 ⟩ $\equiv$ (274)
   double $\phi = sp * \texttt{M\_PI}/12.0$;
   double $p = cos(\phi)/(sin(\phi) + cos(\phi))$;   Used in 275.

As usual, we precompute these factors and put them in the table *intensity_factor*:

⟨ print element 132 ⟩ $+\equiv$ (275)
   void *intensity_factor*(**int** *sp*)
   { ⟨ compute intensity stereo factor p 274 ⟩
    printf (**"%.15f"**, p);
   }

⟨ print table 135 ⟩ $+\equiv$ (276)
   print_array(**"static␣const␣double␣intensity_factor"**, 7, *intensity_factor*);

From this table, we can

⟨ compute p 277 ⟩ $\equiv$ (277)
   const double $p = intensity\_factor[sp]$;   Used in 273.

11.10 Joint Stereo Processing

Joint Stereo Processing is complicated by three facts:

- Short blocks are handled differently than long blocks.
- Granules can contain mixed—long and short—blocks.
- The same granule can combine bands with different stereo modes.

So we choose the following strategy: We determine the boundary between long and short blocks, and consider non mixed blocks as a special case with the boundary being zero or equal to the total number of bands. Then, we determine for each band the correct stereo mode and store it in the array *stereo_mode*. Finally, we iterate first over the long then over the short bands and apply the predetermined *stereo_mode*.

⟨ joint stereo processing 278 ⟩ $\equiv$ (278)
   { **unsigned char** *stereo_mode*[BANDS];
    int *band_limit*, *first_short_band*, *long_limit*;

    ⟨ determine *first_short_band* 279 ⟩
    ⟨ determine *stereo_mode* and *band_limit* 283 ⟩
    long_limit = *min*(*band_limit*, *first_short_band*);

```
{ int i = 0, band = 0;
    while (band < long_limit) ⟨quantization and scaling for long blocks 288⟩
    while (band < band_limit) ⟨quantization and scaling for short blocks 289⟩
    ⟨adjust frequency limits 285⟩
}
}
```
Used in 290.

Note that the standard has avoided at least one complication: in mid/side and intensity stereo mode, both channels of a granule are required to have the same block type.

The *first_short_band* in mixed blocks is version dependent. We take it from an array defined in Appendix A.10. The rest is simple.

⟨determine *first_short_band* 279⟩ ≡ (279)
```
{ if (s→block_type[gr][0] ≡ SHORT_BLOCK)
    { if (s→mixed_block[gr][0]) first_short_band = boundary_table[s→info.version];
      else first_short_band = 0;
    }
    else first_short_band = BANDS;
}
```
Used in 278.

In layer III, for the stereo mode, three choices are available:

⟨private declarations 1⟩ +≡ (280)
```
#define STEREO    0
#define INTENSITY 1
#define MID_SIDE  2
```

Intensity stereo and mid/side stereo, the two joint stereo modes, must be enabled in the header of each frame. For this, the two mode extension bits are used (Tab. 16). We derive the appropriate information when we

⟨process the mode extension bits 97⟩ +≡ (281)
```
    if (info→mode ≡ MP3_JOINT_STEREO)
    { info→ms_stereo = (bits ≫ 1) & 1;
      info→i_stereo = bits & 1;
    }
    else info→ms_stereo = info→i_stereo = 0;
```

and store it as part of the stream information.

⟨infos 31⟩ +≡ (282)
```
    int ms_stereo;
    int i_stereo;
```

If neither mid/side nor intensity stereo is enabled, we have plain stereo, and we deal with this case in the general procedure to ⟨quantize and scale raw samples 290⟩.

We have an other relatively simple case if mid/side stereo is enabled, but intensity stereo is not. Then, the entire spectrum is decoded in mid/side stereo mode.

Bit	Mid/Side Stereo	Intensity Stereo
00	off	off
01	off	on
10	on	off
11	on	on

Tab. 16: Mode extension and joint stereo mode

Using this rule, we can

⟨ determine *stereo_mode* and *band_limit* $_{283}$ ⟩ ≡   (283)
  { **int** *band*;
    int *limit* = *max*(*ulimit*[0], *ulimit*[1]);

    if (¬*s*→*info*.*i_stereo*)
        for (*band* = 0; *start*[*gr*][0][*band*] < *limit*; *band*++)
            stereo_mode[*band*] = MID_SIDE;
    else ⟨ determine intensity stereo mode $_{287}$ ⟩
    band_limit = *band*;
    while (*band* < BANDS) *stereo_mode*[*band*++] = NONE;
  }   Used in 278.

The above code uses the upper bounds on non zero frequencies, *ulimit*, which are set by the Huffman decoder for both channels.

⟨ global variables $_{43}$ ⟩ +≡   (284)
  static int *ulimit*[CHANNELS];

After setting the stereo mode, these values are updated to reflect the fact that the stereo processing may introduce new, non zero values into bands that might have been zero before.

⟨ adjust frequency limits $_{285}$ ⟩ ≡   (285)
  ulimit[0] = *ulimit*[1] = *start*[*gr*][0][*band*];   Used in 278.

Unused places in the *stereo_mode* array are filled with the value NONE.

⟨ private declarations $_1$ ⟩ +≡   (286)
#**define** NONE 3

The complex case is intensity stereo mode. Intensity stereo is used only for the upper part of the spectrum. It requires the transmission of only one channel but is of lesser quality. So it is used only for the high frequencies, where as for the lower frequencies, mid/side stereo or full stereo is used.

If enabled, the decoder switches to intensity stereo as soon as the band in the second channel contains no further data. All bands before this point are encoded in mid/side stereo, if enabled, or two channel stereo. Figure 54 gives a survey of all possibilities. While the value of *ulimit*[1] is not aligned with the boundaries of the frequency bands, it nevertheless can be used to find the first band in intensity stereo mode.

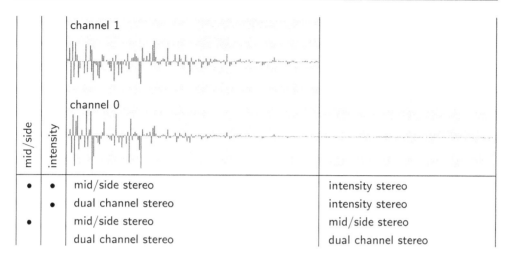

Fig. 54: Combination of joint stereo modes

$\langle$ determine intensity stereo mode $_{287}$ $\rangle \equiv$ (287)
  { **unsigned char** $low\_frequency\_mode = s \rightarrow info.ms\_stereo$? MID_SIDE : STEREO;

  for $(band = 0;\ start[gr][1][band] < ulimit[1];\ band ++)$
     $stereo\_mode[band] = low\_frequency\_mode;$
  if $(s \rightarrow info.version \equiv$ MP3_V1_0$)$
  { **for** $(\ ;\ start[gr][0][band] < ulimit[0];\ band ++)$
      if $(s \rightarrow sfi[1][band] < 7)\ stereo\_mode[band] =$ INTENSITY;
      else $stereo\_mode[band] = low\_frequency\_mode;$
  }
  else $\langle$ version 2 determine intensity stereo mode $_{388}$ $\rangle$
  }
                                                                      Used in 283.

One last special case needs explanation, the test for < 7 in the above code. Scale-factors are transmitted using at least 3 bits; this allows for the value 7 or above to be transmitted. The value 7 is not a valid stereo position. It indicates that the corresponding band is not transmitted in intensity stereo mode. In this case, we use mid/side stereo, if enabled, or plain stereo otherwise.

Now we summarize:

$\langle$ quantization and scaling for long blocks $_{288}$ $\rangle \equiv$ (288)
  { **int** $ch,\ size = width[gr][0][band];$

  if $(stereo\_mode[band] \equiv$ STEREO$)$
  { $ch = 0;\ qs\_band(0, i, i, size, \langle$ long exponent $_{262}$ $\rangle, 1);$
     $ch = 1;\ qs\_band(1, i, i, size, \langle$ long exponent $_{262}$ $\rangle, 1);$
  }
  else if $(stereo\_mode[band] \equiv$ INTENSITY$)$
     $qs\_intensity\_band(i, i, size, (ch = 0, \langle$ long exponent $_{262}$ $\rangle), s \rightarrow sfi[1][band], 1);$

```
    else if (stereo_mode[band] ≡ MID_SIDE)
    { int m_M, m_S;
        ch = 0; m_M = ⟨ long exponent 262 ⟩;
        ch = 1; m_S = ⟨ long exponent 262 ⟩;
        qs_mid_side_band(i, i, size, m_M, m_S, 1);
    }
    else if (stereo_mode[band] ≡ INTENSITY_V2)
        ⟨ process band in version 2 intensity stereo 392 ⟩
    else break;
    i = i + size;
    band ++;
}
```
                                                                    Used in 278.

Similar, but for short blocks, we have:

⟨ quantization and scaling for short blocks 289 ⟩ ≡   (289)

```
    { int ch, k, j = i, size = width[gr][0][band];
        for (k = 0; k < 3; k++, band++, j++, i = i + size)
            if (stereo_mode[band] ≡ STEREO)
            { qs_band(0, i, j, size, (ch = 0, ⟨ short exponent 265 ⟩), 3);
                qs_band(1, i, j, size, (ch = 1, ⟨ short exponent 265 ⟩), 3);
            }
            else if (stereo_mode[band] ≡ INTENSITY)
                qs_intensity_band(i, j, size, (ch = 0, ⟨ short exponent 265 ⟩), s→sfi[1][band], 3);
            else if (stereo_mode[band] ≡ MID_SIDE)
            { int m_M, m_S;
                ch = 0; m_M = ⟨ short exponent 265 ⟩;
                ch = 1; m_S = ⟨ short exponent 265 ⟩;
                qs_mid_side_band(i, j, size, m_M, m_S, 3);
            }
            else if (stereo_mode[band] ≡ INTENSITY_V2)
                ⟨ process short band in version 2 intensity stereo 393 ⟩
            else
            { qs_band(0, i, j, size, (ch = 0, ⟨ short exponent 265 ⟩), 3);
                qs_band(1, i, j, size, (ch = 1, ⟨ short exponent 265 ⟩), 3);
            }
    }
```
                                                                    Used in 278.

The last **else** case will be used if one or two of the remaining short blocks do not have a stereo mode assigned to them because they contain all zeros. In this case it does not matter which stereo mode we use, all of them will produce only zeros. It is, however, important that we use some sort of processing to copy the zeros into z and to increase $band$.

We wrap up this section with the code to

⟨quantize and scale raw samples $_{290}$ ⟩ ≡   (290)
  { **if** $(s{\to}info.mode \equiv$ MP3_JOINT_STEREO $\wedge\,(s{\to}info.i\_stereo \vee s{\to}info.ms\_stereo))$
    ⟨joint stereo processing $_{278}$ ⟩
  else
  { **int** ch;

    for $(ch = 0;\ ch < s{\to}info.channels;\ ch\,{+}{+})$
      if $(s{\to}block\_type[gr][ch] \neq$ SHORT_BLOCK$)\ \ qs(s, gr, ch, 0, 0, ulimit[ch])$;
      else
    { **if** $(s{\to}mixed\_block[gr][ch])$
      { **int** $band = boundary\_table[s{\to}info.version]$;
        int $limit = start[gr][ch][band]$;

        $qs(s, gr, ch, 0, 0, limit)$;
        $band = qs\_short(s, gr, ch, band, limit, ulimit[ch])$;
        $ulimit[ch] = start[gr][ch][band]$;
      }

      else
      { **int** $band = qs\_short(s, gr, ch, 0, 0, ulimit[ch])$;
        $ulimit[ch] = start[gr][ch][band]$;
      }

    }

  }

  }

}
Used in 363.

Note: Scaling normal stereo signals up to the maximum of $ulimit[0]$ and $ulimit[1]$ is not optimal, we could scale both up to the minimum and then continue to scale only one remaining channel. With "normal" signals, however, the difference between both values is usually zero (or very small), and the extra test would be more expensive then the occasional extra scaling.

11.11 Alias Reduction

Aliasing is an effect caused by the reduction of sample rate due to the decimation of subbands after filtering. Recall the example discussed in Section 2.2, where a signal was split into high and low frequencies using a very simple filter. The high frequency signal, sampled at discrete intervals, is shown in Figure 55. After splitting the frequencies into two subbands, it is not necessary to keep the full sample rate. Instead, the original signal can be reconstructed from two subbands at half the sample rate. Decimating the samples, by taking only every second sample, will however allow a new interpretation of the samples as a low frequency signal (Fig. 56). Any further analysis of the decimated high frequency band may therefore interpret the high frequency as a much lower frequency. This lower frequency is called its "alias".

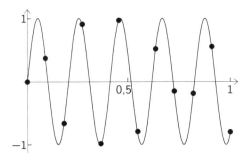

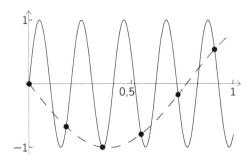

Fig. 55: High frequency output   Fig. 56: Reduced sample rate and alias

The same effect can also be observed in the opposite direction: a low frequency having
a higher frequency as its alias.

   The aliasing effect, which is not caused by the limited quality of filters, but by the
reduction of the sample rate, is usually not a problem. The misinterpretation of a
frequency as its alias can only occur if the input of the frequency analysis contains
both, the frequency and its alias.

   This is the situation, we encounter, when each of the 32 subbands is split into 18
separate frequencies during layer III processing. As can be seen from Figure 27, the
filters used for layer I subband filtering do overlap considerably. A frequency that
belongs to the upper/lower half of one subband is also present in the output of the
next/previous subband, and will be taken there for a higher/lower frequency, its alias.

   Reducing this aliasing improves the coding efficiency of the MPEG encoder. A
closer study of the situation reveals that each frequency and its alias frequency happen
to be symmetric to the boundary between subbands. For example, within the first
subband (frequencies 0 to 17) and the second subband (frequencies 18 to 35) the alias
of frequency 17 will be frequency 18, 16 will pair up with 19, 15 with 21, and so on...
In the encoder, the effect of aliasing is reduced, by computing from each frequency an
estimate of its alias and compensating the appropriate alias frequency. This process
is reversed in the decoder. The standard specifies the exact factors to be used to
compensate for aliasing. So, for a frequency and its alias, we load the two values,
separate them into the estimated original and the alias, using two constants c and d,
compensate each value for the alias, and write the new values back.

⟨ apply alias reduction 291 ⟩ ≡   (291)
    ⟨ determine *sblimit* 292 ⟩
    if $(s \rightarrow block\_type\,[gr][ch] \neq \texttt{SHORT\_BLOCK} \lor s \rightarrow mixed\_block\,[gr][ch])$
    { **int** k;

        if $(s \rightarrow block\_type\,[gr][ch] \equiv \texttt{SHORT\_BLOCK} \land s \rightarrow mixed\_block\,[gr][ch])$ $k = 1$;
        else $k = \texttt{SUBBANDS} - 1$;
        ⟨ increase *sblimit* if needed 293 ⟩
        if $(k > s \rightarrow sblimit\,[ch] - 1)$ $k = s \rightarrow sblimit\,[ch] - 1$;

```
for ( ; k > 0; k--)
{ int i;
  double *zHi = z[ch] + k * SUBFREQUENCIES;
  double *zLo = zHi - 1;

  for (i = 0; i < 8; i++, zLo--, zHi++)
  { double zHi, zLo, c, d;

    zLo = *zLo;
    zHi = *zHi;
    c = alias_coefficients[i].c;
    d = alias_coefficients[i].d;
    *zLo = zLo * c - zHi * d;
    *zHi = zHi * c + zLo * d;
  }

}

}
```
Used in 297.

We do not need to perform alias reduction for all subbands, but only for those subbands that are not zero The number of subbands that contain non zero values is stored in the variable *sblimit* and is computed by rounding up *ulimit* to the next multiple of 18 and dividing by 18. Since the boundaries of layer III bands do not coincide with the subband boundaries, we complete the initialization for the last subband.

⟨ determine *sblimit* 292 ⟩ ≡   (292)
```
  s→sblimit[ch] = (ulimit[ch] + SUBFREQUENCIES - 1)/SUBFREQUENCIES;
  { int i;
    for (i = ulimit[ch]; i < s→sblimit[ch] * SUBFREQUENCIES; i++) z[ch][i] = 0.0;
  }
```
Used in 291.

Due to alias reduction, nonzero values may spread into the next subband. Therefore, after we perform alias reduction, we have to

⟨ increase *sblimit* if needed 293 ⟩ ≡   (293)
```
  { if (s→sblimit[ch] < SUBBANDS ∧
        ulimit[ch] > s→sblimit[ch] * SUBFREQUENCIES + 1 - SUBFREQUENCIES/2)
    { int i;
      for (i = 0; i < SUBFREQUENCIES; i++)
        z[ch][s→sblimit[ch] * SUBFREQUENCIES + i] = 0.0;
      s→sblimit[ch]++;
    }

  }
```
Used in 291.

The *alias_coefficients*, as defined by the standard, are written into a table.

⟨ print element $_{132}$ ⟩ +≡   (294)
  void *alias_coefficients*(**int** *i*)
  { **static const double** $c[8] = \{$ $-0.6, -0.535, -0.33, -0.185, -0.095, -0.041,$
       $-0.0142, -0.0037\}$;

     $printf\,("\{%.16e,\sqcup%.16e\}", 1.0/sqrt\,(1 + c[i] * c[i]), c[i]/sqrt\,(1 + c[i] * c[i]));$
  }

⟨ print table $_{135}$ ⟩ +≡   (295)
  print_array (
       `"static␣const␣struct␣{double␣c;␣double␣d;}␣alias_coefficients"`,
       8, *alias_coefficients*);

One last complication: The simple alias reduction, as described above, will work only, if the phase differences are 0 or 180 degree. To achieve the correct phase difference, the encoder compensates the 32 band polyphase filter for its frequency inversion. This effect must be reversed in the decoder (for details see [9],[8] or[6]).

⟨ compensate for frequency inversion $_{296}$ ⟩ ≡   (296)
  { **int** *i*, *sb*;

     for $(sb = 1; \ sb < $ SUBBANDS$; \ sb = sb + 2)$
        for $(i = 1; \ i < 18; \ i = i + 2)$ $\boldsymbol{y}[i][ch][sb] = -\boldsymbol{y}[i][ch][sb]$;
  }
                                                                  Used in 297.

We conclude this chapter with the code to

⟨ produce subband samples $_{297}$ ⟩ ≡   (297)
  for $(ch = 0; \ ch < s{\rightarrow}info.channels; \ ch\,{+}{+})$
  { ⟨ apply alias reduction $_{291}$ ⟩
     ⟨ IMDCT and overlap add $_{234}$ ⟩
     ⟨ compensate for frequency inversion $_{296}$ ⟩
  }
                                                                  Used in 363.

12 Huffman Coding

Huffman coding is a method to code a sequence of data items with the minimum number of bits necessary. To see how this works, let us look at an example. Consider the text "abbbaabaaabaaa". It can be coded using the ASCII code (7 bit per character) and requires then $14 \cdot 7 = 98$ bits. Alternatively, we can use ISO-8859 Code (8 bit per character) and will need 112 bits. If we care for the minimum amount of bits, we can use a 0-bit for an "a" and a 1-bit for a "b" and get by with only 14 bits.

That was easy. But how about coding "abcdaabaaabaaa"? Now, we can no longer use one bit per character, and we might consider using two bits per character.

Code	Data
00	a
01	b
10	c
11	d

Tab. 17: Encoding 1

Code	Data
0	a
10	b
110	c
111	d

Tab. 18: Encoding 2

Code	Data
0	a
1	b
01	c
11	d

Tab. 19: Encoding 3

Encoding 1 brings us to $14 \cdot 2 = 28$ bits. This, however is not optimal. If we choose encoding 2, we need only 21 bits (9 bits for 9 "a", 6 bits for 3 "b", 3 bits for 1 "c", and 3 bits for 1 "d"). This is a saving of 25 % compared to encoding 1.

The principle is simple. For codes that occur more often, we use short bit sequences and for codes that occur infrequently, we use longer bit sequences. The extra spending for a few long codes is easily recovered with many short codes.

But may be there are still better codings. For instance, we could use encoding 3. This would require a total of only $9 \cdot 1 + 3 \cdot 1 + 1 \cdot 2 + 1 \cdot 2 = 16$ bits. Unfortunately, it won't work. We can encode the text to yield "0101110010001000", and it is only 16 bits long, but we can no longer decode it unambiguously. We could take the leading "01" either for an "ab" or for a "c". Similar for the next two bits. And how should we know that in the first case it is "ab" and in the second "c"?

Let us return to encoding 2, which yields "0101101110010000010000", and study the decoding process in detail. We start reading a 0-bit. How can we know that this is an "a" and not the start of a longer code for a different character? Simple: all the

other codes start with a 1. So it's an "a". We read the second bit: 1. Obviously,
this is not an "a". It is not a code for any character. So we read on and get an other
0-bit. This is a "b". How do we know? The reason is as before: There is no other
code that starts with "10". In summary: to make unambiguous decoding feasible, no
code must be the prefix of an other code.

Codes that have this prefix property can
be depicted as binary decision trees. Encoding 2 is shown in Figure 57 as a binary
tree.

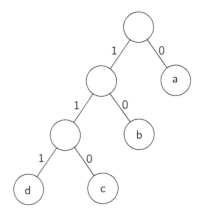

Each code describes a path from the
root of the tree to a leaf node. A 0-
bit selects the branch to the right, a 1-
bit selects a branch to the left. Once we
arrive at a leaf node, we have found the
correct decoded character.

Back to the question of an optimal encoding that allows unambiguous decoding. This is the problem for which Huffman coding is the answer[15]. We omit
the details here and recommend reading
a good book on algorithms (for example
[33] pages 351–357) instead.

Fig. 57: Huffman tree for encoding 2

In our case, the encodings are given by the standard and we just have to use them.
We better focus our curiosity on the problem of optimal decoding of a given encoding.

Naturally, it is possible to choose a representation of the binary Huffman tree and
decode a bit stream by traversing the tree. Each time we encounter a leaf node,
we emit the corresponding character and start over from the root of the tree. The
runtime of this algorithm is proportional to the number of bits in the bit stream, and
this is not bad. Since the most frequent characters will have short codes, they can be
decoded very fast.

An alternative is decoding with a lookup table. The index we want to use is the
Huffman code, and the result is the corresponding character. Our Huffman codes are,
however, of variable length, and we do not even know the exact length before we have
decoded them. We solve this problem, by taking a bit string of maximum code length
from the input and use it as an index. For a short code this means that there must
be many different entries in our table, one for every possible extension of the code up
to the maximum code length.

For encoding 2, the required table is shown in Table 20. Observe, that the character
"a" requires four entries in the table. If the index starts with a 0-bit, it must lead to
the character "a", whatever the next two bits of the index happen to be.

The bit stream "010110111001000010000", which we used above as an example,
starts with "010". We use it as an index to find the first character "a" and the length
of the code: 1 bit. We advance the input by one bit and take the next three bits:
"101". Using these as an index, we obtain the "b" and its code length: 2.

Index	Index (binary)	Code	Bit required
0	000	a	1
1	001	a	1
2	010	a	1
3	011	a	1
4	100	b	2
5	101	b	2
6	110	c	3
7	111	d	3

Tab. 20: Lookup table for encoding 2

The use of the lookup table will yield a faster algorithm but requires more memory. The runtime of the algorithm is now proportional to the number of decoded characters, and all the characters are decoded with the same speed. The space requirements for the tables will grow exponentially with the maximum code length. The maximum code length used in the encodings of the standard is 19, and this would require a table with approximately a half a million entries—too much space wasted for a few very long codes that are not used very often.

Hence, we combine the two approaches. We restrict the lookup tables to a fixed maximum number of bits, HWIDTH, to be used for the index. If this number of bits is enough to decode the character, that is if its code length is less or equal to HWIDTH, the table will immediately reveal the character and its code length. If the code length is greater than HWIDTH, the table will provide a pointer to a new table, called an extension table, and the number of bits required for the index of the extension table. In effect, we replace the binary tree by an n-way tree, where $n = 2^{\text{HWIDTH}}$ is the table size. It provides access to the most common codes with a single table lookup and, for longer codes, has a runtime proportional to the code length.

HWIDTH	Table Entries
1	2726
2	2172
3	2084
4	2176
5	2398
6	2950
7	3746
8	5486

Tab. 21: Total memory usage

HWIDTH	Max. Lookups	Runtime
1	19	100 %
2	10	75.4 %
3	7	61.7 %
4	5	56.5 %
5	4	53.6 %
6	4	51.2 %
7	3	50.5 %
8	3	49.2 %

Tab. 22: Time requirements for encoding 15

The choice of HWIDTH depends on the time/space tradeoff we are willing to make. The total number of table entries for all Huffman encodings used by the standard is given in Table 21. The runtimes in Table 22 are measured with the standard encoding table htab15. This encoding uses codes with up to 15 bits. Of all encodings, it benefits the most from extending table access to 8 bit since 8 bits are just enough to get any value with two lookups. So the relative speed improvement is less pronounced for other tables. On the other hand, there are four encodings with a maximum code length of six or less. These benefit from a choice of HWIDTH $\equiv$ 6, because they can then be decoded with a single lookup, and it seems like 6 would be a good choice.

$\langle$ private declarations $_1\rangle$ $+\equiv$ (298)
#**define** HWIDTH   6

It is interesting to note, that for HWIDTH $=1$, the tables describe a binary tree, and the algorithm traverses this tree just like the simple algorithm does. The algorithm is not that much slower, but the tables are larger. They contain a considerable overhead because they store the more complex structure of a large tree as pointers. The smallest space requirement (HWIDTH $\equiv$ 3) has a tree where each node stores up to 8 leaves or subtrees.

12.1 Decoding Frequencies

We are now prepared to have a detailed look at how Huffman coding is used in coding Layer III bit streams. The data, that is coded, are 576 frequency lines per channel and granule, each stored as a 16 bit signed integer. It would be possible to use one carefully chosen Huffman encoding and just encode the frequency values, but it can be done better. Lets look at a typical frequency spectrum found in an MPEG Layer III file. Figure 58 shows the frequency spectrum of a trumpet with string orchestra (from the Haydn Trumpet Concerto in E flat, Winton Marsalis playing).

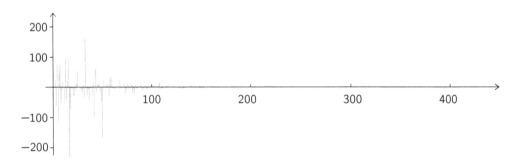

Fig. 58: Typical quantized layer III frequencies

It is instructive to look at the 576 numerical values: 4, 24, −63, 79, −114, 55, 75, −51, −13, 21, −1, −43, 94, −41, 22, 92, −231, −77, −4, −7, −26, −31, −11, 12, 52, 0, 2, −6, −12, −18, 6, −36, 159, −6, −25, −6, −43, −6, 3, −29, 14, −99, 64, −15, 7, 14, 9, −15, −52, −168, 25, 6,

1, 10, 3, 15, −28, 30, 38, 8, −3, −6, −5, 2, 5, 4, −9, 24, −6, −6, −1, 2, 13, −22, −8, 12, 5, −5, −6, 12, −20, −6, −24, 7, −5, −5, 3, 0, 5, 3, −11, −5, −1, 6, −7, −6, 5, −2, 3, 5, 4, 2, 2, −2, 1, 3, −5, 14, 0, −8, −5, 0, 1, −4, 2, 3, 5, −1, 1, −1, 2, 0, 4, −2, 1, 0, 0, −3, −3, −1, 0, −6, −5, −2, −1, 0, −1, −1, 3, 8, 2, 0, 2, 1, 1, 1, 0, 2, −4, −3, −1, 2, 2, −1, −1, 0, 0, 0, 1, 1, 2, 2,

0, −2, 1, 0, −1, 2, 1, −1, 0, −1, 0, −1, −2, −1, 0, 0, 1, 1, −2, −2, 0, 0, 0, −1, 0, 0, 0, 1, −1, −1, 0, 0, 1, 0, 1, 1, −1, −1, 1, −1, 0, 2, 0, 0, −1, 0, 1, 2, 1, 2, −1, 2, 2, 3, −1, 2, 2, 0, 0, −1, 1, 1, 1, 0, −2, 1, 0, 2, 1, 0, 0, −1, 1, 0, −1, 1, 0, −1, 0, 0, 1, 0, −1, −1, 1, 1, 0, 1, 0, −1, 0, 1, 1, −1, 0, 0, 0, −1, −1, −2,

−1, 0, 0, −1, 0, 0, 0, 0, 0, 0, 0, 1, −1, 0, 0, 0, 0, 0, −1, 1, −1, 0, 0, −1, 0, 1, 1, 0, 0, 1, 0, −1, 1, 0, 1, 0, 0, −1, 1, 0, 0, 1, −1, −1, 0, 0, 0, 1, 1, 0, 0, 0, −1, 0, 0, 0, −1, 1, 0, 0, 1, −1, −1, 1, 0, 0, −1, 0, 0, 0, 0, 0, 0, 1, 0, 0, 0, 0, 1, 1, 0, −1, 1, 0, 0, 0, 0, 0, 0, 0, 1, 0, 0, 0, −1, 0, 0, 0, 0, 0, 0, 1, 1, −1, 0, 0, 0, 0, 0, 0, 0, 0, 0, 0, 0, −1, 0, 0, 0, 0, 1, 0, 0, 0, 0, 0, 1, 0, 1, 1, 0, 0, 0, 1, 0, 0, 0, 0, 0, 0, 0, 0, 0, 0, 0, 0, 1, 1, 0, 0, 0, 0, 0, 0, 0, 0, −1, 0, −1, 0, 0, −1, 0, 0, 0, 1, 0, 0, 0, 0, 0, 0, 0, 0, 1, 0, 0, 0, 0, 0, 0, −1, 0, 0, 0, 0, 0, 0, 0, −1, 0, 1, 0, 0, 0, −1, 0, 1, 1, 0, 1, 0, 0, 0, 0, 0, 0, 0, 0, 0, 0, 1, 0, 0, 0, 0, 0, 0, 0, 1, 0, 0, 0, 0, 0, −1, 0, 1, 0, 0, 1, 1, 0, 0, 0, 0, 0, 1, 0, 0, 0, 1, 0, 0, 0, 0, 1, 0, 0, 0, 0, 0, −1, 0,

0, 0, 0, 0, 0, 0, 0, 0, 0, 0, 0, 0, 0, 0, 0, 0, 0, 0, 0, 0, 0, 0, 0, 0, 0, 0, 0, 0, 0, 0, 0, 0, 0, 0, 0, 0, 0, 0, 0, 0, 0, 0, 0, 0, 0, 0, 0, 0, 0, 0, 0, 0, 0, 0, 0, 0, 0, 0

We observe that at the upper end of the spectrum, all values are zero (58 values), preceded by many "small values". The part of the spectrum to the left of the zeros, where the spectrum starts to get populated with ones and minus ones (here 256 values), is called the "small values" part. This phenomenon is easy to understand. For one thing, our hearing is not so good at these frequencies, and encoders therefore often eliminate this frequency content, and the more the available bit rate is constrained the more zeros will be used. Second, the critical bands of our hearing are not equally wide and encompass many more lines in the upper spectrum than in the lower spectrum. This means, individual lines are less important in the upper spectrum as compared to the lower spectrum.

The "small values" are preceded by the "big values". The big values are subdivided by the encoder into three different regions (52 values, 110 values, and 100 values) according to the different statistical distribution of values. For all sections of the frequency spectrum, different methods are used for encoding, each method tailored specifically for the data in question.

The simplest method applies to the zeros at the right end of the spectrum. The most efficient way to code this string of zeros is—its length. This length is implicitly known after we have decoded all the nonzero values and there is no need to store it in the bit stream.

12.2 Decoding Small Values

Small values are either 1, 0 or −1. Not much can be gained by encoding each of these values individually. Even the best Huffman code will require at least one bit per value. Therefore, in this part of the spectrum, we group the values into quadruples $(u0, u1, u2, u3)$ and encode the quadruples. Actually, only the absolute values, 0 or 1, get encoded, and the code for the quadruple is then followed by up to four sign bits. For each non zero value in the quadruple there is one sign bit. If that bit is 0, the value is positive, if it is 1, the value is negative.

The encoder can choose among two different tables for encoding small values, $htabA$ and $htabB$. $htabA$ is a table of bytes, indexed by a 6 bit value. Each byte contains in the leftmost 4 bits the absolute values of $(u0, u1, u2, u3)$ and in the rightmost four bits the number of Huffman bits actually used. The following lines of C-code take the bits from a variable, called $huffman\_cache$, that contains $huffman\_cache\_size$ bits aligned to the left. Here and for the next couple of code snippets, we assume that we did $\langle$ refill the $huffman\_cache$ $_{316}$ $\rangle$ before using it. A refill will make sure that there are at least 16 valid bits in the $huffman\_cache$. Now we are ready to

$\langle$ read four small values with $htabA$ $_{299}$ $\rangle \equiv$ (299)
    $code = htabA[((\textbf{unsigned int})\ huffman\_cache) \gg (\texttt{HUFFMAN\_CACHE\_SIZE} - 6)];$
    $huffman\_cache = huffman\_cache \ll (code\ \&\ {}^{\#}\texttt{F});$
    $huffman\_cache\_size = huffman\_cache\_size - (code\ \&\ {}^{\#}\texttt{F});$
    $\langle$ adjust signs and store four small values $_{300}$ $\rangle$ Used in 302.

After we load the $code$ from $htabA$, the four rightmost bits of $code$ contain the number of bits actually needed. They are used to adjust the $huffman\_cache$. The four leftmost bits of $code$ contain the decoded values.

The values in the variable $code$ need to be adorned with the appropriate sign before they can be stored in the array of raw frequencies $\boldsymbol{u}$. To store the values at the correct position, we maintain a pointer u into $\boldsymbol{u}$. For each decoded value that is not zero, the Huffman code is followed by a sign bit. A 1-bit indicates a negative value of -1, a zero bit indicates a positive value of $+1$. Instead of testing each bit separately, we combine the next four bits from the $huffman\_cache$ and the four bits from $code$ to one 8 bit value which we use as an index into a precomputed table called $signed\_small\_values$, which contains the signed values $u0$, $u1$, $u2$, and $u3$ as well as the number n of actual sign bit used, packed into a structure of bit fields.

$\langle$ adjust signs and store four small values $_{300}$ $\rangle \equiv$ (300)
    $code\ =\ (code\ \&\ {}^{\#}\texttt{F0})\ |\ (((\textbf{unsigned int})$
        $huffman\_cache) \gg (\texttt{HUFFMAN\_CACHE\_SIZE} - 4));$
    $*u\mathord{+}\mathord{+} = signed\_small\_values[code].u0;$
    $*u\mathord{+}\mathord{+} = signed\_small\_values[code].u1;$
    $*u\mathord{+}\mathord{+} = signed\_small\_values[code].u2;$
    $*u\mathord{+}\mathord{+} = signed\_small\_values[code].u3;$
    $huffman\_cache = huffman\_cache \ll (signed\_small\_values[code].n);$
    $huffman\_cache\_size = huffman\_cache\_size - (signed\_small\_values[code].n);$
                                                           Used in 299 and 301.

Things are a simpler when we use $htabB$. A short glance at $htabB$ reveals that the stored values are just the bitwise inverse of the index and there is no need to use a table for this operation.

⟨ read four small values with *htabB* ₃₀₁ ⟩ ≡   (301)
   code = ∼(*huffman_cache* ≫ (HUFFMAN_CACHE_SIZE − 4));
   huffman_cache = *huffman_cache* ≪ 4;
   huffman_cache_size = *huffman_cache_size* − 4;
   code = *code* ≪ 4;
   ⟨ adjust signs and store four small values ₃₀₀ ⟩   Used in 303.

The above code is packaged into two functions. The first one is for decoding small
values using *htabA*. It has as parameters the pointer *u*, indicating where to store the
decoded values, the number of *bits_available* for decoding, and the maximum number
of values to decode *n*.

⟨ auxiliary functions ₆₉ ⟩ +≡   (302)
   static short int
            ∗*decode_small_A*(**stream** ∗*s*, **short int** ∗*u*, **int** *bits_available*, **int** *n*)
   { ⟨ initialize the *huffman_cache* ₃₁₃ ⟩
     bits_available = *bits_available* − *huffman_cache_size*;
     while (*n* ≥ 4)
     { **unsigned char** *code*;

        if (⟨ the *huffman_cache* needs bits ₃₁₅ ⟩)
        { ⟨ refill the *huffman_cache* ₃₁₆ ⟩
          ⟨ adjust and check *bits_available* ₃₁₈ ⟩ }

        ⟨ read four small values with *htabA* ₂₉₉ ⟩
        n = *n* − 4;
     }

     return *u*;
   }

The second one decodes small values pretending to use *htabB*.

⟨ auxiliary functions ₆₉ ⟩ +≡   (303)
   static short int
            ∗*decode_small_B*(**stream** ∗*s*, **short int** ∗*u*, **int** *bits_available*, **int** *n*)
   { ⟨ initialize the *huffman_cache* ₃₁₃ ⟩
     bits_available = *bits_available* − *huffman_cache_size*;
     while (*n* ≥ 4)
     { **unsigned char** *code*;

        if (⟨ the *huffman_cache* needs bits ₃₁₅ ⟩)
        { ⟨ refill the *huffman_cache* ₃₁₆ ⟩
          ⟨ adjust and check *bits_available* ₃₁₈ ⟩ }

        ⟨ read four small values with *htabB* ₃₀₁ ⟩
        n = *n* − 4;
     }

     return *u*;
   }

The tables *htabA* and *signed_small_values* are provided in the file `huffman.h`, which was generated from the data provided in the standard.

⟨ header files ₉ ⟩ +≡   (304)
#**include** "huffman.h"

12.3 Decoding Big Values

The first part of the frequency spectrum contains the "big values". Here values can grow as large as $2^{13} = 8192$ (says the Standard) and putting all these values into an Huffman code table would make for a quite large table—most of which is almost never used. To utilize resources more cleverly, the Huffman coding schema is used only for small "big values", that is values in the range from 0 to 15. To code a larger value, the value 15 is encoded, using the Huffman code table, and is then followed immediately in the bit stream by an unsigned integer, which is added to 15 to yield the desired very big value. To know the number of bits used for coding the unsigned integer, each table is annotated with a value called *"linbits"* which is at most 13. This gives a maximum value for big values of $2^{13} + 15 = 8207$ (see also page 136) and we are on the safe side, if we use this value instead of the value claimed by the standard.

A value in the range 0 to 15 can be encoded with 4 bits and since Huffman codes are at least one bit long, this gives a maximum achievable compression rate of 25 %. Not very much. To improve upon this, big values are encoded in pairs $(u0, u1)$, which brings the achievable compressed size to 12.5 %. Up to two sign bits follow the encoded value pair, as we have seen it for small values.

If *htab* is a Huffman table, as provided by the file `huffman.h`, it is a table of **short int**'s, indexed by HWIDTH bit from the *huffman_cache*. Each **short int** contains in the leftmost 8 bits the number of Huffman bits actually used, then in the next 4 bits the value of $u0$, and in the rightmost 4 bits the value of $u1$. This is very similar to what we have seen for small values.

Since, in general, the Huffman tables use extensions, we can not just assume that every **short int** in the table has the form described above, it might be a pointer to an extension table. In this case, it has a negative value, and the leftmost 12 bits give the difference between the start index of the base table and the extension table. This difference is negative since extension tables are located after the base tables. The remaining 4 bits give the number of index bits used to access the extension table. Putting everything together, this is how we

⟨ read two big values with *htab* ₃₀₅ ⟩ ≡   (305)
  { **int** *width* = HWIDTH;
    short int *∗h* = *htab*;

    code = *h*[((**unsigned int**) *huffman_cache*) ≫ (HUFFMAN_CACHE_SIZE − *width*)];
    while (*code* < 0)
    { *huffman_cache* = *huffman_cache* ≪ *width*;
      huffman_cache_size = *huffman_cache_size* − *width*;
      h = *h* − (*code* ≫ 4);
      width = *code* & #OF;

$$code = h[((\textbf{unsigned int})\ \mathit{huffman\_cache}) \gg (\texttt{HUFFMAN\_CACHE\_SIZE} - \mathit{width})];$$
      }
}

Used in 310 and 311.

After we have retrieved the right *code*, we adjust the *huffman_cache* and mask the code to contain only the two 4 bit values *u0* and *u1*.

⟨ read two big values with *htab* ₃₀₅ ⟩ +≡   (306)
   $\mathit{huffman\_cache} = \mathit{huffman\_cache} \ll (code \gg 8);$
   $\mathit{huffman\_cache\_size} = \mathit{huffman\_cache\_size} - (code \gg 8);$
   $code = code\ \&\ {}^{\#}\texttt{FF};$

In the simplest case, where we have a table with *linbits* = 0, we only need to consider the sign bit to

⟨ extract a big value from *code* ₃₀₇ ⟩ ≡   (307)
   { **short int** *value* = $code \gg 4$;

   if $(\mathit{value} \neq 0)$ ⟨ adjust sign of *value* ₃₀₈ ⟩
   $*u{+}{+} = value;$
   }
   $code = (code \ll 4)\ \&\ {}^{\#}\texttt{FF};$ Used in 310.

To read the sign bit, we could just test the leftmost bit in the *huffman_cache*, which happens to be its sign bit, and test it'like this: **if** $(\mathit{huffman\_cache} < 0)$ ⋯ **else** ⋯. It is, however, faster to avoid the extra two-way branch and compute the correct value from the value of the sign bit directly, as we do below. Even if the generated code is one or two instruction longer than the code generated from the **if**-statement (depending on which branch the **if** takes), the code still runs about 10 % faster. Modern pipelined processors prefer a predictable workload, even if it is slightly higher, over an unpredictable schedule. Do computers gradually acquire human work habits?

The following code uses the properties of binary numbers represented in two's complement format (see Section 7.8). Shifting the leftmost bit of the *huffman_cache* all the way to the right produces an **int** value that has all its bits set to one if the leftmost bit was one, or zero if the leftmost bit was zero. We store this value in *tmp* and use it twice: As a mask for the ⊕-operation, and for subtracting it. In case the sign bit was set, this amounts to a binary complement operation and an addition of 1, that is exactly the definition of negation in the two's complement representation, or it amounts to two operations ⊕ 0 − 0 both doing nothing. The rest is straight forward.

⟨ adjust sign of *value* ₃₀₈ ⟩ ≡   (308)
   { **int** $tmp = ((\textbf{signed int})\ \mathit{huffman\_cache}) \gg (\texttt{HUFFMAN\_CACHE\_SIZE} - 1);$

   $value = (value \oplus tmp) - tmp;$
   $\mathit{huffman\_cache} = \mathit{huffman\_cache} \ll 1;$
   $\mathit{huffman\_cache\_size}\ {-}{-};$
   }

Used in 307 and 309.

If a table has $linbits \neq 0$, we

$\langle$ extract a very big value from $code$ $_{309}$ $\rangle \equiv$ (309)
 { **short int** $value = code \gg 4$;

  if $(value \equiv 15 \wedge linbits > 0)$
  { $value = value + (((\textbf{unsigned int})\ huffman\_cache) \gg$
   $(\texttt{HUFFMAN\_CACHE\_SIZE} - linbits))$;
   $huffman\_cache = huffman\_cache \ll linbits$;
   $huffman\_cache\_size = huffman\_cache\_size - linbits$;
   $\langle$ adjust sign of $value$ $_{308}$ $\rangle$
  }

  else if $(value \neq 0)$ $\langle$ adjust sign of $value$ $_{308}$ $\rangle$
  $*u{+\!+} = value$;
  $code = (code \ll 4)\ \&\ {^\#}\texttt{FF}$;
 }
                             Used in 311.

Note that, if $linbits$ is zero, no bits are read and, as expected, nothing is added to 15. Before we use the above code, we should $\langle$ refill the $huffman\_cache$ $_{316}$ $\rangle$. But wait, is it enough to $\langle$ refill the $huffman\_cache$ $_{316}$ $\rangle$ only once? Yes, most of the time. (That means No!) Some tables might need more bits: e.g. $htab13$ may need up to 19 bits and $htab16$ may need 17 bits. For these tables, we $\langle$ extra fill the $huffman\_cache$ $_{317}$ $\rangle$; after a regular refill, this brings the cache to at least 24 bits.

We wrap things up and package the code into two different functions. Both receive the stream s, a pointer u, indicating where to store the decoded values, the number k of the table to use, and the number n of pairs to decode as arguments. The first one is for reading big values from table 1 to 12, where we have no $linbits$ and 16 bits in the $huffman\_cache$ are sufficient for the table lookup and two sign bits.

$\langle$ auxiliary functions $_{69}$ $\rangle$ $+\equiv$ (310)
 static void $decode\_big$(**stream** $*s$, **short int** $*u$, **int** k, **int** n)
 { **short int** $*htab = huffman\_tables[k].h$;

  $\langle$ initialize the $huffman\_cache$ $_{313}$ $\rangle$
  while $(n{-\!-} > 0)$
  { **int** $code$;

   if $((\langle$ the $huffman\_cache$ needs bits $_{315}$ $\rangle))$ $\langle$ refill the $huffman\_cache$ $_{316}$ $\rangle$
   $\langle$ read two big values with $htab$ $_{305}$ $\rangle$
   $\langle$ extract a big value from $code$ $_{307}$ $\rangle$
   $\langle$ extract a big value from $code$ $_{307}$ $\rangle$
  }

  $\langle$ finalize the $huffman\_cache$ $_{314}$ $\rangle$
 }

The second can read big values from any table.

⟨ auxiliary functions $_{69}$ ⟩ +≡   (311)
  static void *decode_very_big*(**stream** *∗s*, **short int** *∗u*, **int** *k*, **int** *n*)
  { **short int** *∗htab* = *huffman_tables*[*k*]*.h*;
   int *linbits* = *huffman_tables*[*k*]*.linbits*;
   ⟨ initialize the *huffman_cache* $_{313}$ ⟩
   while (*n−−* > 0)
   { **int** *code*;
    if (⟨ the *huffman_cache* needs bits $_{315}$ ⟩) ⟨ refill the *huffman_cache* $_{316}$ ⟩
    ⟨ extra fill the *huffman_cache* $_{317}$ ⟩
    ⟨ read two big values with *htab* $_{305}$ ⟩
    if (⟨ the *huffman_cache* needs bits $_{315}$ ⟩) ⟨ refill the *huffman_cache* $_{316}$ ⟩
    ⟨ extract a very big value from *code* $_{309}$ ⟩
    if (⟨ the *huffman_cache* needs bits $_{315}$ ⟩) ⟨ refill the *huffman_cache* $_{316}$ ⟩
    ⟨ extract a very big value from *code* $_{309}$ ⟩
   }
   ⟨ finalize the *huffman_cache* $_{314}$ ⟩
  }

12.4 Efficient Bitwise Access

The *huffman_cache* and the *huffman_cache_size* work together to provide bitwise access to the input buffer. It is advisable to use this kind of cache only in a small loop where the cache and all the other values needed to maintain it are kept in registers. For, otherwise, it is equally fast to reload the bits from the buffer directly. The *huffman_cache* is a regular **int**, which we assume has 32 bits.

⟨ private declarations $_1$ ⟩ +≡   (312)
#**define** HUFFMAN_CACHE_SIZE (**sizeof**(**int**) ∗ 8)

At the beginning of each decoding function, the initial content is loaded, and at the end the *byte_pointer* and *bit_offset* are adjusted.

⟨ initialize the *huffman_cache* $_{313}$ ⟩ ≡   (313)
  unsigned char *∗byte_pointer* = *s→byte_pointer*;
  int *huffman_cache_size* = 8 − *s→bit_offset*;
  int *huffman_cache* = (*∗byte_pointer*++) ≪ (**sizeof**(**int**) ∗ 8 − *huffman_cache_size*);
                        Used in 302, 303, 310, and 311.

⟨ finalize the *huffman_cache* $_{314}$ ⟩ ≡   (314)
  s→bit_offset = (8 − (*huffman_cache_size* % 8)) & $^\#$7;
  s→byte_pointer = *byte_pointer* − ((*huffman_cache_size* + *s→bit_offset*)/8);
                             Used in 310 and 311.

If

⟨ the *huffman_cache* needs bits $_{315}$ ⟩ ≡   (315)
  (16 − *huffman_cache_size* > 0)
                        Used in 302, 303, 310, and 311.

we

⟨ refill the *huffman_cache* $_{316}$ ⟩ ≡   (316)
  { **int** *tmp* = (∗*byte_pointer* ≪ 8) | (∗(*byte_pointer* + 1) & #FF);

    byte_pointer = *byte_pointer* + 2;
    huffman_cache = *huffman_cache* | (*tmp* ≪ (16 − *huffman_cache_size*));
    huffman_cache_size = *huffman_cache_size* + 16;
  }
                                                 Used in 302, 303, 310, and 311.

If 16 bits are not enough, we

⟨ extra fill the *huffman_cache* $_{317}$ ⟩ ≡   (317)
  if (*huffman_cache_size* < 24)
  { *huffman_cache* = *huffman_cache* | (*byte_pointer* [0] ≪ (24 − *huffman_cache_size*));
    byte_pointer ++;
    huffman_cache_size = *huffman_cache_size* + 8;
  }
                                                    Used in 311.

Used after a regular refill, this brings the cache to at least 24 bits.

While decoding small values, there is a bound on the number of *bits_available*. After taking out some bits, we

⟨ adjust and check *bits_available* $_{318}$ ⟩ ≡   (318)
  bits_available = *bits_available* − 16;
  if (*bits_available* < 0)
  { *huffman_cache_size* = *huffman_cache_size* + *bits_available*;
    bits_available = 0;
    if (*huffman_cache_size* ≤ 0) **break**;
  }
                                                Used in 302 and 303.

The code uses a **break** to exit the current reading loop in case the end of all bits is encountered.

13 Advanced Bit Packing: Layer III

A layer III bit stream is subdivided into frames, as we have seen them for layers I and II. Even the first 4 bytes, the header, and the optional two bytes CRC are identical—only the two layer bits (Tab. 6) in the header reveal the difference. Even the *frame_size*, that is the distance between two headers, is still computed from sample rate, bit rate, and padding. Indeed, layer III uses the same formula for the *frame_size* (see page 47) and the same synchronization mechanism. But then, the frame takes a different turn.

Due to the unpredictable nature of Huffman coding, which may need sometimes more sometimes fewer bits to encode the same number of frequency values, it is impractical to use a fixed number of bytes for the coding of frequencies. For variable size data, it would be best to have a bit stream with variable size frames. The solution in layer III is the interleaving of two bit streams, one with fixed frame size and one with variable frame size, into one single bit stream.

The fixed size stream contains the frame header, the optional CRC, and the side information; the variable size stream contains the scalefactors and the Huffman coded samples, collectively called "main data".

⟨ generate output data ₆₆ ⟩ +≡   (319)
case LAYER_III:
    ⟨ decode layer III side information ₃₃₂ ⟩
    ⟨ decode the main data ₃₆₂ ⟩
    $s \rightarrow frame = next\_frame(s)$;
    break;

This chapter continues with the discussion of the main innovation of layer III, the bit reservoir, and then explains the decoding of side information and main data.

13.1 Bit Reservoir

The distance of two frame headers in the fixed size stream is determined as in layers I and II, but the amount of data in the fixed stream is not sufficient to fill the entire frame. Instead there are large gaps left. These gaps are filled with the variable size stream. Because the fixed size frames are fairly easy to find—the header contains synchronization bits, and the location of future headers is predictable— the fixed size frames are used to find the variable size frames. Since fixed and variable frames come in pairs, it is enough to have in each fixed size frame a pointer that directs the decoder

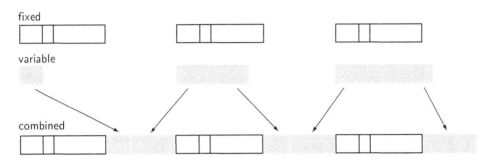

Fig. 59: Merging fixed and variable bit stream

to the beginning of the corresponding variable sized frame. This pointer is located in the first 9 bits of the side information.

$\langle$ read *reservoir_size* $_{320}$ $\rangle \equiv$ (320)
    if $(s{\rightarrow}info.version \equiv$ `MP3_V1_0`$)$ *reservoir_size* $= getbit(s, 9);$ Used in 322.

These 9 bits tell the distance from the start of the fixed size frame to the start of variable size frame. There is one restriction for this pointer: it may never point forward. It can only point back to data already contained in previous frames. This property, together with the limited range of a 9 bit integer, makes the mechanism work like a bit reservoir. Frames that need fewer bytes than available in the gap towards the next frame can donate the extra space to the bit reservoir, and future frames can use these extra bytes for their variable parts by pointing backwards into the reservoir. The bit reservoir allows the encoder to use some extra bits for a difficult to encode frame, provided it was thrifty enough in the past. In the average, however, the actual bit rate can never exceed the bit rate specified in the stream—actually it can only be lower. Unlike modern governments, encoders must maintain a balanced budget.

Because a 9 bit back pointer can not span more than $2^9 - 1 = 511$ bytes, we define

$\langle$ private declarations $_1$ $\rangle$ $+\equiv$ (321)
#**define** `MAX_RESERVOIR` 512

If we start playing a bit stream somewhere in the middle, or if there are missing frames in the stream, a frame might specify a bit reservoir which was actually not read in. In this case, the beginning of the reservoir may be before the *start* of the buffer data. To detect this situation, we

$\langle$ perform additional checks $_{99}$ $\rangle$ $+\equiv$ (322)
    if $(s{\rightarrow}info.layer \equiv 3)$
    { **int** *reservoir_size*;

        $\langle$ read *reservoir_size* $_{320}$ $\rangle$
        $s{\rightarrow}main\_data\_start = s{\rightarrow}frame - reservoir\_size;$
        if $(s{\rightarrow}main\_data\_start < s{\rightarrow}start)$ $\langle$ deal with missing main data $_{323}$ $\rangle$
    }

and occasionally we might have to

⟨ deal with missing main data ₃₂₃ ⟩ ≡   (323)
   { $s{\rightarrow}main\_data\_start = s{\rightarrow}start$;
     $output_mode = $ SKIP;
   }
Used in 322.

Otherwise, the pointer to the main data is stored in the stream.

⟨ stream data ₂ ⟩ +≡   (324)
   unsigned char $*main\_data\_start$;

For the purpose of decoding the variable size stream, the bytes donated to the bit reservoir are considered consecutive bytes of the stream. The interruption by the fixed part does not count. Hence, after reading the fixed part of the frame, we simply remove it, and the variable size frame will remain. We remove the fixed part of the frame by moving the bytes in the reservoir forward. An alternative would be to move the bytes after the fixed part backward, but we expect, on average, fewer bytes in the reservoir than in the input buffer.

⟨ remove fixed part of frame from *buffer* ₃₂₅ ⟩ ≡   (325)
   { **int** $size = s{\rightarrow}frame - s{\rightarrow}main\_data\_start$;

     $memmove(s{\rightarrow}frame - size + s{\rightarrow}info.fixed\_size, s{\rightarrow}frame - size, size)$;
     $s{\rightarrow}main\_data\_start = s{\rightarrow}main\_data\_start + s{\rightarrow}info.fixed\_size$;
     $s{\rightarrow}start = s{\rightarrow}start + s{\rightarrow}info.fixed\_size$;
   }
Used in 326, 401, 403, 405, and 409.

After removing the fixed part, we

⟨ switch to the bit reservoir ₃₂₆ ⟩ ≡   (326)
   int $main\_data\_position = 0$;

   { ⟨ remove fixed part of frame from *buffer* ₃₂₅ ⟩
     $s{\rightarrow}byte\_pointer = s{\rightarrow}main\_data\_start$;
     $s{\rightarrow}bit\_offset = 0$;
   }
Used in 362 and 399.

We initialize the variable $main\_data\_position$ as a bitwise offset to the $main\_data\_start$ pointer. Together with the values in $main\_data\_bit$, it enables us to

⟨ advance the stream to the next granule gr and channel ch ₃₂₇ ⟩ ≡   (327)
   $main\_data\_position = main\_data\_position + main\_data\_bit[gr][ch]$;
   $s{\rightarrow}byte\_pointer = s{\rightarrow}main\_data\_start + main\_data\_position/8$;
   $s{\rightarrow}bit\_offset = main\_data\_position \% 8$;
Used in 364.

Further, it comes in handy when we need to determine the ⟨ main data bits already used ₃₂₈ ⟩ or the opposite, the ⟨ still available main data bits ₃₂₉ ⟩.

⟨ main data bits already used ₃₂₈ ⟩ ≡   (328)
   $((s{\rightarrow}byte\_pointer - s{\rightarrow}main\_data\_start) * 8 + s{\rightarrow}bit\_offset)$
Used in 329.

⟨ still available main data bits $_{329}$ ⟩ ≡   (329)
    $main\_data\_position + main\_data\_bit\,[gr][ch]$
        − ⟨ main data bits already used $_{328}$ ⟩   Used in 369.

When we come to the end of the stream, we did require for layer I and II frames that the whole frame must be in the stream in order to be decoded. For a layer III stream, we can verify whether the fixed part of the frame is in the stream, but it is difficult to tell, unless we are willing to decode the frame, whether the variable frame is there or not. In principle, it might be completely in the bit reservoir. This decoder passes the decision on to the user.

⟨ options $_{20}$ ⟩ +≡   (330)
#**define** MP3_NO_PARTIAL_FRAME   #1000

If the application has set the MP3_NO_PARTIAL_FRAME flag, the decoder will test for a

⟨ partial last frame $_{331}$ ⟩ ≡   (331)
    $(s{\rightarrow}frame + s{\rightarrow}info.fixed\_size < s{\rightarrow}finish \wedge \neg(s{\rightarrow}options.flags$ &
        MP3_NO_PARTIAL_FRAME))   Used in 163.

and will refrain from decoding layer III frames unless the complete frame, up to but not including the next frame header, is in the stream. Otherwise, the last frame will be decoded if at least the fixed part of the frame can be read from the stream.

13.2 Side Information

The fixed part of the stream contains the side information. Some items stored as side information for a frame are already familiar from layers I and II, other items are new, and we will learn about them now.

⟨ decode layer III side information $_{332}$ ⟩ ≡   (332)
    { ⟨ remove padding $_{333}$ ⟩
      ⟨ decode scalefactor sharing $_{335}$ ⟩
      ⟨ decode granule information $_{338}$ ⟩
    }   Used in 319.

Right after the back pointer to the beginning of the bit reservoir, we have either 5 or 3 padding bits. These are not used in any way by the decoder but are just removed.

⟨ remove padding $_{333}$ ⟩ ≡   (333)
    if $(s{\rightarrow}info.mode \equiv$ MP3_MONO) $getbit\,(s,5);$
    else $getbit(s,3);$ Used in 332.

One may wonder why we waste three to five precious bits here, while we fight for every single bit at other places. As can be seen from Table 23, the answer is: The padding bits round up the size of the side information to a sequence of full bytes, and equalize it, making it a "fixed" size (either 17 for mono or 32 for stereo), as required.

We continue here with a closer look at the sharing of scalefactors, which is followed by a detailed discussion of granule information.

Name	single channel	dual channel
reservoir_size	9	9
padding	5	3
share	4	4+4
information for first granule:		
main_data_bit	12	12+12
big_values	9	9+9
global_gain	8	8+8
slength and *slimit*	4	4+4
window_switching	1	1+1
for normal blocks:		
table selection	3*5	3*5+3*5
region 0 pairs	4	4+4
region 1 pairs	3	3+3
subtotal for normal blocks	22	44
preemphasis switch	1	2
fine/coarse scalefactors	1	2
select *htabA* or *htabB*	1	2
subtotal for first granule	59	118
subtotal for second granule	59	118
Total Bit	136	256
Total Byte	17	32

Tab. 23: Layout of side information

The idea of scalefactor sharing is not new (see Section 9.3). As an improvement in layer III, scalefactor sharing is applied to groups of scalefactors instead of single scalefactors. As we have seen before, in layer III there is one scalefactor for each frequency band. Now, we separate the 21 frequency bands into four different groups (Tab. 24).

Group	Scalefactor Band
0	0 – 5
1	6 – 10
2	11 – 15
3	16 – 20

Tab. 24: Groups of scalefactor bands

⟨ private declarations $_1$ ⟩ +≡   (334)
#**define** BANDGROUPS   4

One layer III frame contains two granules, and the encoder can specify separately for each group of scalefactor bands whether the second granule will reuse the scalefactor information of the first granule or not. Therefore, we read for each channel and each group of bands one bit. The value 1 indicates sharing of information.

$\langle$ decode scalefactor sharing $_{335}\,\rangle \equiv$ (335)
    { int ch, $group$;
        for $(ch = 0;\ ch < s{\rightarrow}info.channels;\ ch{+}{+})$
            for $(group = 0;\ group < \texttt{BANDGROUPS};\ group{+}{+})$
                $s{\rightarrow}share\,[ch][group] = getbit\,(s, 1);$
    }
                                                                                                        Used in 332.

The *share* flags are stored in the stream.

$\langle$ stream data $_2\,\rangle \mathrel{+}\equiv$ (336)
    int $share\,[\texttt{CHANNELS}][\texttt{BANDGROUPS}];$

This information is used later, when—as part of the main data—we will

$\langle$ read scalefactors with sharing $_{337}\,\rangle \equiv$ (337)
    { const char $*slength = s{\rightarrow}slength\,[gr][ch];$
        int $band$;
        int $slen = slength\,[0];$
        if $(\neg(s{\rightarrow}share\,[ch][0]))$
            for $(band = 0;\ band < 6;\ band{+}{+})$ $\langle$ read single scalefactor $_{368}\,\rangle$
        if $(\neg(s{\rightarrow}share\,[ch][1]))$
            for $(band = 6;\ band < 11;\ band{+}{+})$ $\langle$ read single scalefactor $_{368}\,\rangle$
        $slen = slength\,[1];$
        if $(\neg(s{\rightarrow}share\,[ch][2]))$
            for $(band = 11;\ band < 16;\ band{+}{+})$ $\langle$ read single scalefactor $_{368}\,\rangle$
        if $(\neg(s{\rightarrow}share\,[ch][3]))$
            for $(band = 16;\ band < 21;\ band{+}{+})$ $\langle$ read single scalefactor $_{368}\,\rangle$
    }
                                                                                                        Used in 365.

Next is the side information that is specific for each granule and channel.

$\langle$ decode granule information $_{338}\,\rangle \equiv$ (338)
    { int ch, gr;
        for $(gr = 0;\ gr < 2;\ gr{+}{+})$
            for $(ch = 0;\ ch < s{\rightarrow}info.channels;\ ch{+}{+})$
                { $\langle$ size of main data $_{339}\,\rangle$
                    $\langle$ number of big value pairs $_{341}\,\rangle$
                    $\langle$ global gain $_{343}\,\rangle$
                    $\langle$ scalefactor bit allocation $_{344}\,\rangle$
                    $\langle$ window dependent layout $_{347}\,\rangle$
                    $\langle$ scalefactor limits $_{345}\,\rangle$
                    $\langle$ preemphasis flag $_{358}\,\rangle$
                    $\langle$ select scalefactor quantization $_{359}\,\rangle$
                    $\langle$ select small values table $_{360}\,\rangle$
                }
    }
                                                                                                        Used in 332.

The main data is partitioned in four or two sections, one for each granule and channel. The size of each of these sections is the first item in the side information. It is a 12 bit unsigned integer indicating the number of bits used for the main data—scalefactors and Huffman code data—for granule gr and channel ch.

$\langle$ size of main data $_{339}$ $\rangle$ $\equiv$ (339)
$\quad$ $main\_data\_bit[gr][ch] = getbit(s, 12);$ Used in 338 and 378.

$\langle$ global variables $_{43}$ $\rangle$ $+\equiv$ (340)
$\quad$ **static int** $main\_data\_bit$[GRANULES][CHANNELS];

Next is the number of big value pairs which should never exceed FREQUENCIES/2.

$\langle$ number of big value pairs $_{341}$ $\rangle$ $\equiv$ (341)
$\quad$ $big\_values[gr][ch] = getbit(s, 9);$
$\quad$ **if** $(big\_values[gr][ch] >$ FREQUENCIES/2$)$
$\quad\quad$ $big\_values[gr][ch] =$ FREQUENCIES/2;   Used in 338 and 378.

$\langle$ global variables $_{43}$ $\rangle$ $+\equiv$ (342)
$\quad$ **static int** big_values[GRANULES][CHANNELS];

The following 8 bits contain the $global\_gain$.

$\langle$ global gain $_{343}$ $\rangle$ $\equiv$ (343)
$\quad$ $global\_gain[gr][ch] = getbit(s, 8);$ Used in 338 and 378.

Using this factor, which is applied to all samples in a granule, the encoder can scale the values to a common value range to achieve a more homogeneous data distribution, which aids Huffman coding.

The next four bits contain the bit allocation information for scalefactors.

$\langle$ scalefactor bit allocation $_{344}$ $\rangle$ $\equiv$ (344)
$\quad$ $s \rightarrow slength[gr][ch] = slength\_v1[getbit(s, 4)];$ Used in 338.

Stored in the bit stream is an index into the array $slength\_v1$ shown in Table 25. It specifies two different bit allocations, one for the low frequency bands and one for the high frequency bands. As one can see, not all combinations are possible. Highly unusual combinations, like 4 bits in the lower bands and 0 bits in the higher bands, are omitted. This combination would be rarely used, because it is unlikely that the scalefactor requirements change so rapidly from one group of bands to the other. The given table lacks this combination, forcing the encoder to use one bit for the second batch of scalefactors, applicable to the high frequency bands, even if none would suffice.

Index	0	1	2	3	4	5	6	7	8	9	10	11	12	13	14	15
low	0	0	0	0	3	1	1	1	2	2	2	3	3	3	4	4
high	0	1	2	3	0	1	2	3	1	2	3	1	2	3	2	3

Tab. 25: Bit allocation for scalefactor information

The split between high and low frequency bands depends on the specific block type and is again different for mixed blocks. A bound on the low frequency bands is taken from the table *slimit_v1* shown in Table 26.

⟨ scalefactor limits ₃₄₅ ⟩ ≡   (345)
$\quad s{\to}slimit[gr][ch] = slimit\_v1\,[s{\to}block\_type[gr][ch] \equiv \texttt{SHORT\_BLOCK}]$
$\quad\quad [s{\to}mixed\_block[gr][ch]];$ Used in 338.

Block Type	Mixed Block	low	high
LONG_BLOCK		0–10	11–20
START_BLOCK		0–10	11–20
SHORT_BLOCK	No	0–5	6–11
SHORT_BLOCK	Yes	0–7 (long) 3–5 (short)	6–11
STOP_BLOCK		0–10	11–20

Tab. 26: Boundaries between high and low frequencies

We see, that the boundary is the same for normal blocks and non normal blocks except for short blocks. For short blocks, we distinguish between mixed blocks and non mixed blocks. In mixed blocks, the 8 lowest bands are actually long blocks. These and the next 3 short bands form the low frequency range. Together with the short bands 6 to 11, they cover the entire frequency range. The C definitions of *slength_v1* and *slimit_v1* are in Appendix A.13. To access the correct part of these tables, pointers are stored in the stream data.

⟨ stream data ₂ ⟩ +≡   (346)
$\quad$ **const char** $*slength[\texttt{GRANULES}][\texttt{CHANNELS}];$
$\quad$ **const char** $*slimit[\texttt{GRANULES}][\texttt{CHANNELS}];$

The next bit, the window switching flag, is of special importance.

⟨ window dependent layout ₃₄₇ ⟩ ≡   (347)
$\quad window\_switching[gr][ch] = getbit(s, 1);$ Used in 338 and 378.

⟨ global variables ₄₃ ⟩ +≡   (348)
$\quad$ **static int** $window\_switching[\texttt{GRANULES}][\texttt{CHANNELS}];$

This flag determines pretty much what comes next.

⟨ window dependent layout ₃₄₇ ⟩ +≡   (349)
$\quad$ **if** $(window\_switching[gr][ch])$
$\quad$ { ⟨ read Huffman decoding information for special block ₃₅₆ ⟩ }
$\quad$ **else** { ⟨ read Huffman decoding information for normal block ₃₅₁ ⟩ }

First, we discuss the decoding information for "normal" blocks. A block is normal, if it is neither a start, stop, or a short block. These blocks are "special".

To decode the Huffman coded bits, which are part of the main data, we need to know which tables to use. For the big values 32 different Huffman tables are available.

We know already that the frequency lines are grouped together in scalefactor bands, now we subdivide the sequence of scalefactor bands into three regions.

⟨ private declarations $_1$ ⟩ +≡ (350)
#define REGIONS 3

For each region, we can pick one Huffman table. The table numbers are stored in the bit stream as 5 bit numbers.

⟨ read Huffman decoding information for normal block $_{351}$ ⟩ ≡ (351)
{ **int** *region*;

$s{\rightarrow}block\_type\,[gr][ch] =$ LONG_BLOCK;
$s{\rightarrow}mixed\_block\,[gr][ch] = 0$;
⟨ select layer III band *width* $_{245}$ ⟩
for (*region* = 0; *region* < REGIONS; *region*++)
    $s{\rightarrow}bigtable\,[gr][ch][region] = getbit\,(s, 5)$;
}
Used in 349.

We store them in the stream.

⟨ stream data $_2$ ⟩ +≡ (352)
int *bigtable* [GRANULES][CHANNELS][REGIONS];

How do we figure out the boundaries of the regions? Easy. We take the number of pairs in each region from the stream.

⟨ stream data $_2$ ⟩ +≡ (353)
int *bigpairs* [GRANULES][CHANNELS][REGIONS];

And how do they get there? The sizes of the first two regions are in the bit stream as a 4 bit and a 3 bit number. The region boundaries are aligned with the partitioning of the spectrum in bands. The numbers contained in the bit stream are one less than the number of bands in the respective region.

⟨ read Huffman decoding information for normal block $_{351}$ ⟩ +≡ (354)
{ **int** *region0*, *region1*;

$region0 = getbit\,(s, 4) + 1$;
$region1 = getbit\,(s, 3) + 1$;
⟨ determine pairs $_{355}$ ⟩
}

From the number of bands, we can get the number of pairs in each region using the *start* table. The size of the third region can be computed from the total number of big value pairs and the sizes of the two other regions.

⟨ determine pairs $_{355}$ ⟩ ≡ (355)
{ **int** *∗pairs* = $s{\rightarrow}bigpairs\,[gr][ch]$;

$pairs\,[0] = start\,[gr][ch][region0]/2$;
if ($pairs\,[0] \geq big\_values\,[gr][ch]$)
{ $pairs\,[0] = big\_values\,[gr][ch]$;
  $pairs\,[1] = pairs\,[2] = 0$;

```
    }
    else
    { pairs[1] = start[gr][ch][region0 + region1]/2;
      if (pairs[1] ≥ big_values[gr][ch])
      { pairs[1] = big_values[gr][ch] − pairs[0];
        pairs[2] = 0;
      }
      else
      { pairs[1] = pairs[1] − pairs[0];
        pairs[2] = big_values[gr][ch] − pairs[0] − pairs[1];
      }
    }
  }
}
```

Used in 354.

This completes the Huffman decoding information for normal blocks. The side information for special blocks and its layout is shown in Table 27, supplementing Table 23.

Name	single channel	dual channel
for start, stop and short blocks:		
block type	2	2+2
mixed block flag	1	1+1
table selection for two regions	2*5	2*5+2*5
subblock gain	3*3	3*3+3*3
subtotal for not normal blocks	22	44

Tab. 27: Layout of side information for special blocks

According to this table, we can

⟨ read Huffman decoding information for special block $_{356}$ ⟩ ≡   (356)
$\quad s{\rightarrow}block\_type[gr][ch] = getbit(s,2);$
$\textbf{if } (s{\rightarrow}block\_type[gr][ch] \equiv \texttt{SHORT\_BLOCK})$
$\{\ s{\rightarrow}share[ch][0] = s{\rightarrow}share[ch][1] = s{\rightarrow}share[ch][2] = s{\rightarrow}share[ch][3] = 0;$
$\}$
$s{\rightarrow}mixed\_block[gr][ch] = getbit(s,1);$
⟨ select layer III band *width* $_{245}$ ⟩
$s{\rightarrow}bigtable[gr][ch][0] = getbit(s,5);$
$s{\rightarrow}bigtable[gr][ch][1] = getbit(s,5);$
$\{\ \textbf{int } i;$
$\quad \textbf{for } (i = 0;\ i < \texttt{SUBBLOCKS};\ i{+}{+})\ subblock\_gain[gr][ch][i] = getbit(s,3);\ \}$
⟨ determine special pairs $_{357}$ ⟩

Used in 349.

There is no region information for special blocks, because they have a fixed subdivision into regions. Region 0 comprises always the first 8 scalefactor bands, except for pure short blocks, where it is 9. The rest of the big values are in region 1. There is no region 2.

$\langle$ determine special pairs $_{357}\rangle \equiv$ (357)
   { **int** $*pairs = s{\rightarrow}bigpairs[gr][ch]$;
    int max_pairs;

    if $(s{\rightarrow}block\_type[gr][ch] \equiv$ SHORT_BLOCK $\land \neg s{\rightarrow}mixed\_block[gr][ch])$
      $max\_pairs = start[gr][ch][9]/2$;
    else $max\_pairs = start[gr][ch][8]/2$;
    if $(big\_values[gr][ch] \leq max\_pairs)$
    { $pairs[0] = big\_values[gr][ch]$;
      $pairs[1] = 0$;
      $pairs[2] = 0$;
    }

    else
    { $pairs[0] = max\_pairs$;
      $pairs[1] = big\_values[gr][ch] - max\_pairs$;
      $pairs[2] = 0$;
    }

   }   Used in 356.

The side information closes with three bits, one to switch *preemphasis* off or on, one to select fine or coarse scalefactor quantization, and one to select *htabA* or *htabB* for the Huffman decoding of small values.

$\langle$ preemphasis flag $_{358}\rangle \equiv$ (358)
   if $(getbit(s, 1) \equiv 0)$ $\langle$ switch *preemphasis* off $_{260}\rangle$
   else $\langle$ switch *preemphasis* on $_{259}\rangle$ Used in 338.

$\langle$ select scalefactor quantization $_{359}\rangle \equiv$ (359)
   if $(getbit(s, 1) \equiv 0)$ $\langle$ select fine scalefactor quantization $_{254}\rangle$
   else $\langle$ select coarse scalefactor quantization $_{255}\rangle$ Used in 338 and 378.

$\langle$ select small values table $_{360}\rangle \equiv$ (360)
   $s{\rightarrow}smalltable\_A[gr][ch] = (getbit(s, 1) \equiv 0)$;   Used in 338 and 378.

$\langle$ stream data $_{2}\rangle +\equiv$ (361)
   int $smalltable\_A[$GRANULES$][$CHANNELS$]$;

13.3 Main Data

After we switch to the bit reservoir, we find the main data. It consists of two granules and possibly some ancillary bits.

$\langle$ decode the main data $_{362}\rangle \equiv$ (362)
   { **int** gr;

⟨ switch to the bit reservoir $_{326}$ ⟩
  for $(gr = 0;\ gr <$ GRANULES; gr ++) ⟨ decode the granule $_{363}$ ⟩
⟨ process ancillary bits $_{141}$ ⟩;
}

Used in 319.

For each granule, we read scalefactors and raw samples u, quantize and scale them to get z, produce subband samples y, and finally output blocks of PCM samples x.

⟨ decode the granule $_{363}$ ⟩ ≡   (363)
  { **int** ch;

    ⟨ read scalefactors and raw samples $_{364}$ ⟩
    ⟨ quantize and scale raw samples $_{290}$ ⟩
    ⟨ produce subband samples $_{297}$ ⟩
    $output\_blocks(s, buffer + s{\rightarrow}info.samples,$ SUBFREQUENCIES$);$
  }

Used in 362 and 399.

For each granule and channel, the stream contains first the scalefactors, then the Huffman coded raw samples.

⟨ read scalefactors and raw samples $_{364}$ ⟩ ≡   (364)
  for $(ch = 0;\ ch < s{\rightarrow}info.channels;\ ch$ ++)
  { ⟨ read scalefactors for granule gr and channel ch $_{365}$ ⟩
    ⟨ read raw samples $_{369}$ ⟩
    ⟨ advance the stream to the next granule gr and channel ch $_{327}$ ⟩
  }

Used in 363.

Before reading scalefactors, we have to decide first whether the scalefactors are shared or not. They are definitely not shared in the first granule of a frame. Further, a short block in either the first or the second granule prevents sharing.

⟨ read scalefactors for granule gr and channel ch $_{365}$ ⟩ ≡   (365)
  { **if** $(gr \equiv 0 \lor s{\rightarrow}block\_type[gr][ch] \equiv$ SHORT_BLOCK $\lor$
          $s{\rightarrow}block\_type[0][ch] \equiv$ SHORT_BLOCK$)$
    ⟨ read scalefactors without sharing $_{367}$ ⟩
  else ⟨ read scalefactors with sharing $_{337}$ ⟩
  }

Used in 364.

Stored in the stream, we do not find scalefactors but scalefactor indices. We store the index along with the maximum scalefactor index into two arrays. We expect to reuse most of it for the second granule.

⟨ stream data $_2$ ⟩ +≡   (366)
  char sfi[CHANNELS][BANDS];
  char sfi_{max}[CHANNELS][BANDS];

The array with the maximum values is not needed for version 1 but will come in handy in version 2 intensity stereo processing.

    Reading of scalefactor indices is determined by two arrays *slength* and *slimit*. All scalefactor indices less than *slimit* are stored using the same number of bits given by *slength*. We continue reading until a negative value of *slength* indicates that all scalefactor indices are read.

⟨ read scalefactors without sharing ₃₆₇ ⟩ ≡   (367)

```
{ const char *slength = s→slength[gr][ch];
  const char *slimit = s→slimit[gr][ch];
  int band = 0, slen = *slength, slim = *slimit;

  do
  { if (band ≥ slim)
    { slen = *++slength;
      slim = *++slimit;
    }
    else
    { ⟨ read single scalefactor ₃₆₈ ⟩
      band++;
    }
  } while (slen ≥ 0);
}
```
               Used in 365.

Using the current value *slen*, we can determine *sfi* and the maximum value sfi_{max}.

⟨ read single scalefactor ₃₆₈ ⟩ ≡   (368)

```
{ int m;
  if (slen ≡ 0) m = 0;
  else m = getbit(s, slen);
  s→sfi_max[ch][band] = (2 ≪ slen) − 1;
  s→sfi[ch][band] = m;
}
```
               Used in 337 and 367.

We turn now our attention to the Huffman code bits. First, we decode three regions of big values, then the small values. We record a bound on the last nonzero frequency in the variable *ulimit*. Frequencies at or above *ulimit* are set to zero.

⟨ read raw samples ₃₆₉ ⟩ ≡   (369)

```
{ short int *u = u[ch];
  int region;

  for (region = 0; region < REGIONS; region++) ⟨ decode a region ₃₇₀ ⟩
  if (s→smalltable_A[gr][ch])
    u = decode_small_A(s, u, ⟨ still available main data bits ₃₂₉ ⟩,
        FREQUENCIES − (u − u[ch]));
  else u = decode_small_B(s, u, ⟨ still available main data bits ₃₂₉ ⟩,
        FREQUENCIES − (u − u[ch]));
  ulimit[ch] = u − u[ch];
  while (u < &(u[ch][FREQUENCIES])) *u++ = 0;
}
```
               Used in 364.

We strictly need to initialize the values of u with zeros only up to the next band boundary. For simplicity, we initialize all the remaining values.

Using the functions defined in Section 12.3, decoding is simply a matter of calling the right function with the right parameters. After decoding, the pointer u is advanced to the next region.

$\langle$ decode a *region* $_{370}\,\rangle \equiv$ (370)
   { **int** $k = s{\rightarrow}bigtable[gr][ch][region]$;

     if $(k \equiv 0)$ $\langle$ use table 0 $_{371}\,\rangle$
     else if $(k \le 12)$ $decode\_big(s, u, k, s{\rightarrow}bigpairs[gr][ch][region])$;
     else $decode\_very\_big(s, u, k, s{\rightarrow}bigpairs[gr][ch][region])$;
     $u = u + 2 * s{\rightarrow}bigpairs[gr][ch][region]$;
   }
Used in 369.

Decoding with table 0 is a special case. Table 0 contains only zeros, and decoding with this table is very simple.

$\langle$ use table 0 $_{371}\,\rangle \equiv$ (371)
   { **int** n;

     for $(n = 0;\ n < s{\rightarrow}bigpairs[gr][ch][region];\ n{+}{+})\ u[2 * n] = u[2 * n + 1] = 0$;
   }
Used in 370.

14 Low Sample Frequencies

MPEG Version 1 allows for sample frequencies of 32 kHz, 44.1 kHz, and 48 kHz. The sample frequency of 44.1 kHz is the sample frequency used for music CD's, 48 kHz is common for digital studio equipment, and the sample frequency of 32 kHz is there mostly because of historic reasons. The main selection criterion for the sample frequency is—aside from compatibility considerations—the maximum frequency of the source sound signal. An important theorem of digital sound processing states that with sample frequency f, one can represent signals with frequencies up to $f/2$ but not higher. Good studio sound recording equipment will even employ analog filters in the input chain to ensure that no frequency components above a certain cut-off frequency can enter the sound processing equipment. The common music CD format can represent frequencies up to 22.050 kHz, which should be more than enough for audible sound. It leaves even some headroom between the maximum audible frequency and the absolute threshold of the maximum representable frequency. This headroom should be used by a filter to suppress any signal content above 22.05 kHz without disturbing any audible frequency components. If a high frequency signal above half of the sample frequency is allowed to enter the system, it can have disastrous effects. While not even audible as part of an analog signal, once sampled, it manifests itself as an alias within the representable frequency range, as demonstrated in Figure 55 and Figure 56 in Section 11.11.

Frequency Index	Sample Rate in Hz		
	Version 1	Version 2	Version 2.5
11	reserved	reserved	reserved
10	32000	16000	8000
01	48000	24000	12000
00	44100	22050	11025

Tab. 28: Version 1, 2, and 2.5 sample rates

If audio quality is the only concern, there is no reason to use any sample rate lower than those provided by MPEG Version 1. If, however, there is a limitation on the available bit rate, the encoder will remove high frequency content anyway to fit the sound data within the available bandwidth. In this case, reducing the sample rate may be justified. It even helps to further reduce the necessary bit rate, since fewer samples to encode means fewer data to transmit. With the Internet as the preferred medium for the dissemination of digital audio, the bandwidth became a limiting factor. To give the distributor more flexibility to trade transmission speed for audio quality, MPEG Version 2, as standardized in ISO/IEC 13818-3.2[3], introduced three new sample rates: 16 kHz, 22.050 kHz, and 24 kHz. These frequencies are just half of the version 1 frequencies.

Even lower sample frequencies, 8 kHz, 11.025 kHz, and 12 kHz, where later introduced by Sieler and Sperschneider from the Fraunhofer Gesellschaft and termed MPEG Version 2.5[29]. These sample rates can be used if the bandwidth is severely restricted and the audio material is suitable, like for instance voice transmission over telephone lines.

Bit	Version 2		Version 2.5
	Layer I	Layer II/III	Layer III
0000	free	free	free
0001	32	8	8
0010	48	16	16
0011	56	24	24
0100	64	32	32
0101	80	40	40
0110	96	48	48
0111	112	56	56
1000	128	64	64
1001	144	80	—
1010	160	96	—
1011	176	112	—
1100	192	128	—
1101	224	144	—
1110	256	160	—
1111	—	—	—

Tab. 29: Version 2 and 2.5 bit rate index

14.1 Frequencies, Bit Rates, and Bands

The new frequencies are part of the *frequency_table* defined in Appendix A.7. As a consequence of the new frequencies, new bit rate tables, shown in Table 29, are needed (see Appendix A.6). In comparison to the bit rate table for version 1 (Tab. 7 on page 46), the new table contains a better selection of small bit rates and none of the very large bit rates. As explained above, these large bit rates are not needed for signals that are of minor quality due to the reduced sample rate.

- Layer I needs no further changes to accommodate the new sample rates except the extended *bit_rate_tables*.

- Layer II uses a more sophisticated schema for the encoding of bit allocation and scalefactors. To accommodate all the necessary changes, it is sufficient to supplement the four tables used in version 1 with a fifth bit allocation table (see Section 9.1 and Appendix A.8).

  $\langle$ select layer II bit allocation table $_{192}\rangle +\equiv$ (372)
      if $(s{\rightarrow}info.version \neq$ MP3_V1_0$)$ $\langle$ select version 2 table $_{420}\rangle$

- Layer III requires more substantial changes.

14.2 Decoding Version 2 Layer III Side Information

The layout of version 2, layer III, side information is shown in Table 30. If we compare it to the corresponding tables for version 1 (Tab. 23 and Tab. 27), we find the following changes:

- The size of the side information for version 2 and version 2.5 is either exactly 9 (mono) or 17 (stereo) bytes. We use this in Appendix A.11.

- The *reservoir_size* has only 8 bits not 9.

  $\langle$ read *reservoir_size* $_{320}\rangle +\equiv$ (373)
      if $(s{\rightarrow}info.version \neq$ MP3_V1_0$)$ *reservoir_size* $= getbit(s, 8)$;

- Because of the different layout of the side information, the padding is different.

  $\langle$ remove version 2 padding $_{374}\rangle \equiv$ (374)
      if $(s{\rightarrow}info.mode \equiv$ MP3_MONO$)$ $getbit(s, 1)$;
      else $getbit(s, 2)$;   Used in 377.

- There is only one granule per frame. Consequently there are only half as many PCM samples stored per frame. This cuts the *frame_size* in half, if we assume the same *bit_rate*.

  $\langle$ determine *frame_size* $_{90}\rangle +\equiv$ (375)
      if $(info{\rightarrow}layer \equiv 3 \wedge info{\rightarrow}version \neq$ MP3_V1_0$)$
          $info{\rightarrow}frame\_size = 1*(info{\rightarrow}padding + 72*info{\rightarrow}bit\_rate/info{\rightarrow}sample\_rate)$;

  Or, in reverse, doubles the *bit_rate* for the same *frame_size*.

  $\langle$ determine free format *bit_rate* $_{91}\rangle +\equiv$ (376)
      if $(s{\rightarrow}info.layer \equiv 3 \wedge s{\rightarrow}info.version \neq$ MP3_V1_0$)$ $s{\rightarrow}info.bit\_rate =$
          $((s{\rightarrow}info.frame\_size - s{\rightarrow}info.padding)*s{\rightarrow}info.sample\_rate + 71)/72$;

Name	single channel	dual channel
reservoir_size	8	8
padding	1	2
information for granule:		
main_data_bit	12	12+12
big_values	9	9+9
global_gain	8	8+8
slength, *slimit*, and preflag	9	9+9
window_switching	1	1+1
for normal blocks:		
table selection	3*5	3*5+3*5
region 0 pairs	4	4+4
region 1 pairs	3	3+3
subtotal for normal blocks	22	44
for special blocks:		
block type	2	2+2
mixed block flag	1	1+1
table selection for two regions	2*5	2*5+2*5
subblock gain	3*3	3*3+3*3
subtotal for special blocks	22	44
fine/coarse scalefactors	1	1+1
select *htabA* or *htabB*	1	1+1
Total Bit	72	136
Total Byte	9	17

Tab. 30: Layout of layer III version 2 and version 2.5 side information

- Because there is only one granule, there is no sharing information for scalefactors, and after the padding follows immediately the granule specific information.

  ⟨ decode version 2 layer III side information $_{377}$ ⟩ ≡   (377)
    ⟨ remove version 2 padding $_{374}$ ⟩
    ⟨ decode version 2 granule information $_{378}$ ⟩   Used in 398.

- The bit allocation information for scalefactors, characterized by *slength* and *slimit*, is combined with the preemphasis flag and occupies now 9 bits instead of 4 + 1 bits.

To decode the side information for the one and only granule, we reuse most of the processing from version 1. Only for the decoding of *slength*, *slimit*, and the preemphasis flag, version 2 specific code is substituted.

⟨ decode version 2 granule information $_{378}$ ⟩ ≡   (378)
  { **const int** $gr = 0$;
   int ch;

   for $(ch = 0;\ ch < s{\to}info.channels;\ ch{+}{+})$
   { ⟨ size of main data $_{339}$ ⟩
    ⟨ number of big value pairs $_{341}$ ⟩
    ⟨ global gain $_{343}$ ⟩
    ⟨ version 2 scalefactor bit allocation $_{379}$ ⟩
    ⟨ window dependent layout $_{347}$ ⟩
    ⟨ version 2 scalefactor limits $_{385}$ ⟩
    ⟨ version 2 preemphasis flag $_{380}$ ⟩
    ⟨ select scalefactor quantization $_{359}$ ⟩
    ⟨ select small values table $_{360}$ ⟩
   }
  }   Used in 377.

14.3 Bit Allocation for Scalefactors

The allocation information for scalefactors changes in version 2 in two ways: Scale-factors are allocated in four blocks, not two, and the length of each scalefactor block is not fixed, but varies depending on stereo mode and sample frequency (compare this to Section 13.2 on page 173). In version 2, instead of the fixed separation in low and high frequencies, a complicated algorithm determines up to four groups of scalefactors, each of them with its own bit allocation.

Clearly, intensity stereo, where the scalefactors of the second channel are used to indicate the stereo position, is a "special" case. The requirements for an optimal bit allocation for the scalefactors is very different in this "special" case from the "normal" case. Hence, throughout this section, we have to consider two cases, the normal case first and then, with slightly modified code, the special case.

The bit allocation for scalefactors is contained in nine bits, stored in the bit stream. They are used as an index into the array $slength\_v2$ to obtain the correct $slength$ table. For the second channel in intensity stereo mode, only the first eight bits are used as an index, the ninth bit is used to specify the granularity of intensity stereo positions and stored in the variable i_scale (see Section 14.4).

⟨ version 2 scalefactor bit allocation $_{379}$ ⟩ ≡   (379)
  { **int** $sfc = getbit(s, 9)$;
   if $(s{\to}info.i\_stereo \wedge ch \equiv 1)$
   { $i\_scale = sfc\ \&\ 1$;
    $s{\to}slength[0][ch] = slength\_v2i[sfc \gg 1];$ }
   else $s{\to}slength[0][ch] = slength\_v2[sfc];$
  }   Used in 378.

Each $slength$ table contains four values to indicate the number of bits used to store scalefactors in each of the four blocks, then a zero because no bits are allocated to the remaining bands, next a -1 to indicate the end of the length information, and a seventh value to determine the *preflag*.

⟨ version 2 preemphasis flag 380 ⟩ $\equiv$ (380)
    if $(s{\rightarrow}slength\,[0][ch][6] \equiv 0)$ ⟨ switch *preemphasis* off 260 ⟩
    else ⟨ switch *preemphasis* on 259 ⟩   Used in 378.

Finaly, the eighth value is used to select the correct *slimit* table.

⟨ slimit index 381 ⟩ $\equiv$ (381)
    $(\textbf{int})(s{\rightarrow}slength\,[0][ch][7])$ Used in 385.

The following function prints for each index i the corresponding *slength* table.

⟨ print element 132 ⟩ $+\equiv$ (382)
    void *slength_v2* (**int** i)
    { **if** $(i < 400)$ *printf* ("{%d,␣%d,␣%d,␣%d,␣0,␣-1,0,␣0}", $(i \gg 4)/5, (i \gg 4)\,\%\,5,$
        $(i\,\%\,16) \gg 2, i\,\%\,4$);
    else if $(i < 500)$
    { $i = i - 400$;
      printf ("{%d,␣%d,␣%d,␣0,␣0,␣-1,␣0,␣1}", $(i \gg 2)/5, (i \gg 2)\,\%\,5, i\,\%\,4$);
    }
    else
    { $i = i - 500$;
      printf ("{%d,␣%d,␣0,␣0,␣0,␣-1,␣1,␣2}", $i/3, i\,\%\,3$);
    }
    }

For the "special" case, a similar function is used.

⟨ print element 132 ⟩ $+\equiv$ (383)
    void *slength_v2i* (**int** i)
    { **if** $(i < 180)$
      printf ("{%d,␣%d,␣%d,␣0,␣0,␣-1,␣0,␣0}", $i/36, (i\,\%\,36)/6, (i\,\%\,36)\,\%\,6$);
    else if $(i < 244)$
    { $i = i - 180$;
      printf ("{%d,␣%d,␣%d,␣0,␣0,␣-1,␣0,␣1}", $(i\,\%\,64) \gg 4, (i\,\%\,16) \gg 2, i\,\%\,4$);
    }
    else
    { $i = i - 244$;
      printf ("{%d,␣%d,␣0,␣0,␣0,␣-1,␣0,␣2}", $i/3, i\,\%\,3$);
    }
    }

With these functions the tables are generated.

⟨ print table 135 ⟩ $+\equiv$ (384)
    printf ("static␣const␣char␣slength_v2[512][8]␣=");
    print_array (NULL, 512, *slength_v2*);

$printf\,("\,;\n");$
$printf\,("\texttt{static}_\sqcup\texttt{const}_\sqcup\texttt{char}_\sqcup\texttt{slength\_v2i[256][8]}_\sqcup=");$
$print\_array\,(\texttt{NULL},256,slength\_v2i\,);$
$printf\,("\,;\n");$

With the $\langle$ slimit index $_{381}\,\rangle$, stored as part of the *slength* table, the subdivision of the scalefactors into four blocks can be tailored to the individual needs of the current frame. The selection of the *slimit* array depends not only on the $\langle$ slimit index $_{381}\,\rangle$, but also on whether the block is a SHORT_BLOCK or not, and whether the block is a *mixed_block*.

$\langle$ version 2 scalefactor limits $_{385}\,\rangle\equiv$ (385)
    if $(s{\rightarrow}info.i\_stereo \land ch \equiv 1)$ $s{\rightarrow}slimit\,[0][ch] = slimit\_v2i\,[\langle\,\text{slimit index}\ _{381}\,\rangle]$
        $[s{\rightarrow}block\_type\,[0][ch] \equiv \texttt{SHORT\_BLOCK}][s{\rightarrow}mixed\_block\,[0][ch]];$
    else $s{\rightarrow}slimit\,[0][ch] = slimit\_v2\,[\langle\,\text{slimit index}\ _{381}\,\rangle]$
        $[s{\rightarrow}block\_type\,[0][ch] \equiv \texttt{SHORT\_BLOCK}][s{\rightarrow}mixed\_block\,[0][ch]];$ Used in 378.

The *slimit* tables are as follows:

$\langle$ global variables $_{43}\,\rangle\ +\equiv$ (386)
  static const char $slimit\_v2\,[6][2][2][6] =$
    $\{\ \{\ \{\ \{\ 6,11,16,21,22,0\ \},\{\ 6,11,16,21,22,0\ \}\ \},$
        $\{\ \{\ 9,18,27,36,39,0\ \},\{\ 6,15,24,33,36,0\ \}\ \}\ \},$
    $\{\ \{\ \{\ 6,11,18,21,22,0\ \},\{\ 6,11,18,21,22,0\ \}\ \},$
        $\{\ \{\ 9,18,30,36,39,0\ \},\{\ 6,15,27,33,36,0\ \}\ \}\ \},$
    $\{\ \{\ \{\ 11,21,21,21,22,0\ \},\{\ 11,21,21,21,22,0\ \}\ \},$
        $\{\ \{\ 18,36,36,36,39,0\ \},\{\ 15,33,33,33,36,0\ \}\ \}\ \}\ \};$
  static const char $slimit\_v2i\,[6][2][2][6] =$
    $\{\ \{\ \{\ \{\ 7,14,21,21,22,0\ \},\{\ 7,14,21,21,22,0\ \}\ \},$
        $\{\ \{\ 12,24,36,36,39,0\ \},\{\ 6,21,33,33,36,0\ \}\ \}\ \},$
    $\{\ \{\ \{\ 6,12,18,21,22,0\ \},\{\ 6,12,18,21,22,0\ \}\ \},$
        $\{\ \{\ 12,21,30,36,39,0\ \},\{\ 6,18,27,33,36,0\ \}\ \}\ \},$
    $\{\ \{\ \{\ 8,16,21,21,22,0\ \},\{\ 8,16,21,21,22,0\ \}\ \},$
        $\{\ \{\ 15,27,36,36,39,0\ \},\{\ 6,24,33,33,36,0\ \}\ \}\ \}\ \};$

14.4 Intensity Stereo

In regard to the decoding of the granule, only the processing of intensity stereo is different in version 2. We indicate this using a special constant for the *stereo_mode*.

$\langle$ private declarations $_1\,\rangle\ +\equiv$ (387)
#**define** INTENSITY_V2   3

    In version 1, intensity stereo could be selectively switched off for a single band, by using the value 7 as intensity stereo position. In version 2, a more flexible mechanism is used. For each band, the reserved value that switches off intensity stereo mode is the maximum value for the scalefactor index, which is dependent of course on the number of bits used to store the scalefactor index. For this purpose, we have stored the possible maximum value sfi_{max} together with the scalefactor index sfi.

⟨ version 2 determine intensity stereo mode $_{388}$ ⟩ ≡   (388)
  { ⟨ adjust mode for short blocks $_{394}$ ⟩
    for (; $start[gr][0][band] < ulimit[0]$; $band{+}{+}$)
      if $(s{\rightarrow}sfi[1][band] < s{\rightarrow}sfi_{\max}[1][band])$ $stereo\_mode[band] =$ `INTENSITY_V2`;
      else $stereo\_mode[band] = low\_frequency\_mode$;
  }
                                                                              Used in 287.

The scalefactors f_L and f_R for the right and the left channel are computed by reducing the scalefactor $2^{m/4}$ of the first channel. The scalefactor of the second channel, stored in sp, determines the reduction. If the rightmost bit of sp is 1, the left channel is reduced, otherwise the right channel is reduced. The reduction is by the factor $2^{sp/2}$ or $2^{sp/4}$, depending on i_scale. The variable i_scale was taken from the $slength$ table.

⟨ global variables $_{43}$ ⟩ +≡   (389)
  static char i_scale;

Instead of dividing $2^{m/4}$, it is of course easier to subtract from the exponent m.

⟨ compute version 2 f_L and f_R $_{390}$ ⟩ ≡   (390)
  double f_L, f_R;
  if $(sp \equiv 0)$ $f_L = f_R = 2^{m/4}$;
  else if $(sp \mathbin{\&} 1)$
  { $f_R = 2^{m/4}$;
    if $(i\_scale \equiv 0)$ $sp = (sp + 1) \gg 1$;
    else $sp = sp + 1$;
    $f_L = 2^{m-sp/4}$;
  }
  else
  { $f_L = 2^{m/4}$;
    if $(i\_scale \equiv 0)$ $sp = sp \gg 1$;
    $f_R = 2^{m-sp/4}$;
  }
                                                                              Used in 391.

This code is used in the function $qs\_intensity\_v2\_band$, applying version 2 intensity stereo to one band.

⟨ auxiliary functions $_{69}$ ⟩ +≡   (391)
  static void $qs\_intensity\_v2\_band$(**int** i, **int** j, **int** $width$, **int** m, **int** sp, **int** $step$)
  { ⟨ compute version 2 f_L and f_R $_{390}$ ⟩
    while $(width\, \text{--} > 0)$
    { ⟨ assign intensity stereo values $_{272}$ ⟩
      $i = i + 1$;
      $j = j + step$;
    }
  }

It can be called two ways to process either a short or a long block.

⟨ process band in version 2 intensity stereo $_{392}$ ⟩ ≡   (392)
   $qs\_intensity\_v2\_band$ (
      $i, i, size, (ch = 0, ⟨$ long exponent $_{262}$ ⟩), s{→}sfi\,[1][band], 1)$;   Used in 288.

⟨ process short band in version 2 intensity stereo $_{393}$ ⟩ ≡   (393)
   $qs\_intensity\_v2\_band$ (
      $i, j, size, (ch = 0, ⟨$ short exponent $_{265}$ ⟩), s{→}sfi\,[1][band], 3)$;   Used in 289.

One last complication remains: In version 2 for all three parts of a short block, the last block before switching to intensity stereo is determined independently. Hence, going up to $ulimit[1]$, a common upper bound for the interleaved frequencies of all three short blocks, is possibly too much for two of the three short blocks. We have to go back for these two blocks and change the mode to intensity stereo as long as the bands are completely empty.

⟨ adjust mode for short blocks $_{394}$ ⟩ ≡   (394)
  { **int** k;

    $k = band - 2$;
    while $(k \geq first\_short\_band \wedge is\_zero\_band(k))$
    { **if** $(s{→}sfi\,[1][k] < s{→}sfi_{max}[1][k])$ $stereo\_mode[k] =$ `INTENSITY_V2`;
      else $stereo\_mode[k] = low\_frequency\_mode$;
      $k = k - 3$;
    }

    $k = band - 3$;
    while $(k \geq first\_short\_band \wedge is\_zero\_band(k))$
    { **if** $(s{→}sfi\,[1][k] < s{→}sfi_{max}[1][k])$ $stereo\_mode[k] =$ `INTENSITY_V2`;
      else $stereo\_mode[k] = low\_frequency\_mode$;
      $k = k - 3$;
    }

  }   Used in 388.

To check if a $band$ is all zero, we use this function:

⟨ auxiliary functions $_{69}$ ⟩ +≡   (395)
  static int is_zero_band (**int** $band$)
  { **int** i;

    for $(i = 0;\ i < width[0][1][band];\ i{+}{+})$
      if $(u[1][start[0][1][band] + i] \neq 0)$ **return** 0;
    return 1;
  }

14.5 Generating Output

For version 2 and version 2.5 layer III streams, we define a new *output_mode*.

⟨ private declarations $_1$ ⟩ +≡   (396)
#**define** LAYER_III_V2   4

⟨ derive further information $_{65}$ ⟩ +≡   (397)
  if (*output_mode* ≡ LAYER_III ∧ *s→info.version* ≠ MP3_V1_0)
    output_mode = LAYER_III_V2;

The processing of this *output_mode* just uses the code presented above.

⟨ generate output data $_{66}$ ⟩ +≡   (398)
case LAYER_III_V2:
  ⟨ decode version 2 layer III side information $_{377}$ ⟩
  ⟨ decode version 2 main data $_{399}$ ⟩
  s→frame = *next_frame*(*s*);
  break;

The decoding of the main data is the same as for version 1 (see page 177), only the
loop over two granules has been removed.

⟨ decode version 2 main data $_{399}$ ⟩ ≡   (399)
  { **const int** *gr* = 0;

    ⟨ switch to the bit reservoir $_{326}$ ⟩
    ⟨ decode the granule $_{363}$ ⟩
    ⟨ process ancillary bits $_{141}$ ⟩;
  }   Used in 398.

Appendix

A Tables and Special Code

A.1 Special Output Modes

We have several special output modes.

⟨ private declarations ₁ ⟩ +≡   (400)
#define MUTE   5
#define REPEAT   6
#define REPAIR   7
#define SKIP   8

SKIP will do just that, skip the current frame without any output. It is easy to implement.

⟨ generate output data ₆₆ ⟩ +≡   (401)
case SKIP: **default**:
  if $(s \rightarrow info.layer \equiv 3)$ ⟨ remove fixed part of frame from *buffer* ₃₂₅ ⟩
  $s \rightarrow frame = next\_frame(s);$
  break;

MUTE outputs a frame of silence.

⟨ generate output data ₆₆ ⟩ +≡   (402)
case MUTE:
  { **int** n;
    ⟨ determine number n of blocks per frame ₄₀₄ ⟩
    $output\_silence(s, buffer + s \rightarrow info.samples, n);$
    break; }

MUTE and SKIP can be combined to replace the current frame by a frame of silence.

⟨ generate output data ₆₆ ⟩ +≡   (403)
case MUTE | SKIP:
  { **int** n;

    if ($s{\rightarrow}info.layer \equiv 3$) ⟨ remove fixed part of frame from *buffer* ₃₂₅ ⟩
    ⟨ determine number n of blocks per frame ₄₀₄ ⟩
    output_silence(s, *buffer* + $s{\rightarrow}info.samples$, n);
    $s{\rightarrow}frame$ = *next_frame*(s);
    break;
  }

To imitate a silent frame, we use the function *output_silence* and provide as a parameter the number of blocks per frame depending on version and layer.

⟨ determine number n of blocks per frame ₄₀₄ ⟩ ≡   (404)
  if ($s{\rightarrow}info.layer \equiv 1$) $n = 12$;
  else if ($s{\rightarrow}info.layer \equiv 2$) $n = 12 * $ GROUPS;
  else if ($s{\rightarrow}info.version \equiv $ MP3_V1_0) $n = 18 * $ GRANULES;
  else $n = 18$;   Used in 402, 403, 405, and 409.

Repeating the last frame is similar.

⟨ generate output data ₆₆ ⟩ +≡   (405)
case REPEAT:
  { **int** n;

    ⟨ determine number n of blocks per frame ₄₀₄ ⟩
    output_repeat(s, *buffer* + $s{\rightarrow}info.samples$, n, n);
    break;
  }
case REPEAT | SKIP:
  { **int** n;

    if ($s{\rightarrow}info.layer \equiv 3$) ⟨ remove fixed part of frame from *buffer* ₃₂₅ ⟩
    ⟨ determine number n of blocks per frame ₄₀₄ ⟩
    output_repeat(s, *buffer* + $s{\rightarrow}info.samples$, n, n);
    $s{\rightarrow}frame$ = *next_frame*(s);
    break;
  }

We use the function *output_repeat*, which works similar to the function *output_blocks* (see Section 6.4), to generate n blocks of subband samples by repeating the last d blocks of subband samples.

⟨ auxiliary functions ₆₉ ⟩ +≡   (406)
  static void *output_repeat*(**stream** *$*s$, **mp3_sample** *$*buffer$, **int** n, **int** d)
  { **int** i;

    for ($i = 0$; $i < n$; i++) ⟨ repeat a single block of samples ₄₀₈ ⟩

```
    if (s→options.flags & MP3_TWO_CHANNEL_MONO)
      s→info.samples += n * 2 * SUBBANDS;
    else  s→info.samples += n * s→info.channels * SUBBANDS;
}
```

The effect of a frame is to compute a sequence of subband samples, treat them with a CosDFT and store the result in v, from where windowing does generate the PCM samples. If a frame is repeated, all the computations up to and including the storing of transformed samples in v is repeated. The windowing is usually different, since the content of v depends on previous frames. So repeating a frame is not the same as duplicating the PCM samples produced by the frame.

We can simulate the effect of the repeated frame by putting the transformed subband samples from the first frame again into v and apply windowing. From where do we get the transformed samples of the first frame? Here we reap the benefit of setting the constant SHIFTBLOCKS to $51 = 36 + 15$. While layer I frames produce only 12 blocks of subband samples, layer II and layer III frames produce 36 blocks of subband samples—and they are all still present in v.

The decoders memory of the past, determined by the constant SHIFTBLOCKS $-$ (WINDOWBLOCKS $- 1$), sets an upper bound on the possible exact reproduction of a past frame. As long as the parameter n of the *output_repeat* function is less or equal to SHIFTBLOCKS $-$ (WINDOWBLOCKS $- 1$) there is enough data available for exact reconstruction.

If we have to repeat n blocks, we find the data from the previous frame just $d = n$ blocks to the right—almost. We have to make sure that d blocks to the right is not past the end of the vector, in which case we subtract SHIFTSIZE $-$ (WINDOWBLOCKS $-$ 1) $*$ SUBBANDS to get the proper place at the beginning of the vector.

⟨ copy previous block ₄₀₇ ⟩ ≡   (407)
```
    { int previous_offset;
      previous_offset = s→offset[ch] + d * SUBBANDS;
      if (previous_offset ≥ SHIFTSIZE)
        previous_offset = previous_offset − SHIFTSIZE + (WINDOWBLOCKS − 1) * SUBBANDS;
      memmove(v, s→w[ch] + previous_offset, sizeof(double) * SUBBANDS);
    }
```
                                                                 Used in 408.

The code to ⟨ repeat a single block of samples ₄₀₈ ⟩ is similar to the code to ⟨ output a single block of samples ₇₀ ⟩. Only equalization and the call to *dct32* is replaced by the copying of previous data.

⟨ repeat a single block of samples ₄₀₈ ⟩ ≡   (408)
```
    { int ch;
      double *v;

      { ch = 0;
        ⟨ shift vector v  ₄ ⟩
        ⟨ copy previous block  ₄₀₇ ⟩
        windowing(v, buffer);
```

```
      }
      if (s→info.channels > 1)
      { ch = 1;
        ⟨shift vector v 4⟩
        ⟨copy previous block 407⟩
        windowing(v, buffer + 1);
        buffer = buffer + 2 * SUBBANDS;
      }
      else ⟨post-process single channel output 71⟩
  }
```
                                                                          Used in 406.

To supply a frame of silence or to repeat the last frame are two simple mechanisms to repair a data stream in case a damaged frame is encountered. While repeating the frame is already better than inserting silence, both methods are far from perfect. Especially the discontinuities in the transition from the end of the frame to its beginning causes a distortion which, if repeated for several frames, produces a distinct tonal noise. One idea to produce a better repair is to search the past of the signal for a block of samples that is as similar as possible to the last block of samples and hope that the continuation of both blocks is similar as well.

To judge the similarity of two sample vectors, we can either use the distance or, more sophisticated, the angle between the two vectors. Using the angle as a measure of similarity could be combined with scaling of the past samples to approximate as good as possible the future signal. Using the distance as a measure will allow a simple repetition of the past sample block. We decide (at least in this version of the decoder) for the simple method and hope that in the future someone will come up with an even better method of repair which can replace the following code.

⟨generate output data 66⟩ +≡   (409)
```
case REPAIR:
  { int n, d;
    ⟨determine number n of blocks per frame 404⟩
    ⟨determine optimal distance 410⟩
    output_repeat(s, buffer + s→info.samples, n, d);
    break;
  }
case REPAIR | SKIP:
  { int n, d;
    if (s→info.layer ≡ 3) ⟨remove fixed part of frame from buffer 325⟩
    ⟨determine number n of blocks per frame 404⟩
    ⟨determine optimal distance 410⟩
    output_repeat(s, buffer + s→info.samples, n, d);
    s→frame = next_frame(s);
    break;
  }
```

⟨determine optimal distance $_{410}$⟩ ≡   (410)
  { **int** i, k, *previous_offset*;
    double $*p$, *sum*, *distance*, $*v = s{\rightarrow}w[0] + s{\rightarrow}offset[0]$;

    distance = SUBBANDS $*$ ⟨output scalefactor $_{136}$⟩ $*$ ⟨output scalefactor $_{136}$⟩;
    for $(d = 1, i = 1;\ i <$ SHIFTBLOCKS $-$ WINDOWBLOCKS $+ 1;\ i{+}{+})$
    { *previous_offset* $= s{\rightarrow}offset[0] + i *$ SUBBANDS;
      if (*previous_offset* $\geq$ SHIFTSIZE) *previous_offset* $=$
           previous_offset $-$ SHIFTSIZE $+$ (WINDOWBLOCKS $- 1) *$ SUBBANDS;
      $p = s{\rightarrow}w[0] + previous\_offset$;
      for (*sum* $= 0.0, k = 0;\ k <$ SUBBANDS; $k{+}{+}$)
        sum $=$ *sum* $+ (p[k] - v[k]) * (p[k] - v[k])$;
      if (*sum* $<$ *distance*)
      { *distance* $=$ *sum*; $d = i$; }

    }

  }
                                             Used in 409.

A.2 32 Point CosDFT

The code for the Cosine Discrete Fourier Transform, short CosDFT, was generated
by spiral[30] with the commands

```
POST := SPLSymbol("I",[32,64]);
PRE1 := DirectSumSPL(SPLSymbol("I",32),SPLSymbol("J",32));
PRE2 := TensorSPL(SPLMat([[1],[1]]),SPLSymbol("I",32));
T := Transform("CosDFT",64);
C := POST * T * PRE1 * PRE2;
S := DP(C);
Implement(C);
```

⟨32 point CosDFT $_{411}$⟩ ≡   (411)
  { **double** $f0$, $f1$, $f2$, $f3$, $f4$, $f5$, $f6$, $f7$, $f8$, $f9$, $f10$, $f11$, $f12$, $f13$, $f14$, $f15$, $f16$,
      $f17$, $f18$, $f19$, $f20$, $f21$, $f22$, $f23$, $f24$, $f25$, $f26$, $f27$, $f28$, $f29$, $f30$, $f31$, $f32$,
      $f33$, $f34$, $f35$, $f36$, $f37$, $f38$, $f39$, $f40$, $f41$, $f42$, $f43$, $f44$, $f45$, $f46$, $f47$, $f48$,
      $f49$, $f50$, $f51$, $f52$, $f53$, $f54$, $f55$, $f56$, $f57$, $f58$, $f59$, $f60$, $f61$, $f62$, $f63$, $f64$,
      $f65$, $f66$, $f67$, $f68$, $f69$, $f70$, $f71$, $f72$, $f73$, $f74$, $f75$, $f76$, $f77$, $f78$, $f79$, $f80$,
      $f81$, $f82$, $f83$, $f84$, $f85$, $f86$, $f87$, $f88$, $f89$, $f90$, $f91$, $f92$, $f93$, $f95$, $f96$, $f97$,
      $f98$, $f99$, $f100$, $f101$, $f102$, $f103$, $f104$, $f105$, $f106$, $f107$, $f108$, $f109$, $f110$,
      $f111$, $f112$, $f113$, $f114$, $f115$, $f116$, $f117$, $f118$, $f119$, $f120$, $f121$, $f122$, $f123$,
      $f124$, $f125$, $f126$, $f127$, $f128$, $f129$, $f130$, $f131$, $f132$, $f133$, $f134$, $f135$, $f151$,
      $f152$, $f153$, $f154$, $f155$, $f156$, $f157$, $f158$, $f159$, $f160$, $f161$, $f162$, $f163$, $f164$,
      $f165$, $f166$, $f167$, $f168$, $f169$, $f170$, $f171$, $f172$, $f173$, $f174$, $f175$, $f176$, $f177$,
      $f178$, $f179$, $f180$, $f181$, $f182$, $f183$, $f184$, $f185$, $f186$, $f187$, $f188$, $f189$, $f190$,
      $f191$, $f192$, $f193$, $f194$, $f195$, $f196$, $f197$, $f198$, $f199$, $f200$, $f201$, $f202$, $f203$,
      $f204$, $f205$, $f206$, $f207$, $f208$, $f209$, $f210$, $f211$, $f212$, $f213$, $f214$, $f215$, $f216$,
      $f217$, $f218$, $f219$, $f220$, $f221$, $f222$, $f223$, $f224$, $f225$, $f226$, $f227$, $f228$, $f229$,
      $f230$, $f231$, $f232$, $f233$, $f234$, $f235$, $f236$, $f237$, $f238$, $f239$, $f240$, $f241$, $f242$,
      $f243$, $f244$, $f245$, $f246$, $f247$;

$$f0 = (y[31]) + (y[30]);$$
$$f1 = (y[30]) + (y[29]);$$
$$f2 = (y[29]) + (y[28]);$$
$$f3 = (y[28]) + (y[27]);$$
$$f4 = (y[27]) + (y[26]);$$
$$f5 = (y[26]) + (y[25]);$$
$$f6 = (y[25]) + (y[24]);$$
$$f7 = (y[24]) + (y[23]);$$
$$f8 = (y[23]) + (y[22]);$$
$$f9 = (y[22]) + (y[21]);$$
$$f10 = (y[21]) + (y[20]);$$
$$f11 = (y[20]) + (y[19]);$$
$$f12 = (y[19]) + (y[18]);$$
$$f13 = (y[18]) + (y[17]);$$
$$f14 = (y[17]) + (y[16]);$$
$$f15 = (y[16]) + (y[15]);$$
$$f16 = (y[15]) + (y[14]);$$
$$f17 = (y[14]) + (y[13]);$$
$$f18 = (y[13]) + (y[12]);$$
$$f19 = (y[12]) + (y[11]);$$
$$f20 = (y[11]) + (y[10]);$$
$$f21 = (y[10]) + (y[9]);$$
$$f22 = (y[9]) + (y[8]);$$
$$f23 = (y[8]) + (y[7]);$$
$$f24 = (y[7]) + (y[6]);$$
$$f25 = (y[6]) + (y[5]);$$
$$f26 = (y[5]) + (y[4]);$$
$$f27 = (y[4]) + (y[3]);$$
$$f28 = (y[3]) + (y[2]);$$
$$f29 = (y[2]) + (y[1]);$$
$$f30 = (y[1]) + (y[0]);$$
$$f46 = (y[0]) - (y[31]);$$
$$f47 = (y[0]) + (y[31]);$$
$$f31 = f23 - f7;$$
$$f32 = f24 - f6;$$
$$f33 = f22 - f8;$$
$$f34 = f25 - f5;$$
$$f35 = f21 - f9;$$
$$f36 = f26 - f4;$$
$$f37 = f20 - f10;$$
$$f38 = f27 - f3;$$
$$f39 = f19 - f11;$$
$$f40 = f28 - f2;$$
$$f41 = f18 - f12;$$
$$f42 = f29 - f1;$$
$$f43 = f17 - f13;$$
$$f44 = f30 - f0;$$
$$f45 = f16 - f14;$$

$f48 = f30 + f0;$
$f49 = f28 + f2;$
$f50 = f26 + f4;$
$f51 = f24 + f6;$
$f52 = f22 + f8;$
$f53 = f20 + f10;$
$f54 = f18 + f12;$
$f55 = f16 + f14;$
$f56 = f29 + f1;$
$f57 = f25 + f5;$
$f58 = f21 + f9;$
$f59 = f17 + f13;$
$f60 = f27 + f3;$
$f61 = f19 + f11;$
$f62 = f47 - f15;$
$f63 = f47 + f15;$
$f64 = f23 + f7;$
$f65 = f63 + f64;$
$f66 = f63 - f64;$
$f67 = f60 - f61;$
$f68 = f60 + f61;$
$f69 = 0.7071067811865476 * f67;$
$f70 = f65 + f68;$
$f75 = f56 + f59;$
$f76 = f57 - f58;$
$f77 = f57 + f58;$
$f79 = f75 + f77;$
$v[16] = f70 - f79;$
$f78 = f75 - f77;$
$f71 = f62 - f69;$
$f72 = f62 + f69;$
$f73 = f65 - f68;$
$f74 = f56 - f59;$
$f80 = 0.7071067811865476 * f78;$
$f81 = f74 + f76;$
$f82 = 1.3065629648763766 * f74;$
$f83 = (-0.9238795325112866) * f81;$
$f84 = (-0.5411961001461967) * f76;$
$f85 = f82 + f83;$
$f86 = f84 - f83;$
$f87 = f70 + f79;$
$f88 = f71 - f85;$
$f90 = f66 - f80;$
$f91 = f66 + f80;$
$f89 = f72 + f86;$
$f92 = f72 - f86;$
$f93 = f71 + f85;$
$f95 = f48 - f55;$

$f96 = f48 + f55;$
$f97 = f49 - f54;$
$f98 = f49 + f54;$
$f99 = f50 - f53;$
$f100 = f50 + f53;$
$f101 = f51 - f52;$
$f102 = f51 + f52;$
$f103 = f96 - f102;$
$f104 = f96 + f102;$
$f105 = f98 - f100;$
$f106 = f98 + f100;$
$f107 = f104 - f106;$
$f108 = f104 + f106;$
$\mathbf{v}[0] = f87 + f108;$
$f109 = 0.7071067811865476 * f107;$
$\mathbf{v}[24] = f73 - f109;$
$\mathbf{v}[8] = f73 + f109;$
$f110 = f103 + f105;$
$f111 = 1.3065629648763766 * f103;$
$f112 = (-0.9238795325112866) * f110;$
$f113 = (-0.5411961001461967) * f105;$
$f114 = f111 + f112;$
$\mathbf{v}[20] = f90 - f114;$
$\mathbf{v}[12] = f90 + f114;$
$f115 = f113 - f112;$
$\mathbf{v}[4] = f91 + f115;$
$\mathbf{v}[28] = f91 - f115;$
$f116 = f97 - f99;$
$f117 = f97 + f99;$
$f118 = 0.7071067811865476 * f117;$
$f119 = 0.7071067811865476 * f116;$
$f120 = f95 - f118;$
$f121 = f95 + f118;$
$f122 = f101 - f119;$
$f123 = f101 + f119;$
$f124 = f123 + f121;$
$f126 = 0.9807852804032304 * f124;$
$f125 = (-0.7856949583871021) * f123;$
$f127 = 1.1758756024193588 * f121;$
$f128 = f125 + f126;$
$\mathbf{v}[2] = f89 + f128;$
$\mathbf{v}[30] = f89 - f128;$
$f129 = f127 - f126;$
$\mathbf{v}[18] = f92 - f129;$
$\mathbf{v}[14] = f92 + f129;$
$f130 = f122 + f120;$
$f132 = 0.5555702330196022 * f130;$
$f131 = 0.2758993792829431 * f122;$

$f133 = 1.3870398453221475 * f120;$
$f134 = f131 + f132;$
$\boldsymbol{v}[22] = f88 - f134;$
$\boldsymbol{v}[10] = f88 + f134;$
$f135 = f133 - f132;$
$\boldsymbol{v}[6] = f93 + f135;$
$\boldsymbol{v}[26] = f93 - f135;$
$f151 = 0.7071067811865476 * f31;$
$f152 = f46 - f151;$
$f153 = f46 + f151;$
$f154 = f38 + f39;$
$f155 = 1.3065629648763766 * f38;$
$f156 = (-0.9238795325112866) * f154;$
$f157 = (-0.5411961001461967) * f39;$
$f158 = f155 + f156;$
$f159 = f157 - f156;$
$f160 = f153 - f159;$
$f161 = f153 + f159;$
$f162 = f152 - f158;$
$f163 = f152 + f158;$
$f164 = f34 - f35;$
$f165 = f34 + f35;$
$f166 = 0.7071067811865476 * f165;$
$f167 = 0.7071067811865476 * f164;$
$f168 = f42 - f166;$
$f169 = f42 + f166;$
$f170 = f43 - f167;$
$f171 = f43 + f167;$
$f172 = f171 + f169;$
$f173 = (-0.7856949583871021) * f171;$
$f174 = 0.9807852804032304 * f172;$
$f175 = 1.1758756024193588 * f169;$
$f176 = f173 + f174;$
$f177 = f175 - f174;$
$f178 = f170 + f168;$
$f179 = 0.2758993792829431 * f170;$
$f180 = 0.5555702330196022 * f178;$
$f181 = 1.3870398453221475 * f168;$
$f182 = f179 + f180;$
$f183 = f181 - f180;$
$f184 = f161 - f176;$
$f185 = f161 + f176;$
$f186 = f163 - f183;$
$f187 = f163 + f183;$
$f188 = f162 - f182;$
$f189 = f162 + f182;$
$f190 = f160 - f177;$
$f191 = f160 + f177;$

$f192 = f44 - f40;$
$f193 = f36 - f40;$
$f194 = f36 - f32;$
$f195 = f33 - f32;$
$f196 = f33 - f37;$
$f197 = f41 - f37;$
$f198 = f41 - f45;$
$f199 = f196 - f194;$
$f200 = f196 + f194;$
$f201 = 0.7071067811865476 * f200;$
$f202 = f198 - f201;$
$f203 = f198 + f201;$
$f204 = 0.7071067811865476 * f199;$
$f205 = f204 - f192;$
$f206 = f204 + f192;$
$f207 = f206 + f203;$
$f208 = (-0.7856949583871021) * f206;$
$f209 = 0.9807852804032304 * f207;$
$f210 = 1.1758756024193588 * f203;$
$f211 = f208 + f209;$
$f212 = f210 - f209;$
$f213 = f205 + f202;$
$f214 = (-0.2758993792829429) * f205;$
$f215 = 0.8314696123025452 * f213;$
$f216 = 1.3870398453221475 * f202;$
$f217 = f214 + f215;$
$f218 = f216 - f215;$
$f219 = f193 + f197;$
$f222 = 0.5411961001461961 * f197;$
$f221 = (-0.3826834323650904) * f219;$
$f220 = 1.3065629648763770 * f193;$
$f223 = f220 + f221;$
$f224 = f222 - f221;$
$f225 = 0.7071067811865476 * f195;$
$f226 = f225 + f45;$
$f227 = f225 - f45;$
$f228 = f224 - f227;$
$f229 = f224 + f227;$
$f232 = f211 + f229;$
$f233 = f211 - f229;$
$f244 = 0.5024192861881557 * f232;$
$v[17] = f184 - f244;$
$v[15] = f184 + f244;$
$f240 = 5.1011486186891641 * f233;$
$v[31] = f185 - f240;$
$v[1] = f185 + f240;$
$f230 = f223 - f226;$
$f231 = f223 + f226;$

$f234 = f231 - f217;$
$f235 = f217 + f231;$
$f241 = 1.7224470982383342 * f235;$
$v[29] = f187 + f241;$
$v[3] = f187 - f241;$
$f236 = f218 + f230;$
$f237 = f218 - f230;$
$f242 = 1.0606776859903475 * f237;$
$v[27] = f189 - f242;$
$v[5] = f189 + f242;$
$f238 = f228 - f212;$
$f239 = f212 + f228;$
$f243 = 0.7881546234512502 * f239;$
$v[25] = f191 + f243;$
$v[7] = f191 - f243;$
$f247 = 0.6468217833599901 * f238;$
$v[23] = f190 - f247;$
$v[9] = f190 + f247;$
$f245 = 0.5224986149396889 * f234;$
$v[19] = f186 - f245;$
$v[13] = f186 + f245;$
$f246 = 0.5669940348163577 * f236;$
$v[21] = f188 - f246;$
$v[11] = f188 + f246;$
}

Used in 6.

A.3 Windowing

The following code was produced using Mathematica[28]. First, it was used to produce a matrix that incorporated the necessary permutations of the input variables, the multiplications with the windowing coefficients, and the summing up to form the output values. Then, the same tool was used to generate from this matrix the following C code. The output values are written in every second element of x, because we will produce stereo output where both channels are interleaved, that is values for the left and right channel alternate. Rounding from **double** to **mp3_sample** is packaged into the function mk_sample.

$\langle$ apply windowing $_{412}$ $\rangle \equiv$ (412)

{ $x[2 * 0] = mk\_sample(0.0003128982862089532 * v[48] + 0.00229818330588584 *$
        $v[80] + 0.004952423160365843 * v[112] + 0.021978401160177793 * v[144] +$
        $0.055987738287977 * v[176] + 0.07093078561039573 * v[208] + 0.4044910600631663 *$
        $v[240] + 0.8096294961834989 * v[272] - 0.4044910600631663 * v[304] +$
        $0.07093078561039573 * v[336] - 0.055987738287977 * v[368] + 0.021978401160177793 *$
        $v[400] - 0.004952423160365843 * v[432] + 0.00229818330588584 * v[464] -$
        $0.0003128982862089532 * v[496]);$

    $x[2 * 1] = mk\_sample(-0.00011360878959224075 * v[17] + 0.00031919919129172973 *$
        $v[47] + 0.002476637364442382 * v[81] + 0.005344017796184724 * v[111] +$
        $0.02272144372414786 * v[145] + 0.0568072144837296 * v[175] + 0.06769854183592361 *$

$v[209] + 0.405032784854463 * v[239] + 0.8519632570908607 * v[273] -$
$0.36697645997870415*v[303]+0.08104738996801669*v[337]-0.049300877952645254*$
$v[367] + 0.0234371694196013 8 * v[401] - 0.004128999734678011 * v[431] +$
$0.0023630300639226835 * v[465] - 0.00026771603849710295 * v[495]);$

$x[2 * 2] = mk\_sample(-0.000012026451399242627 * v[18] + 0.0003454403479776696 *$
$v[46] + 0.002669835167364561 * v[82] + 0.005734305378041188 * v[110] +$
$0.023475308411616744 * v[146] + 0.058024067210062064 * v[174] +$
$0.06359499620678986*v[210]+0.4063954732221264*v[238]+0.9002396009802017*$
$v[274] - 0.3335076121914026 * v[302] + 0.09188081818496067 * v[338] -$
$0.04367349866115977 * v[366] + 0.025014672910544967 * v[402] -$
$0.003424791978534475 * v[430] + 0.0024293092919982022 * v[466] -$
$0.0002368 7325210604534 * v[494]);$

$x[2 * 3] = mk\_sample(-0.0000128076362393955 24 * v[19] + 0.00036094905567626167 *$
$v[45] + 0.0028816787044306583 * v[83] + 0.006126635156083047 * v[109] +$
$0.024244520500667208*v[147]+0.05924313659295743*v[173]+0.05841482143352409*$
$v[211] + 0.4084993331613 2825 * v[237] + 0.9558206795039699 * v[275] -$
$0.30345366228164333*v[301]+0.10363795967934386*v[339]-0.03859305196361568*$
$v[365] + 0.026729167517774474 * v[403] - 0.0027926057862843277 * v[429] +$
$0.0025102622895860605 * v[467] - 0.00019947210866493324 * v[493]);$

$x[2 * 4] = mk\_sample(-0.000013732737188838566 * v[20] + 0.0003762073747154337 *$
$v[44] + 0.0031172881430076437 * v[84] + 0.006523990077013419 * v[108] +$
$0.02502070156719418*v[148]+0.06045931174897625*v[172]+0.05185409834400458*$
$v[212] + 0.4112682982520986 5 * v[236] + 1.0205067915868626 * v[276] -$
$0.27630153237206495*v[300]+0.11661679235020145*v[340]-0.033996319386491995*$
$v[364] + 0.028632361049190227 * v[404] - 0.0022388942 09067779 * v[428] +$
$0.00260918406683 0402 * v[468] - 0.0001743401055855475 * v[492]);$

$x[2 * 5] = mk\_sample(-0.000014804 1874153566 * v[21] + 0.000400269964178869 *$
$v[43] + 0.003383568789794713 * v[85] + 0.006929113044274127 *$
$v[107] + 0.02580713125 8987214 * v[149] + 0.0616860046209525 6 *$
$v[171] + 0.043556026986667926 * v[213] + 0.4146527011613699 * v[235] +$
$1.0968105060105893 * v[277] - 0.2516273090155306 * v[299] + 0.13118748783541162 *$
$v[341] - 0.02980674854717961 5 * v[363] + 0.03079344290379831 * v[405] -$
$0.0017522914386632425 * v[427] + 0.002715758699539749 * v[469] -$
$0.00015121274781770293 * v[491]);$

$x[2 * 6] = mk\_sample(-0.00001618488081052 6708 * v[22] + 0.00042389328289552916 *$
$v[42] + 0.003690101912 2711613 * v[86] + 0.007335945692136624 * v[106] +$
$0.026607575997348865*v[150]+0.06290054423507843*v[170]+0.03296814611963793*$
$v[214] + 0.418616056131 4836 * v[234] + 1.1881965990501728 * v[278] -$
$0.22909258929059503*v[298]+0.14791158074082497*v[342]-0.025987241635379382*$
$v[362] + 0.033291839493137715 * v[406] - 0.0013235847089620946 * v[426] +$
$0.0028484997775783186 * v[470] - 0.0001384142836041004 * v[490]);$

$x[2 * 7] = mk\_sample(-0.0000356889678885047 8 * v[23] + 0.00044730397038539186 *$
$v[41] + 0.004050641722228487 * v[87] + 0.007756080247117002 * v[105] +$
$0.0273909039558 8898*v[151]+0.06411636834739066*v[169]+0.019307464995376257*$
$v[215] + 0.4231410221445687 * v[233] + 1.2996850208044854 * v[279] -$
$0.20840984504257087*v[297]+0.1675395442615175*v[343]-0.022474909442567505*$
$v[361] + 0.0362594896849 8941 * v[407] - 0.0009368064494148356 * v[425] +$
$0.0030156756867410497 * v[471] - 0.00011815571358256615 * v[489]);$

$x[2*8] = mk\_sample(-0.00003987368562097255 * v[24] + 0.0004789639659038583 *$
$v[40] + 0.004465791710495543 * v[88] + 0.008183675180516712 * v[104] +$
$0.028190308457639226 * v[152] + 0.06532075706446365 * v[168] +$
$0.0013955595012289305 * v[216] + 0.428201925227916 * v[232] + 1.438802225110984 *$
$v[280] - 0.18934761605173117 * v[296] + 0.19123156716694048 * v[344] -$
$0.019241133583379637 * v[360] + 0.03989307403680713 * v[408] -$
$0.0005945758950919168 * v[424] + 0.0032097875061080226 * v[472] -$
$0.00010735382320940022 * v[488]);$

$x[2*9] = mk\_sample(-0.0000452937357607573 * v[25] + 0.000510493366984739 * v[39] +$
$0.00500488045817701 * v[89] + 0.0086216633933471 * v[103] + 0.028987590162386057 *$
$v[153] + 0.0665180758030911 * v[167] - 0.022601260985843145 * v[217] +$
$0.43378958256256167 * v[231] + 1.6174169450737852 * v[281] - 0.17169588389745313 *$
$v[295] + 0.220803908066784 * v[345] - 0.016254752237246636 * v[359] +$
$0.04443254033707173 * v[409] - 0.00029171019196707585 * v[423] +$
$0.003487570160304309 * v[473] - 0.000089133905786647 * v[487]);$

$x[2*10] = mk\_sample(-0.00005256564054403748 5 * v[26] + 0.0005421435178641913 *$
$v[38] + 0.00565072884836460 8 * v[90] + 0.009064955437752093 * v[102] +$
$0.029725458062796715 * v[154] + 0.06769616305329242 * v[166] -$
$0.055771372960923764 * v[218] + 0.43991742826671476 * v[230] +$
$1.8552786357645104 * v[282] - 0.15529217543776508 * v[294] + 0.2592238736529565 *$
$v[346] - 0.013489801838191559 * v[358] + 0.05043603451092918 * v[410] -$
$0.00001594561273072942 6 * v[422] + 0.00386352118412671 * v[474] -$
$0.0000797270186564172 4 * v[486]);$

$x[2*11] = mk\_sample(-0.0000941969835116273 3 * v[27] + 0.0005741526349443321 *$
$v[37] + 0.00653104298725841 4 * v[91] + 0.009516773268488255 * v[101] +$
$0.03045726817284568 5 * v[155] + 0.06885896591478574 * v[165] - 0.1036175132063181 *$
$v[219] + 0.446564748376332 5 * v[229] + 2.1878680874779404 * v[283] -$
$0.1399909467378425 * v[293] + 0.31195151197178694 * v[347] - 0.01091676115086594 *$
$v[357] + 0.0587165916400259 9 * v[411] + 0.00022808801187731097 * v[421] +$
$0.004364495904242906 * v[475] - 0.0000707858636243641 * v[485]);$

$x[2*12] = mk\_sample(-0.0001173200175358151 5 * v[28] + 0.000614530022057634 *$
$v[36] + 0.00782139772096872 1 * v[92] + 0.009980281306807181 * v[100] +$
$0.0310509482858878 1 * v[156] + 0.06999421114046105 * v[164] - 0.1772719689146902 *$
$v[220] + 0.453764427232256 6 * v[228] + 2.686337095474546 * v[284] -$
$0.12566753494641256 * v[292] + 0.38974022501082417 * v[348] - 0.008517855199218877 *$
$v[356] + 0.0710573946300317 4 * v[412] + 0.0004433952147214215 4 * v[420] +$
$0.005162121778223031 * v[476] - 0.00006223074634124471 * v[484]);$

$x[2*13] = mk\_sample(-0.0002079833798212382 5 * v[29] + 0.0006555943185742344 *$
$v[35] + 0.00982723940171454 2 * v[93] + 0.010458658182621363 * v[99] +$
$0.0314575654248580 2 * v[157] + 0.07110499217425234 * v[163] - 0.3025126011809063 *$
$v[221] + 0.46152299958705484 * v[227] + 3.516436002235974 * v[285] -$
$0.11220690178333473 * v[291] + 0.5178279446177007 * v[349] - 0.006278279899935265 *$
$v[355] + 0.0914609255494682 9 * v[413] + 0.0006401683558200812 * v[419] +$
$0.006499498509357893 * v[477] - 0.00005399036416857643 5 * v[483]);$

$x[2*14] = mk\_sample(-0.0003113486059416926 * v[30] + 0.000697634299836563 5 *$
$v[34] + 0.01377721279624738 3 * v[94] + 0.010947490659780413 * v[98] +$
$0.0312906139649436 96 * v[158] + 0.07218597419618838 * v[162] - 0.5568484074977561 *$
$v[222] + 0.469860468079733 4 * v[226] + 5.175716801105264 * v[286] -$

$0.09950870260152139 * v[290] + 0.771835168273 9714 * v[350] - 0.00417813888071215 * v[354] + 0.1321678224486 3165 * v[414] + 0.000812629030897881 * v[418] + 0.009106968403676138 * v[478] - 0.00005366440879632929 * v[482]);$

$x[2 * 15] = mk\_sample(-0.0007774364797779736 * v[31] + 0.0007409439994969087 * v[33] + 0.02534414974750568 * v[95] + 0.011442616132258705 * v[97] + 0.02876512937176878 * v[159] + 0.0732159383041 6676 * v[161] - 1.3278605597900235 * v[223] + 0.47881772391819916 * v[225] + 10.151758277274979 * v[287] - 0.08750011221721796 * v[289] + 1.5296829232042684 * v[351] - 0.0021999153944375154 * v[353] + 0.2540660561332939 * v[415] + 0.0009701015297780469 * v[417] + 0.017259081699064517 * v[479] - 0.00004583170629742692 6 * v[481]);$

$x[2 * 16] = mk\_sample(0.000793457 * v[32] + 0.011955261 * v[96] + 0.0742111205 * v[160] + 0.4884262085 * v[224] - 0.0761032105 * v[288] - 0.000343323 * v[352] + 0.0011138915 * v[416] - 0.000038147 * v[480]);$

$x[2 * 17] = mk\_sample(0.000932925813735193 * v[31] + 0.00084788431378890 6 * v[33] - 0.0197468702823475 3 * v[95] + 0.012481464971181395 * v[97] + 0.04478030658918366 * v[159] + 0.07514850316317577 * v[161] + 1.781105701420322 * v[223] + 0.49872390378363474 * v[225] - 9.746558677486934 * v[287] - 0.06523360623560533 * v[289] - 1.4903446617835223 * v[351] + 0.0014131401892461 78 * v[353] - 0.23291980222534767 * v[415] + 0.0012450912669596103 * v[417] - 0.015082261593687814 * v[479] - 0.00003819300514735606 4 * v[481]);$

$x[2 * 18] = mk\_sample(0.0005448638862594261 * v[30] + 0.0008969580984074182 * v[34] - 0.008250761012623637 * v[94] + 0.01301739431162627 * v[98] + 0.04242135595896376 * v[158] + 0.07601912888371658 * v[162] + 1.0103288125631422 * v[222] + 0.5097636111201113 * v[226] - 4.77057339081518 * v[286] - 0.05484478111165616 * v[290] - 0.732916495609436 * v[350] + 0.003081856481314591 * v[354] - 0.1111517379855069 * v[414] + 0.001356937022652688 * v[418] - 0.007083199914480826 * v[478] - 0.00003066516113249408 5 * v[482]);$

$x[2 * 19] = mk\_sample(0.00036397347039348086 * v[29] + 0.00096410952988962 * v[35] - 0.00431566450221384 5 * v[93] + 0.01356694671255165 * v[99] + 0.04232472513328717 * v[157] + 0.0768125195398193 * v[163] + 0.7564374879314253 * v[221] + 0.5216140070070716 * v[227] - 3.111335335720492 * v[285] - 0.04487350543896398 * v[291] - 0.4793509205301274 * v[349] + 0.0046662890328484875 * v[355] - 0.07050654636264594 * v[413] + 0.001457733261429084 9 * v[419] - 0.004419657895928673 * v[477] - 0.0000308514200373465 8 * v[483]);$

$x[2 * 20] = mk\_sample(0.00031285508870580557 * v[28] + 0.0010268098636084333 * v[36] - 0.002229098273588622 * v[92] + 0.014134194585690216 * v[100] + 0.0428221498312425 3 * v[156] + 0.07752415081998365 * v[164] + 0.6317733613142048 * v[220] + 0.5343456712406365 * v[228] - 2.2812278251465887 * v[284] - 0.0352615870068741 8 * v[292] - 0.3518846618866347 * v[348] + 0.006176417632929279 * v[356] - 0.0501742623562371 * v[412] + 0.0015557727368957506 * v[420] - 0.003089451048987311 * v[476] - 0.0000233364024290719 88 * v[484]);$

$x[2 * 21] = mk\_sample(0.0002825930083158919 6 * v[27] + 0.001093249311821209 * v[37] - 0.0009105783858094341 * v[91] + 0.014707740552704334 * v[101] + 0.0435821535082242 7 * v[155] + 0.07813978596089458 * v[165] + 0.5588751870793057 * v[219] + 0.5480324265319146 * v[229] - 1.782786409461297 * v[283] - 0.02595483590563307 8 * v[293] - 0.2749004014508211 * v[347] + 0.00762914852034751 5 * v[357] - 0.03799308858720617 * v[411] + 0.0016359411047571037 * v[421] - 0.0022921458047390248 * v[475] - 0.0000235951160590180 58 * v[485]);$

$x[2 * 22] = mk\_sample\,(0.0002628247578259909 * v[26] + 0.0011719863382515497 *$
$v[38] + 0.00005256564054403\,7485 * v[90] + 0.015299603803195833 * v[102] +$
$0.044469916986641635 * v[154] + 0.07863470238447309 * v[166] + 0.5119296957232544 *$
$v[218] + 0.5627926213267186 * v[230] - 1.4502134094076737 * v[282] -$
$0.016918061027924428 * v[294] - 0.2231643420269582 * v[346] + 0.009017119122058518 *$
$v[358] - 0.029883153261981734 * v[410] + 0.0017141298561157408 * v[422] -$
$0.0017872076642378991 * v[474] - 0.000015945612730729426 * v[486]);$

$x[2 * 23] = mk\_sample\,(0.00024911257835448383 * v[25] + 0.0012478725568426936 *$
$v[39] + 0.0008152753703752325 * v[89] + 0.015898217145142637 *$
$v[103] + 0.04542898916632\,5054 * v[153] + 0.07900490189542053 * v[167] +$
$0.479857849300644 * v[217] + 0.5787210366984598 * v[231] - 1.2123606659191597 *$
$v[281] - 0.008086860489657418 * v[295] - 0.18590556785657805 * v[345] +$
$0.010371925607222346 * v[359] - 0.024095934971805434 * v[409] +$
$0.0017907775773322414 * v[423] - 0.001426733382321273 * v[473] -$
$0.000016206357794878032 * v[487]);$

$x[2 * 24] = mk\_sample\,(0.0002591750559647375 * v[24] + 0.00132953751736565\,7 *$
$v[40] + 0.0014354331897910278 * v[88] + 0.01652425231079951 * v[104] +$
$0.046452205652427546 * v[152] + 0.07921070867440823 * v[168] +$
$0.45712558267510284 * v[216] + 0.5959713952135566 * v[232] - 1.0337708953195046 *$
$v[280] + 0.0005780596725076552 * v[296] - 0.15769825760950626 *$
$v[344] + 0.011676808090635137 * v[360] - 0.01975713961085953 * v[408] +$
$0.0018497914932205967 * v[424] - 0.0011563212895452418 * v[472] -$
$0.000016516222584261643 * v[488]);$

$x[2 * 25] = mk\_sample\,(0.00024981926689973314 * v[23] + 0.0014263083753403834 *$
$v[41] + 0.0019807108206935462 * v[87] + 0.017149461412794647 *$
$v[105] + 0.04751920351830151\,6 * v[151] + 0.0792403030045825\,1 * v[169] +$
$0.440645594906755\,2 * v[215] + 0.6147052345940991 * v[233] - 0.8946565235162459 *$
$v[279] + 0.00913175085456763\,8 * v[297] - 0.13556267108171202 * v[343] +$
$0.012954932750957705 * v[361] - 0.016398853873420858 * v[407] +$
$0.001915810854369827 * v[425] - 0.0009457447852061088 * v[471] -$
$0.000016879624699179178 * v[489]);$

$x[2 * 26] = mk\_sample\,(0.00025895491093536933 * v[22] + 0.0015225548518689649 *$
$v[42] + 0.0024762528223246346 * v[86] + 0.01779485894536847 * v[106] +$
$0.048618709485169304 * v[150] + 0.07906038704205563 * v[170] +$
$0.4286020886788143 * v[214] + 0.6351043138911755 * v[234] - 0.7831755560842464 *$
$v[278] + 0.017621841232599356 * v[298] - 0.11767864129376937 * v[342] +$
$0.014222045671239966 * v[362] - 0.013724589066020854 * v[406] +$
$0.001972400564902248 * v[426] - 0.0007930485529389487 * v[470] -$
$8.650999027262802 \cdot 10^{-6} * v[490]);$

$x[2 * 27] = mk\_sample\,(0.0002522832283331547\,5 * v[21] + 0.0016277631219501435 *$
$v[43] + 0.002923521644216535 * v[85] + 0.018456879385188026 * v[107] +$
$0.04972955559714183 * v[149] + 0.07863075419622369 * v[171] + 0.41981480246462693 *$
$v[213] + 0.6574029179227462 * v[235] - 0.6918062372106849 * v[277] +$
$0.0261064778986361\,4 * v[299] - 0.10291688110521781 * v[341] + 0.01546819920113868 *$
$v[363] - 0.0115605266984652\,7 * v[405] + 0.0020280330861290126 * v[427] -$
$0.0006678100902549639 * v[469] - 8.895004679857398 \cdot 10^{-6} * v[491]);$

$x[2 * 28] = mk\_sample\,(0.000260918406683040\,2 * v[20] + 0.0017434010558554753 * v[44] +$
$0.00335074197528923 * v[84] + 0.01913153200626151\,5 * v[108] + 0.0508790875032403\,9 *$

$$v[148] + 0.07792084947107533 * v[172] + 0.4135144655813375 * v[212] +$$
$$0.6818808379899038 * v[236] - 0.6155065051657198 * v[276] + 0.03464780080203036 *$$
$$v[300] - 0.09048375437030715 * v[340] + 0.016718298292953078 * v[364] -$$
$$0.009763841144830749 * v[404] + 0.0020829053453968282 * v[428] -$$
$$0.00056303412495637 * v[468] - 9.175921629741856 \cdot 10^{-6} * v[492]);$$

$$x[2 * 29] = mk\_sample(0.00026895700362872434 * v[19] + 0.0018617373983575926 *$$
$$v[45] + 0.0037653930147042687 * v[83] + 0.01982370169095419 * v[109] +$$
$$0.0520367067180179 * v[147] + 0.07686314941070457 * v[173] + 0.40915989856270835 *$$
$$v[211] + 0.7088849290922274 * v[237] - 0.5507975895314607 * v[275] +$$
$$0.04332338422655655 * v[301] - 0.0798801226409765 * v[339] + 0.0179809618734234 *$$
$$v[365] - 0.00826081122858336 * v[403] + 0.0021371985853214895 * v[429] -$$
$$0.0004866834622998666 * v[467] - 9.49879041340121 \cdot 10^{-6} * v[493]);$$

$$x[2 * 30] = mk\_sample(0.0002886308928087058 * v[18] + 0.0019936826123059135 * v[46] +$$
$$0.004173121100249679 * v[82] + 0.0205290115172049 * v[110] + 0.05321631209338495 *$$
$$v[146] + 0.07540463876838151 * v[174] + 0.40638020126565166 * v[210] +$$
$$0.7388075471885076 * v[238] - 0.49519431690415505 * v[274] + 0.052191064589741536 *$$
$$v[302] - 0.07070253046441433 * v[338] + 0.019265687721575508 * v[366] -$$
$$0.0069872713199412816 * v[402] + 0.002191077096864582 * v[430] -$$
$$0.0004209202818911278 * v[466] - 9.869853592290089 \cdot 10^{-6} * v[494]);$$

$$x[2 * 31] = mk\_sample(0.0002953791302584709 * v[17] + 0.0021417256087434577 *$$
$$v[47] + 0.004555649177065818 * v[81] + 0.02124221215327783 * v[111] +$$
$$0.05439513647513115 * v[145] + 0.07345707245390273 * v[175] + 0.4048961286830606 *$$
$$v[209] + 0.7721744861726333 * v[239] - 0.4468853573225977 * v[273] +$$
$$0.06135838173971364 * v[303] - 0.06267710257781978 * v[337] + 0.02059351619540377 *$$
$$v[367] - 0.005896215025383755 * v[401] + 0.0022446932639493943 * v[431] -$$
$$0.0003521820359820493 * v[465] - 0.000010296900482261932 * v[495]);$$

}

Used in 6.

A.4 18 Point DCT

The following code was generated by the `genfft` code generator from the FFTW Project[10][11] version 3.0.1 with the command line:

```
gen_r2r -compact -variables 4 -redft01 -n 18 -name dct18
  -with-istride 1 -with-ostride 1
```

It was then modified to include preprocessing with S_{18}, according to equation (7). Some small additional modifications were needed because `genfft` uses a different definition of DCT^{III}. Still a scaling factor of 2 remains and is compensated by a factor $1/2$ each time the function is used.

$\langle$ `perform.c` $_6$ $\rangle$ $+\equiv$ (413)
```
#define DK(name, value) const double name = ((double)(value))
  void dct18(const double *I, double *O)
  { double I17, I16, I15, I14, I13, I12, I11, I10, I9, I8, I7, I6, I5, I4, I3, I2,
      I1, I0;

    DK(KP173648177, +0.173648177666930348851716626769314796000375677);
    DK(KP984807753, +0.984807753012208059366743024589523013670643252);
    DK(KP642787609, +0.642787609686539326322643409907263432907559884);
    DK(KP766044443, +0.766044443118978035202392650555416673935832457);
```

DK(KP939692620, +0.939692620785908384054109277324731469936208135);
DK(KP342020143, +0.342020143325668733044099614682259580763083368);
DK(KP1_732050807, +1.732050807568877293527446341505872366942805254);
DK(KP1_224744871, +1.224744871391589049098642037352945695982973740);
DK(KP707106781, +0.707106781186547524400844362104849039284835938);
DK(KP1_414213562, +1.414213562373095048801688724209698078569671875);
I17 = $I[17] + I[16]$;
I16 = $I[16] + I[15]$;
I15 = $I[15] + I[14]$;
I14 = $I[14] + I[13]$;
I13 = $I[13] + I[12]$;
I12 = $I[12] + I[11]$;
I11 = $I[11] + I[10]$;
I10 = $I[10] + I[9]$;
I9 = $I[9] + I[8]$;
I8 = $I[8] + I[7]$;
I7 = $I[7] + I[6]$;
I6 = $I[6] + I[5]$;
I5 = $I[5] + I[4]$;
I4 = $I[4] + I[3]$;
I3 = $I[3] + I[2]$;
I2 = $I[2] + I[1]$;
I1 = $I[1] + I[0]$;
I0 = $I[0]$;
{ **double** $f0$, $f1$, $f2$, $f3$, $f4$, $f5$, $f6$, $f7$, $f8$, $f9$, $f10$, $f11$, $f12$, $f13$, $f14$, $f15$, $f16$, $f17$, $f18$, $f19$, $f20$, $f21$, $f22$, $f23$;

   $f22$ = I0 + I0;
   $f23$ = KP1_414213562 ∗ I9;
   $f0$ = $f22 - f23$;
   $f1$ = $f22 + f23$;
   { **double** $g0$, $g1$;

      $g0$ = KP707106781 ∗ (I17 + I1);
      $g1$ = KP707106781 ∗ (I17 − I1);
      $f2$ = I8 − $g0$;
      $f3$ = $g1$ + I10;
      $f4$ = I8 + $g0$;
      $f5$ = $g1$ − I10;
   }
   { **double** $g1$, $g2$, $g3$;

      $g1$ = KP1_732050807 ∗ I6;
      $g2$ = KP707106781 ∗ (I15 − I3);
      $g3$ = KP1_224744871 ∗ (I15 + I3);
      $f6$ = $g2$ + I12;
      $f7$ = $g3$ − $g1$;
      $f8$ = $g2$ − I12;
      $f9$ = $g3$ + $g1$;
   }

```
{ double g4, g5, g6, g7;
  g4 = KP707106781 * (I7 − I11);
  g5 = KP707106781 * (I7 + I11);
  g6 = KP707106781 * (I5 + I13);
  g7 = KP707106781 * (I13 − I5);
  f10 = g6 − I4;
  f11 = I16 − g4;
  f12 = f10 + f11;
  f13 = g5 − I2;
  f14 = g7 + I14;
  f15 = f13 + f14;
  f16 = I4 + g6;
  f17 = I16 + g4;
  f18 = f16 − f17;
  f19 = g5 + I2;
  f20 = g7 − I14;
  f21 = f19 + f20;
}
{ double g0, g1, g2, g3;
  g0 = KP1_732050807 * (f15 + f3);
  g1 = f0 − f6 − f6;
  g2 = f2 + f12;
  g3 = g1 − g2;
  O[13] = g1 + g2 + g2;
  O[10] = g3 + g0;
  O[1] = g3 − g0;
}
{ double g0, g1, g2, g3;
  g0 = KP1_732050807 * (f21 + f5);
  g1 = f1 + f8 + f8;
  g2 = f4 − f18;
  g3 = g1 − g2;
  O[4] = g1 + g2 + g2;
  O[16] = g3 + g0;
  O[7] = g3 − g0;
}
{ double g0, g1, g2, g3, g4, g5, g6;
  g6 = f1 − f8;
  g0 = g6 + f9;
  g1 = g6 − f9;
  { double h0, h1, h2, h3;
    h0 = f18 + f4 + f4;
    h1 = KP1_732050807 * (f19 − f20);
    g2 = h0 + h1;
    g3 = h0 − h1;
    h2 = f5 + f5 − f21;
```

```
      h3 = KP1_732050807 * (f16 + f17);
      g4 = h2 - h3;
      g5 = h3 + h2;
    }
    O[11] = g0 - KP342020143 * g4 - KP939692620 * g2;
    O[0]  = g0 + KP766044443 * g2 - KP642787609 * g4;
    O[8]  = g1 + KP766044443 * g3 + KP642787609 * g5;
    O[15] = g1 + KP342020143 * g5 - KP939692620 * g3;
    O[3]  = g1 + KP173648177 * g3 - KP984807753 * g5;
    O[12] = g0 + KP173648177 * g2 + KP984807753 * g4;
  }
  { double g0, g1, g2, g3, g4, g5, g6;

    g6 = f0 + f6;
    g0 = g6 + f7;
    g1 = g6 - f7;
    { double h0, h1, h2, h3;

      h0 = f2 + f2 - f12;
      h1 = KP1_732050807 * (f14 - f13);
      g2 = h0 - h1;
      g3 = h0 + h1;
      h2 = f15 - f3 - f3;
      h3 = KP1_732050807 * (f10 - f11);
      g4 = h2 - h3;
      g5 = h3 + h2;
    }
    O[2]  = g0 + KP342020143 * g4 - KP939692620 * g2;
    O[14] = g0 + KP173648177 * g2 - KP984807753 * g4;
    O[5]  = g1 + KP173648177 * g3 + KP984807753 * g5;
    O[17] = g1 + KP766044443 * g3 - KP642787609 * g5;
    O[6]  = g1 - KP342020143 * g5 - KP939692620 * g3;
    O[9]  = g0 + KP766044443 * g2 + KP642787609 * g4;
  }
 }
}
```

A.5 6 Point DCT

The following function computes $\mathrm{DCT}_6^{\mathrm{III}} \boldsymbol{S}_6$. After multiplying the result with $\boldsymbol{R}_6$, it is used to compute $\mathrm{DCT}_6^{\mathrm{IV}}$ according to equation (7) on page 125. For $\mathrm{DCT}_6^{\mathrm{III}}$ the matrix product from equation (6), derived in Section 10.12, was used. The matrix calculations were executed with Mathematica[28], which was also used to translate the sequence of all seven matrices to spl code. The spl code was then fed to the spl compiler of the spiral[30] tool and translated into the following C code.

⟨ `perform.c` ₆ ⟩ +≡   (414)
  void $dct6$ (const double $*z$, double $*t$)
  { double $f0$, $f1$, $f2$, $f3$, $f4$, $f5$, $f6$, $f7$, $f8$, $f9$, $f10$, $f11$, $f12$, $f13$, $f14$, $f15$, $f16$,
     $f17$, $f18$, $f19$, $f20$;

$f0 = z[0 * 3] + z[1 * 3]$;
$f1 = z[1 * 3] + z[2 * 3]$;
$f2 = z[2 * 3] + z[3 * 3]$;
$f3 = z[3 * 3] + z[4 * 3]$;
$f4 = z[4 * 3] + z[5 * 3]$;
$f5 = f0 + f4$;
$f6 = f4 - f0$;
$f7 = f2 + f2$;
$f8 = f7 - f6$;
$f9 = f2 + f6$;
$f10 = z[0 * 3] - f3$;
$f11 = 0.5000000000000000 * f3$;
$f12 = z[0 * 3] + f11$;
$f13 = (-0.8660254037844386) * f1$;
$f14 = f13 + f12$;
$f15 = f12 - f13$;
$f16 = 0.3535533905932737 * f8$;
$f17 = (-0.7071067811865475) * f9$;
$f18 = 0.6123724356957945 * f5$;
$f19 = f16 + f18$;
$f20 = f18 - f16$;
$t[0] = f19 + f15$;
$t[1] = f17 + f10$;
$t[2] = f20 + f14$;
$t[3] = f14 - f20$;
$t[4] = f10 - f17$;
$t[5] = f15 - f19$;
  }

A.6 Bit Rate Table

The following table is indexed by the version, the layer, and the bit rate index (see
pages 46 and 182) and gives the bit rate in bit/s.

⟨ global variables ₄₃ ⟩ +≡   (415)
  static const int bit_rate_table[3][3][16] = {
  {   /* MP3_V1_0 */
  { 0, 32000, 64000, 96000, 128000, 160000, 192000, 224000, 256000, 288000, 320000, 352000,
    384000, 416000, 448000, −1 },
  { 0, 32000, 48000, 56000, 64000, 80000, 96000, 112000, 128000, 160000, 192000, 224000,
    256000, 320000, 384000, −1 },
  { 0, 32000, 40000, 48000, 56000, 64000, 80000, 96000, 112000, 128000, 160000, 192000,
    224000, 256000, 320000, −1 } },
  {   /* MP3_V2_0 */

$\{\ 0, 32000, 48000, 56000, 64000, 80000, 96000, 112000, 128000, 144000, 160000, 176000,$
$\qquad 192000, 224000, 256000, -1\ \},$
$\{\ 0, 8000, 16000, 24000, 32000, 40000, 48000, 56000, 64000, 80000, 96000, 112000, 128000,$
$\qquad 144000, 160000, -1\ \},$
$\{\ 0, 8000, 16000, 24000, 32000, 40000, 48000, 56000, 64000, 80000, 96000, 112000, 128000,$
$\qquad 144000, 160000, -1\ \}\ \},$
$\{$ $/* \mathtt{MP3\_V2\_5} */$
$\{\ 0, 32000, 48000, 56000, 64000, 80000, 96000, 112000, 128000, 144000, 160000, 176000,$
$\qquad 192000, 224000, 256000, -1\ \},$
$\{\ 0, 8000, 16000, 24000, 32000, 40000, 48000, 56000, 64000, 80000, 96000, 112000, 128000,$
$\qquad 144000, 160000, -1\ \},$
$\{\ 0, 8000, 16000, 24000, 32000, 40000, 48000, 56000, 64000, 80000, 96000, 112000, 128000,$
$\qquad 144000, 160000, -1\ \}\ \},$
$\};$

A.7 Frequency Table

This table is indexed by the MPEG version and by the *frequency_index* (see pages 46 and 181) and gives the sample rate in Hz.

$\langle$ global variables $_{43}\rangle\ +\equiv$ (416)
   static const int *frequency_table* $[3][3] =$
      $\{\ \{\ 44100, 48000, 32000\ \}, \{\ 22050, 24000, 16000\ \}, \{\ 11025, 12000, 8000\ \}\ \};$

A.8 Layer II Bit Allocation Tables

For each of the following tables, we have a specific value of *sblimit*, which determines also the number of rows in the *nbit* array; a table for *nbal*, which gives the number of bits to read to get the bit allocation; and a table *nbit*, which gives the number of bits to read per sample or group of samples from the stream. A more detailed description of these tables can be found in Section 9.1.

$\langle$ select table a $_{417}\rangle\ \equiv$ (417)
   $\{$ **static const char** *nbal* $[32] = \{\ 4, 4, 4, 4, 4, 4, 4, 4, 4, 4, 4, 3, 3, 3, 3, 3, 3, 3, 3, 3, 3, 3, 2, 2,$
      $2, 2\ \};$
   static const char *nbit* $[27][16] = \{$
      $\{\ 0, -5, 3, 4, 5, 6, 7, 8, 9, 10, 11, 12, 13, 14, 15, 16\ \},$
      $\{\ 0, -5, 3, 4, 5, 6, 7, 8, 9, 10, 11, 12, 13, 14, 15, 16\ \},$
      $\{\ 0, -5, 3, 4, 5, 6, 7, 8, 9, 10, 11, 12, 13, 14, 15, 16\ \},$
      $\{\ 0, -5, -7, 3, -10, 4, 5, 6, 7, 8, 9, 10, 11, 12, 13, 16\ \},$
      $\{\ 0, -5, -7, 3, -10, 4, 5, 6, 7, 8, 9, 10, 11, 12, 13, 16\ \},$
      $\{\ 0, -5, -7, 3, -10, 4, 5, 6, 7, 8, 9, 10, 11, 12, 13, 16\ \},$
      $\{\ 0, -5, -7, 3, -10, 4, 5, 6, 7, 8, 9, 10, 11, 12, 13, 16\ \},$
      $\{\ 0, -5, -7, 3, -10, 4, 5, 6, 7, 8, 9, 10, 11, 12, 13, 16\ \},$
      $\{\ 0, -5, -7, 3, -10, 4, 5, 6, 7, 8, 9, 10, 11, 12, 13, 16\ \},$
      $\{\ 0, -5, -7, 3, -10, 4, 5, 6, 7, 8, 9, 10, 11, 12, 13, 16\ \},$
      $\{\ 0, -5, -7, 3, -10, 4, 5, 6, 7, 8, 9, 10, 11, 12, 13, 16\ \},$
      $\{\ 0, -5, -7, 3, -10, 4, 5, 6, 7, 8, 9, 10, 11, 12, 13, 16\ \},$
      $\{\ 0, -5, -7, 3, -10, 4, 5, 16\ \},$

```
      { 0, -5, -7, 3, -10, 4, 5, 16 },
      { 0, -5, -7, 3, -10, 4, 5, 16 },
      { 0, -5, -7, 3, -10, 4, 5, 16 },
      { 0, -5, -7, 3, -10, 4, 5, 16 },
      { 0, -5, -7, 3, -10, 4, 5, 16 },
      { 0, -5, -7, 3, -10, 4, 5, 16 },
      { 0, -5, -7, 3, -10, 4, 5, 16 },
      { 0, -5, -7, 3, -10, 4, 5, 16 },
      { 0, -5, -7, 3, -10, 4, 5, 16 },
      { 0, -5, -7, 3, -10, 4, 5, 16 },
      { 0, -5, -7, 3, -10, 4, 5, 16 },
      { 0, -5, -7, 16 },
      { 0, -5, -7, 16 },
      { 0, -5, -7, 16 },
      { 0, -5, -7, 16 }
    };
  s→sblimit[0] = 27;
  s→nbal = nbal;
  s→nbit = nbit;
  }
```
                                                                                   Used in 192.

⟨ select table b 418 ⟩ ≡   (418)
  { **static const char** $nbal[32]$ = { 4, 4, 4, 4, 4, 4, 4, 4, 4, 4, 4, 3, 3, 3, 3, 3, 3, 3, 3, 3, 3, 3, 3, 2, 2,
      2, 2, 2, 2, 2 };
  static const char $nbit[30][16]$ = {
      { 0, -5, 3, 4, 5, 6, 7, 8, 9, 10, 11, 12, 13, 14, 15, 16 },
      { 0, -5, 3, 4, 5, 6, 7, 8, 9, 10, 11, 12, 13, 14, 15, 16 },
      { 0, -5, 3, 4, 5, 6, 7, 8, 9, 10, 11, 12, 13, 14, 15, 16 },
      { 0, -5, -7, 3, -10, 4, 5, 6, 7, 8, 9, 10, 11, 12, 13, 16 },
      { 0, -5, -7, 3, -10, 4, 5, 6, 7, 8, 9, 10, 11, 12, 13, 16 },
      { 0, -5, -7, 3, -10, 4, 5, 6, 7, 8, 9, 10, 11, 12, 13, 16 },
      { 0, -5, -7, 3, -10, 4, 5, 6, 7, 8, 9, 10, 11, 12, 13, 16 },
      { 0, -5, -7, 3, -10, 4, 5, 6, 7, 8, 9, 10, 11, 12, 13, 16 },
      { 0, -5, -7, 3, -10, 4, 5, 6, 7, 8, 9, 10, 11, 12, 13, 16 },
      { 0, -5, -7, 3, -10, 4, 5, 6, 7, 8, 9, 10, 11, 12, 13, 16 },
      { 0, -5, -7, 3, -10, 4, 5, 16 },
      { 0, -5, -7, 3, -10, 4, 5, 16 },
      { 0, -5, -7, 3, -10, 4, 5, 16 },
      { 0, -5, -7, 3, -10, 4, 5, 16 },
      { 0, -5, -7, 3, -10, 4, 5, 16 },
      { 0, -5, -7, 3, -10, 4, 5, 16 },
      { 0, -5, -7, 3, -10, 4, 5, 16 },
      { 0, -5, -7, 3, -10, 4, 5, 16 },
      { 0, -5, -7, 3, -10, 4, 5, 16 },
      { 0, -5, -7, 3, -10, 4, 5, 16 },
      { 0, -5, -7, 3, -10, 4, 5, 16 },
```
```

```
        { 0, −5, −7, 3, −10, 4, 5, 16 },
        { 0, −5, −7, 16 },
        { 0, −5, −7, 16 },
        { 0, −5, −7, 16 },
        { 0, −5, −7, 16 },
        { 0, −5, −7, 16 },
        { 0, −5, −7, 16 },
        { 0, −5, −7, 16 }
    };
```

$s \rightarrow sblimit[0] = 30;$

$s \rightarrow nbal = nbal;$

$s \rightarrow nbit = nbit;$

```
}
```
Used in 192.

⟨ select table d $_{419}$ ⟩ ≡   (419)
```
    { static const char nbal[32] = { 4, 4, 3, 3, 3, 3, 3, 3, 3, 3, 3, 3 };
      static const char nbit[12][16] = {
        { 0, −5, −7, −10, 4, 5, 6, 7, 8, 9, 10, 11, 12, 13, 14, 15 },
        { 0, −5, −7, −10, 4, 5, 6, 7, 8, 9, 10, 11, 12, 13, 14, 15 },
        { 0, −5, −7, −10, 4, 5, 6, 7 },
        { 0, −5, −7, −10, 4, 5, 6, 7 },
        { 0, −5, −7, −10, 4, 5, 6, 7 },
        { 0, −5, −7, −10, 4, 5, 6, 7 },
        { 0, −5, −7, −10, 4, 5, 6, 7 },
        { 0, −5, −7, −10, 4, 5, 6, 7 },
        { 0, −5, −7, −10, 4, 5, 6, 7 },
        { 0, −5, −7, −10, 4, 5, 6, 7 },
        { 0, −5, −7, −10, 4, 5, 6, 7 },
        { 0, −5, −7, −10, 4, 5, 6, 7 }
    };
```

$s \rightarrow sblimit[0] = 12;$

$s \rightarrow nbal = nbal;$

$s \rightarrow nbit = nbit;$

```
}
```
Used in 192.

For MPEG version 2, the following table is needed (see [3] table B.1).

⟨ select version 2 table $_{420}$ ⟩ ≡   (420)
```
    { static const char nbal[32] = { 4, 4, 4, 4, 3, 3, 3, 3, 3, 3, 3, 2, 2, 2, 2, 2, 2, 2, 2, 2, 2, 2, 2, 2, 2,
        2, 2, 2, 2, 2 };
      static const char nbit[30][16] = {
        { 0, −5, −7, 3, −10, 4, 5, 6, 7, 8, 9, 10, 11, 12, 13, 14 },
        { 0, −5, −7, 3, −10, 4, 5, 6, 7, 8, 9, 10, 11, 12, 13, 14 },
        { 0, −5, −7, 3, −10, 4, 5, 6, 7, 8, 9, 10, 11, 12, 13, 14 },
        { 0, −5, −7, 3, −10, 4, 5, 6, 7, 8, 9, 10, 11, 12, 13, 14 },
        { 0, −5, −7, −10, 4, 5, 6, 7 },
        { 0, −5, −7, −10, 4, 5, 6, 7 },
        { 0, −5, −7, −10, 4, 5, 6, 7 },
```

```
    { 0, −5, −7, −10, 4, 5, 6, 7 },
    { 0, −5, −7, −10, 4, 5, 6, 7 },
    { 0, −5, −7, −10, 4, 5, 6, 7 },
    { 0, −5, −7, −10, 4, 5, 6, 7 },
    { 0, −5, −7, −10 },
    { 0, −5, −7, −10 },
    { 0, −5, −7, −10 },
    { 0, −5, −7, −10 },
    { 0, −5, −7, −10 },
    { 0, −5, −7, −10 },
    { 0, −5, −7, −10 },
    { 0, −5, −7, −10 },
    { 0, −5, −7, −10 },
    { 0, −5, −7, −10 },
    { 0, −5, −7, −10 },
    { 0, −5, −7, −10 },
    { 0, −5, −7, −10 },
    { 0, −5, −7, −10 },
    { 0, −5, −7, −10 },
    { 0, −5, −7, −10 },
    { 0, −5, −7, −10 },
    { 0, −5, −7, −10 },
    { 0, −5, −7, −10 }
  };
```

$s{\rightarrow}sblimit\,[0] = 30;$

$s{\rightarrow}nbal = nbal;$

$s{\rightarrow}nbit = nbit;$

```
}
```

Used in 372.

A.9 Computing the Degrouping Tables

The global tables to look up the individual parts of grouped sample values (see Section 9.2) consist of four tables. The basic degrouping tables come first.

⟨ print table $_{135}$ ⟩ +≡   (421)

     $print\_degroup\_table\,(5, 3, 2);$

     $print\_degroup\_table\,(7, 5, 3);$

     $print\_degroup\_table\,(10, 9, 4);$

The three tables generated are:

- *degroup5* for *bit_allocation* $= -5$, that works for 3 levels coded as 2 bit integers.

- *degroup7* for *bit_allocation* $= -7$, that works for 7 levels coded as 3 bit integers. and

- *degroup10* for *bit_allocation* $= -10$, that works for 9 levels coded as 4 bit integers.

The actual printing uses the following function

⟨ printing prerequisites $_{130}$ ⟩ +≡   (422)
```
static int scale(int s, int nbit)
{ s = s ≪ (sizeof(int) * 8 − nbit);         /* make it a binary fraction */
  s = s + (3 ≪ (sizeof(int) * 8 − 2));             /* add −0.5 */
  return −s;
}
static void print_degroup_table(int n, int nlevels, int nbit)
{ int s0, s1, s2, c, size;
  size = 1 ≪ n;
  printf("static␣const␣int␣degroup%d[%d][3]␣=␣{\n", n, size);
  for (c = 0; c < size; c++)
  { ⟨ degrouping c ₂₀₀ ⟩
    printf("{%d,␣%d,␣%d}", scale(s0, nbit), scale(s1, nbit), scale(s2, nbit));
    if (c ≠ size − 1) printf(",\n");
  }
  printf("\n};\n\n");
}
```

The last array, *degroup*, is used to map a negative number n, obtained as the *bit_allocation*, to the correct degrouping table.

⟨ print table $_{135}$ ⟩ +≡   (423)
```
printf("static␣const␣int␣(*degroup[6])[3]="
"{degroup5,NULL,degroup7,NULL,NULL,degroup10};\n");
```

⟨ read three grouped samples $_{424}$ ⟩ ≡   (424)
```
{ int c;
{ unsigned int bits;
  n = −n;
  ⟨ get n bits ₁₄₂ ⟩
  bits = (bits ≫ (sizeof (bits) * 8 − n));
  n = −n;
  c = bits;
}
```
                                                                   Used in 201.

It is used to

⟨ read three grouped samples $_{424}$ ⟩ +≡   (425)
```
{ const int (*table)[3];
  table = degroup[−n − 5];
```

by first finding the right *table*, which is then indexed by the group code c to get the correct triplet of degrouped samples.

⟨ read three grouped samples $_{424}$ ⟩ +≡   (426)
```
y[i][ch][sb] = table[c][0] * f;
```

$y[i+1][ch][sb] = table[c][1] * f;$
$y[i+2][ch][sb] = table[c][2] * f; \}$ $\}$

A.10 Mixed Block Boundary

In mixed blocks, the lower bands are encoded as long blocks and the higher bands as three short blocks. The boundary differs for the different MPEG versions. The following table, indexed by the version, gives the number of long bands in a mixed block. Invariably these long bands replace the first 3 short bands.

$\langle$ boundary table $_{427}\rangle \equiv$ (427)
  static const int $boundary\_table[3] = \{\ 8, 6, 6\ \};$
#**define** FIRST_MIXED_SHORT   3   Used in 428 and 433.

$\langle$ global variables $_{43}\rangle\ +\equiv$ (428)
  $\langle$ boundary table $_{427}\rangle$

Note that for version 2.5 mixed blocks, the transition from long to short is not between the second and the third subband (after 36 frequencies) but between the fourth and the fifth (after 72 frequencies).

Using the boundary table and the information about the start of each subband, it is possible to compute the

$\langle$ number of long subbands $_{429}\rangle \equiv$ (429)
  $start[gr][ch][boundary\_table[s{\rightarrow}info.version]]/$SUBFREQUENCIES   Used in 234.

A.11 Layer III Fixed Part Length

Layer III frames are divided into a fixed and a variable length part. The size of the fixed part depends on the number of channels, the version, and the presence of a CRC. It is computed by adding to the size of the side information, as given in Tables 23 and 30, the size of the header (4 bytes), and the size of the CRC (2 bytes).

$\langle$ derive further information $_{65}\rangle\ +\equiv$ (430)
  $\{$ **static const int** $side\_info\_size[2][2] = \{$
    $\{\ 17, 9\ \},$ /* MP3_V2_0 or MP3_V2_5 */
    $\{\ 32, 17\ \}\ \};$ /* MP3_V1_0 */

    $s{\rightarrow}info.fixed_size\ =\ $HEADER_SIZE$\ +\ 2 * s{\rightarrow}info.crc_protected\ +$
      $side_info_size[s{\rightarrow}info.version \equiv $MP3_V1_0$]$
      $[s{\rightarrow}info.mode \equiv $MP3_MONO$];$
  $\}$

$\langle$ infos $_{31}\rangle\ +\equiv$ (431)
  int $fixed\_size;$

A.12 Layer III Scalefactor Bands

Layer III groups the 576 frequencies into 22 bands, each resembling, as close as possible, a critical band of the human auditory system. The following tables give the number of frequency lines in each band, called its width. The band width depends on the sample rate and is different for long blocks and short blocks. The right table can be selected from one of the arrays below by using first the *version* and then the $layer - 1$ as index.

⟨ bandwidth tables $_{432}$ ⟩ ≡   (432)

  const int *bandwidth_table*$[3][3][22] = \{$

  $\{$ $\{$ $4, 4, 4, 4, 4, 4, 6, 6, 8, 8, 10, 12, 16, 20, 24, 28, 34, 42, 50, 54, 76, 158\,\}$,   /∗ 44.1 kHz ∗/

  $\{$ $4, 4, 4, 4, 4, 4, 6, 6, 6, 8, 10, 12, 16, 18, 22, 28, 34, 40, 46, 54, 54, 192\,\}$,   /∗ 48.0 kHz ∗/

  $\{$ $4, 4, 4, 4, 4, 4, 6, 6, 8, 10, 12, 16, 20, 24, 30, 38, 46, 56, 68, 84, 102, 26\,\}$ $\}$,   /∗ 32.0 kHz ∗/

  $\{$ $\{$ $6, 6, 6, 6, 6, 6, 8, 10, 12, 14, 16, 20, 24, 28, 32, 38, 46, 52, 60, 68, 58, 54\,\}$,   /∗ 22.05 kHz ∗/

  $\{$ $6, 6, 6, 6, 6, 6, 8, 10, 12, 14, 16, 18, 22, 26, 32, 38, 46, 54, 62, 70, 76, 36\,\}$,   /∗ 24.00 kHz ∗/

  $\{$ $6, 6, 6, 6, 6, 6, 8, 10, 12, 14, 16, 20, 24, 28, 32, 38, 46, 52, 60, 68, 58, 54\,\}$ $\}$,   /∗ 16.00 kHz ∗/

  $\{$ $\{$ $6, 6, 6, 6, 6, 6, 8, 10, 12, 14, 16, 20, 24, 28, 32, 38, 46, 52, 60, 68, 58, 54\,\}$,   /∗ 11.025 kHz ∗/

  $\{$ $6, 6, 6, 6, 6, 6, 8, 10, 12, 14, 16, 20, 24, 28, 32, 38, 46, 52, 60, 68, 58, 54\,\}$,   /∗ 12.000 kHz ∗/

  $\{$ $12, 12, 12, 12, 12, 12, 16, 20, 24, 28, 32, 40, 48, 56, 64, 76, 90, 2, 2, 2, 2, 2\,\}$ /∗ 8.000 kHz ∗/

  $\}$ $\}$;

  const int *bandwidth_table_short*$[3][3][13] = \{$

  $\{$ $\{$ $4, 4, 4, 4, 6, 8, 10, 12, 14, 18, 22, 30, 56\,\}$,   /∗ 44.1 kHz ∗/

  $\{$ $4, 4, 4, 4, 6, 6, 10, 12, 14, 16, 20, 26, 66\,\}$,   /∗ 48.0 kHz ∗/

  $\{$ $4, 4, 4, 4, 6, 8, 12, 16, 20, 26, 34, 42, 12\,\}$ $\}$,   /∗ 32.0 kHz ∗/

  $\{$ $\{$ $4, 4, 4, 6, 6, 8, 10, 14, 18, 26, 32, 42, 18\,\}$,   /∗ 22.05 kHz ∗/

  $\{$ $4, 4, 4, 6, 8, 10, 12, 14, 18, 24, 32, 44, 12\,\}$,   /∗ 24.00 kHz ∗/

  $\{$ $4, 4, 4, 6, 8, 10, 12, 14, 18, 24, 30, 40, 18\,\}$ $\}$,   /∗ 16.00 kHz ∗/

  $\{$ $\{$ $4, 4, 4, 6, 8, 10, 12, 14, 18, 24, 30, 40, 18\,\}$,   /∗ 11.025 kHz ∗/

  $\{$ $4, 4, 4, 6, 8, 10, 12, 14, 18, 24, 30, 40, 18\,\}$,   /∗ 12.000 kHz ∗/

  $\{$ $8, 8, 8, 12, 16, 20, 24, 28, 36, 2, 2, 2, 26\,\}$ $\}$ /∗ 8.000 kHz ∗/

  $\}$;   Used in 433.

From this information, we generate two tables, the *width_table* and the *start_table*. These tables, indexed by version, frequency index, *mixed_block*, and *block_type* ≡ SHORT_BLOCK, contain pointers into an auxiliar array *sw*, where the actual data is stored.

⟨ printing prerequisites $_{130}$ ⟩ +≡   (433)

  ⟨ bandwidth tables $_{432}$ ⟩

  ⟨ boundary table $_{427}$ ⟩

  void *print_start_width*(**void**)

  $\{$ **int** *width_table*$[3][3][2][2] = \{$ 0 $\}$;

    int *start_table*$[3][3][2][2] = \{$ 0 $\}$;

    int *version*, *f*, *mixed_block*, *short_block*, *k*, *width*, *band*;

    int $i = 0$;

    printf("static␣const␣short␣int␣sw[]␣␣=␣{\n");

    for (*version* = 0; *version* < 3; *version*++)

```
for (f = 0;  f < 3;  f++)
{  short_block = 0;
   width_table[version][f][0][short_block]  =
       width_table[version][f][1][short_block] = i;
   for (band = 0;  band < 22;  band++, i++)
     printf("%d,␣", bandwidth_table[version][f][band]);
   start_table[version][f][0][short_block]  =
       start_table[version][f][1][short_block] = i;
   k = 0;
   printf("\n%d,␣", k);
   i++;
   for (band = 0;  band < 22;  band++, i++)
   {  k = k + bandwidth_table[version][f][band];
     printf("%d,␣", k);
   }
   short_block = 1;
   mixed_block = 0;
   width_table[version][f][mixed_block][short_block] = i;
   for (band = 0;  band < 13;  band++, i = i + 3)
   {  k = bandwidth_table_short[version][f][band];
     printf("%d,␣%d,␣%d,\n", k, k, k);
   }
   start_table[version][f][mixed_block][short_block] = i;
   k = 0;
   printf("%d,␣", k);
   i++;
   for (band = 0;  band < 13;  band++, i = i + 3)
   {  width = bandwidth_table_short[version][f][band];
     printf("%d,␣%d,␣%d,\n", k + width, k + 2 * width, k + 3 * width);
     k = k + 3 * width;
   }
   short_block = mixed_block = 1;
   width_table[version][f][mixed_block][short_block] = i;
   for (band = 0;  band < boundary_table[version];  band++, i++)
     printf("%d,␣", bandwidth_table[version][f][band]);
   for (band = FIRST_MIXED_SHORT;  band < 13;  band++, i = i + 3)
   {  k = bandwidth_table_short[version][f][band];
     printf("%d,␣%d,␣%d,\n", k, k, k);
   }
   start_table[version][f][mixed_block][short_block] = i;
   k = 0;
   printf("%d,␣", k);
   i++;
```

```
        for (band = 0; band < boundary_table[version]; band++, i++)
        { k = k + bandwidth_table[version][f][band];
          printf("%d,␣", k);
        }

        for (band = FIRST_MIXED_SHORT; band < 13; band++, i = i + 3)
        { width = bandwidth_table_short[version][f][band];
          printf("%d,␣%d,␣%d,\n", k + width, k + 2 * width, k + 3 * width);
          k = k + 3 * width;
        }

      }

  printf("␣0};\n");
  printf("static␣const␣short␣int␣*width_table[3][3][2][2]={");
  for (version = 0; version < 3; version++)
  { printf("{");
    for (f = 0; f < 3; f++)
    { printf("{{&sw[%d],&sw[%d]},{&sw[%d],&sw[%d]}}",
            width_table[version][f][0][0], width_table[version][f][0][1],
            width_table[version][f][1][0], width_table[version][f][1][1]);
      if (f < 2) printf(",\n");
    }
    if (version < 2) printf("}\n,\n");
    else printf("}\n};\n");
  }

  printf("static␣const␣short␣int␣*start_table[3][3][2][2]={");
  for (version = 0; version < 3; version++)
  { printf("{");
    for (f = 0; f < 3; f++)
    { printf("{{&sw[%d],&sw[%d]},{&sw[%d],&sw[%d]}}",
            start_table[version][f][0][0], start_table[version][f][0][1],
            start_table[version][f][1][0], start_table[version][f][1][1]);
      if (f < 2) printf(",\n");
    }
    if (version < 2) printf("}\n,\n");
    else printf("}\n};\n");
  }

}
```

⟨ print table $_{135}$ ⟩ +≡   (434)
  $print\_start\_width(\,);$

A.13 Layer III Scalefactor Bits

The number of bits used to encode scalefactors is stored in the bit stream as an index into the following table:

$\langle$ global variables $_{43}$ $\rangle$ $+\equiv$ (435)
 static const char $slength\_v1$ [16][4] = { { 0,0,0,−1 },{ 0,1,0,−1 },{ 0,2,0,
  −1 },{ 0,3,0,−1 },{ 3,0,0,−1 },{ 1,1,0,−1 },{ 1,2,0,−1 },{ 1,3,0,−1 },
  { 2,1,0,−1 },{ 2,2,0,−1 },{ 2,3,0,−1 },{ 3,1,0,−1 },{ 3,2,0,−1 },{ 3,
  3,0,−1 },{ 4,2,0,−1 },{ 4,3,0,−1 } };

The first number gives the number of bits used to store a scalefactor for bands 0 to 10, and the second gives the number of bits used for bands 11 to 20 (see *slimit_v1* below). The following zero indicates no bits for the last band. The extra −1 is used to indicate the end of the array.

$\langle$ global variables $_{43}$ $\rangle$ $+\equiv$ (436)
 static const char $slimit\_v1$ [2][2][4] = { { { 11,21,22,0 },{ 11,21,22,0 } },
  { { 18,36,39,0 },{ 17,35,38,0 } } };

The array *slimit_v1* is indexed by *block_type* $\equiv$ SHORT_BLOCK and *mixed_block*. A zero entry marks the end of each row.

A.14 Minimum and Maximum

Unfortunately *max*, *min*, and M_PI are not part of standard C. So, we define them.

$\langle$ private declarations $_1$ $\rangle$ $+\equiv$ (437)
#**ifndef** *max*
#**define** *max*(a,b) $((a) > (b)$? $(a) : (b))$
#**endif**
#**ifndef** *min*
#**define** *min*(a,b) $((a) > (b)$? $(b) : (a))$
#**endif**
#**ifndef** M_PI
#**define** M_PI   3.14159265358979323846264338328
#**endif**

B Theory and Practice of CRCs

This section is devoted to the general theory and practice of CRCs. The problem that we try to solve with the use of CRCs is the following: Given a long sequence of bits, compute from it a short sequence of bits such that two short sequences are different if they were computed from two different long sequences. The solution of this problem can be used to check a long sequence of bits for transmission errors simply by comparing two short sequences, one computed before the transmission and one after. But, of course, this problem has no solution since there are many more long sequences than short sequences, and hence, not all long sequences can be mapped to different short sequences. So we have to modify the problem in order to solve it. We can not really expect to be able to detect any kind of transmission error with only the very limited information provided by a short sequence of check bits. But we can reasonably expect to be able to find at least the most common errors, and the most common errors are small errors. Therefore we have a new problem: Given a long sequence of bits, compute from it a short sequence of bits such that two short sequences are different if they are computed from two long sequences that differ only by a few bits.

This is a rather difficult problem because of its combinatory complexity. Even if we consider only two single bit errors, there are already many, many different possibilities how these two errors can occur, for example in the 38 protected bytes of a version 1, layer III frame. Hence, without some mathematical theory, there is no way of deriving a solution. The theory we will use is the theory of polynoms over the Field of two numbers, 0 and 1.

B.1 Fields and Rings

When we do computations with numbers like 1, -3, $\frac{1}{7}$, or 3.1415, we use certain rules of computation, like $a + b = b + a$, $a \cdot 1 = a$, or $a + (-a) = 0$. The complete set of rules does not matter for our informal discussion here, but a good book on algebra (e.g. the timeless classic [32] or [13]) is recommended for those with a deeper interest in the subject. Sets of numbers that fulfill these rules are called Fields. For example, the set of real numbers is such a Field. It might come as a surprise that there are small finite sets of numbers that satisfy all the normal rules of computation and therefore are Fields.

To further investigate the topic, think, for example, about the numbers from 1 to 12, as we use them for the 12 hours on a clock. We can do all the normal computations on these, because we restart with 1 each time a number gets bigger than 12. For example, 10 plus 4 is 2 o'clock. Multiples of 12 hours do not matter in regard to the hour shown on a clock and are neglected. We only care for the remainder after discarding any multiples of 12, and two numbers are considered equal if they differ only by a multiple of 12. The number 12 itself is like 0. Mathematically we say: we compute "modulo 12".

But, do we have negative numbers? Look at the equation $10 + 4 = 2$ that we stated above. In this equation, the number 4 behaves like -8. Instead of going 8 hours backward, we can always go 4 hours forward and the clock will show he same time. It is easy to see that for each number on the clock there is also the negative number present.

How about fractions? Is there a number like $\frac{1}{5}$ with the property $5 \cdot \frac{1}{5} = 1$? In this case the answer is yes. We have $5 \cdot 5 = 25 = 12 + 12 + 1 = 1$, and the number 5 takes the role of $\frac{1}{5}$. We should not expect to find a number for $\frac{1}{12}$ since $12 = 0$ and there is no such thing as $\frac{1}{0}$. There is, however, also no number for $\frac{1}{2}$. Whatever number a we choose, $2 * a$ will always be an even number and it can never be 1 or a multiple of 12 plus 1 which is always an odd number. We conclude that the numbers modulo 12 are not a Field; they constitute what mathematicians call a Ring. A Ring is an algebraic structure, where we can do addition, subtraction, and multiplication as usual, but division is limited. Division might leave a remainder. The whole numbers, for example, constitute a Ring. A deeper investigation reveals, that the whole numbers modulo n constitute a Field, if and only if n is a prime number. The numbers modulo 2 constitute the simplest and smallest Field. It is called G_2 and consists only of the two numbers 0 and 1, which we can also interpret as the boolean values "false" and "true". Multiplication and addition can then be written as $\wedge$ (and) and $\oplus$ (exclusive or), because the rules of computation are the same for these operations.

The Field G_2 offers us a new mathematical model for sequences of bits: bit vectors. So far, we have seen vectors only as vectors of real numbers, but now, we know that the boolean values 0 and 1 obey the same rules of computation as the real numbers, and we can easily reuse the theory of vectors for vectors of booleans, or in general vectors over an arbitrary Field. Unfortunately, linear algebra is not sufficient for the theory of CRCs, and we have to go one step further. We have to consider polynoms.

B.2 Polynom Rings

A polynom p over the variable x is an expressions of the form

$$p = a_n x^n + a_{n-1} x^{n-1} + \cdots + a_1 x^1 + a_0 x^0.$$

The numbers $a_n, a_{n-1}, \ldots, a_1, a_0$ are taken from a fixed but otherwise arbitrary Field and are called "coefficients". If $a_n \neq 0$ we call n the degree of the polynom. Most people know polynoms like $x^2 - 2x + 1$ from school. Here, we consider polynoms with coefficients from the Field G_2.

Since polynoms are added componentwise and multiplication by numbers from the Field is again componentwise, we know that polynoms form a vector space. The polynom above can be equally well written as the vector $(a_n, a_{n-1}, \ldots, a_1, a_0)$. There is, however, much more we can do with a polynom: We can multiply polynoms, and we can evaluate polynoms for any value of x taken from the Field. We can even divide one polynom by another, but usually, this leaves a remainder, and hence, polynoms are not a Field but a Ring.

The Ring of polynoms over the Field G_2 is the right algebraic model to use if we want to study CRCs. A sequence of bits, like 101101, is modeled by the polynom $1x^5 + 0x^4 + 1x^3 + 1x^2 + 0x^1 + 1x^0$, which we can write shorter as $x^5 + x^3 + x^2 + 1$.

The CRC of a bit sequence is defined using a so called generator polynom. In the case of MPEG streams this generator polynom is

$$g = x^{16} + x^{15} + x^2 + 1.$$

The definition of the CRC for a bit sequence is now very simple: We take the polynom p that belongs to the given bit sequence, divide it by g, and obtain a remainder. The bit sequence that corresponds to this remainder is the CRC.

This definition of the CRC is a clever move: it yields a code that can be computed efficiently in hardware and in software, as we will see below, and lends itself to a thorough investigation of the properties of such a code.

B.3 Properties

Without too much mathematics, we can derive some of the properties of CRCs with simple means. More elaborate techniques can be found in the classic CRC paper [26] or in books like [31] and [20].

Assume a polynom p and a polynom $\tilde{p} \neq p$, which differ by some bits caused by a transmission error. We investigate the question: Under what circumstances will that error pass by undetected, that is, under what circumstances will both polynoms have the same remainder when divided by the generator polynom g? We can write $p = qg + r$ and $\tilde{p} = \tilde{q}g + \tilde{r}$, for suitable factors q and $\tilde{q}$ and remainders r and $\tilde{r}$. If both polynoms yield the same CRC, we have $r = \tilde{r}$ and we can conclude $p - \tilde{p} = (qg + r) - (\tilde{q}g + \tilde{r}) = (q - \tilde{q})g + (r - \tilde{r}) = (q - \tilde{q})g$.

The last equation states the first important property of CRCs:

Property 1: Two bit sequences yield the same CRC, if and only if the difference of the two sequences is a multiple of the generator polynom g.

Now we apply this to the case of a single bit error. The situation is as follows:

$$
\begin{array}{cc}
 & \downarrow \\
p & \ldots 011010101 \ldots \\
-\tilde{p} & -\ldots 011000101 \ldots \\
\hline
p - \tilde{p} & \ldots 000010000 \ldots
\end{array}
$$

Subtracting $\tilde{p}$ from p will zero out all the coefficients, except at the position (indicated by the arrow) where the two bit sequences differ. So we have $p - \tilde{p} = x^k$ where k is the position of the bit error, and we have reduced our investigation to the simple mathematical question: is x^k a multiple of g. In our case, where $g = x^{16} + x^{15} + x^2 + 1$, the answer is: No. The only factors of x^k are $1, x, x^2, \ldots, x^k$ and nothing else. We conclude:

Property 2: Any generator polynom g with more than one term can detect any single bit error.

How about two error bits? Can one error bit cancel out the effect of the other error bit on the CRC? If p and $\tilde{p}$ differ by two bits, we have $p - \tilde{p} = x^k + x^\ell$, where k and ℓ are the positions of the error bits. Then the equation $x^k + x^\ell = (x^{k-\ell} + 1) \cdot x^\ell$ reveals that the two errors will go by undetected, if g either divides $x^{k-\ell} + 1$ or x^ℓ. If we exclude, as above, the second possibility, we can conclude that two single bit errors will remain undetected if the distance $d = k - \ell$ between the two error bits is such that $x^d + 1$ is a multiple of g. One idea to determine the smallest such d would be to try successively $d = 1, 2, 3, \ldots$, compute the remainder, and see whether it is 0. Unfortunately, this would take a long long time. Some more mathematics—learning it will take some time too, but is a lot more fun—reveals that our g has two factors, $g = (x + 1)(x^{15} + x^{14} + x + 1)$, of which the second factor $x^{15} + x^{14} + x + 1$ is a so called primitive polynom. Primitive polynoms have a nice property: for them, the smallest d such that $x^d + 1$ is a multiple of the primitive polynom is $d = 2^n - 1$, where n is the degree of the primitive polynom. And this is as good as it can get, because for all polynoms of degree n, the minimal d is a factor of $2^n - 1$ and hence can not be larger.

Property 3: If the generator polynom g is a primitive polynom of degree n, it can detect two single bit errors as long as the distance between the two errors is less than $2^n - 1$.

In our case, the smallest d such that $x^d + 1$ is a multiple of $x^{15} + x^{14} + x + 1$ is $d = 2^{15} - 1 = 32767$. As long as the distance of the two single bit errors is less than 32767 bits (≈ 4 kbyte), our CRC will detect them. Since an MPEG audio frame easily fits into 4 kbyte, the CRC guards them against two single bit errors.

How about three error bits? A general method, used often with polynoms, can help us to gain clarity. If we have $x^k + x^\ell + x^j = hg$, we can evaluate the polynoms on both sides of the equation for the same value x and get the same result. If we evaluate both sides for the value $x = 1$, we have: $1^k + 1^\ell + 1^j = 1 + 1 + 1 = 1$ and $h(1) \cdot g(1) = h(1) \cdot (1^{16} + 1^{15} + 1^2 + 1) = h(1) \cdot (1 + 1 + 1 + 1) = h(1) \cdot 0 = 0$. And we conclude, that the two sides must be different for any polynom h. So all three bit errors are detectable, and in general, all errors with an odd number of error bits are detectable.

Property 4: If the generator polynom g has an even number of terms, it can detect any odd number of bit errors.

How about four or more bits? Don't expect too much. Since the error pattern $1\,1000\,0000\,0000\,0101$ corresponds exactly to the generator polynom $x^{16} + x^{15} + x^2 + x$, it is obviously a multiple of g and we have a simple example of a four bit error that can not be detected. On the other hand, any error pattern that is shorter than this is represented by a polynom of degree 15 or less and therefore can not be a multiple of g, since multiplying with a polynom (except with the polynom $x^0 = 1$) will increase the degree. So our CRC will detect all error pattern that are confined within 16 bits (or 2 consecutive bytes) and the only undetectable error pattern of length 17 is g itself.

Property 5: If the generator polynom g has degree n, it can detect any burst of error bits that is confined to a single stretch of no more then n bits. The only burst error pattern of length $n+1$ that can not be detected is the generator polynom itself.

If our error pattern is spread out more than 17 bits, some pattern, but not very many, are undetectable.

Property 6: If the generator polynom g has degree n, it will fail to detect a random burst of error bits longer than $n + 1$ bits with a likelihood of only 2^{-n}.

For our generator polynom of degree 16, the fraction of undetectable error patterns is exactly $1/2^{16}$ or 0.0015 %.

Now that we have seen that our CRC provides the best error protection we can buy with only 16 bits, we study how to compute it efficiently.

B.4 Bitwise Computation

To compute the CRC, we have to divide the polynom p representing the given bit sequence by g, the generator polynom, and take the remainder. As we do when we manually perform a division, we use an incremental algorithm. An example will illustrate this: Assume we divide, using decimal numbers, 2301 by 19. How do we go about it?

First, we look at the head of the number: 2 and decide how often $19 \cdots$ will "fit in" $20 \cdots$. Once! So we subtract 19 from 20 and obtain the remainder 01 Actually, we were subtracting 1900, a multiple of 19, from 2000 and get a remainder of 100. But we don't care about the thousands, hundreds, or $\cdots$, all we care about is that we are now done with the thousands and continue with the hundreds. That is, we can now shift the result 01 one place to the left and get 1, computing now in units of one hundred, not one thousand. We consider the next digit 3 (hundred). Before we use it, we add the remainder from the previous computation: $3+1 = 4$ (hundred). Then the algorithm repeats: We look at the 4 and decide how often $19 \cdots$ will "fit in" $40 \cdots$. Two times! We subtract 38 and obtain the remainder 2. We add this remainder with the next digit $2 + 0 = 2$ (actually $20 + 00 = 20$) and continue. We look at 2 and decide that we should again subtract 19 from 20, and get the remainder 1. We add the remainder 1 and the next digit 1, to give a total remainder of 2. We stop here, since shifting is no longer possible because we have reached the end of the dividend. 2 is the final result.

With polynoms, we follow the same algorithm. Lets divide

$$1x^5 + 0x^4 + 0x^3 + 1x^2 + 0x + 0 \quad \text{by} \quad 1x^2 + 0x + 1.$$

We consider the leading "digit" $1x^5$ and see that $1x^2 + 0x + 1$ will fit in x^3 times. This is simple, we just need to compare the two leading exponents. We subtract $(1x^2 + 0x + 1)x^3$ from $1x^5$ and get $0x^5 + 0x^4 + 1x^3$. Note that the highest exponent has disappeared. We shift, that is discard the $0x^5$, add $0x^4$, the next "digit" from the dividend, to $0x^4 + 1x^3$ and repeat. We look at $0x^4 + 1x^3$ and see that no subtraction is necessary. We shift again, add $0x^3$ (the next "digit"), and repeat. We have $1x^3$ and decide that we must subtract $(1x^2 + 0x + 1)x^1$. The result is: $0x^3 + 0x^2 + 1x$. We shift, add the next "digit", and we have: $1x^2 + 1x$. A last time, we subtract $(1x^2 + 0x + 1)x^0$ and get $0x^2 + 1x + 1$. Shifting is no longer possible and we stop here with the remainder $1x+1$. We were lucky so, that the dividend did not contain further non zero coefficients for x^1 and x^0. Otherwise, we should have added them to the final result. One way to avoid this unnecessary complication, is the multiplication of the original polynom by x^{d-1}, where d is the degree of the generator polynom, before computing the remainder. This will ensure that the last d coefficients are always zero and avoids the extra addition. The loop can then terminate exactly after dealing with the last digit of the original polynom. The properties of the CRC do not change through this modification. Like most applications, the MPEG standard uses the CRC in this modified way.

Computing with polynoms and binary coefficients is even easier than computing with decimal numbers. Whether the dividing polynom "fits in" is decided purely by the leading coefficient. If it is 1, we subtract, otherwise, we don't. We do not really need to compute multiples either. We subtract once or not at all. As an intermediate result, we need to carry along only one polynom, the remainder so far, and its degree is always smaller than the degree of the generator polynom.

The algorithm to compute the (modified) CRC for a bit sequence of length n as the remainder of the corresponding modified polynom is now as follows:

- Shift the variable crc, the remainder so far, one bit to the left..

- Align the next input bit with bit d of the crc, where d is the degree of the generator polynom g, and add.

- Consider bit d, the most significant bit (msb) of the sum.

- If it is 1, subtract the generator polynom from the sum otherwise leave it untouched.

- Repeat for all n bits.

$\langle$ compute the CRC for n bits $_{438}$ $\rangle$ $\equiv$ (438)
    static unsigned short int
        $bitcrc$(**unsigned short int** crc, **unsigned short int** $bits$, **int** n)
  { $bits = bits \ll (16 - n)$;
    while $(n-- > 0)$
    { **unsigned short int** $msb = (bits \oplus crc)$ & $^\#8000$;
      $crc = crc \ll 1$;
      $bits = bits \ll 1$;
      if (msb) $crc = crc \oplus {}^\#8005$;
    }
    return crc;
  }
Used in 439 and 440.

The given code uses some optimizations. We do not really need the sum of the shifted *crc* and the next input bit. The addition affects only the *msb* (most significant bit) and if it is not zero anyway, it will be zero after the subtraction. So all we need the *msb* for is to decide about the subtraction. After the subtraction, the highest bit is always zero and is shifted out in the next step. If we change the order of shifting and subtraction, we do not need to compute this highest bit, and can restrict the subtraction to the lower bits. Hence it is sufficient to represent the generator polynom without the leading coefficient as #8005.

We need this as auxiliar function,

⟨ auxiliary functions $_{69}$ ⟩ +≡ (439)
    ⟨ compute the CRC for n bits $_{438}$ ⟩

and for printing.

⟨ printing prerequisites $_{130}$ ⟩ +≡ (440)
    ⟨ compute the CRC for n bits $_{438}$ ⟩

B.5 Bytewise Computation

For performance, we need a faster algorithm that operates on bytes, not on bits. The algorithm presented here goes back to A. Perez[25]; good tutorials are [34] and [27]. We do not present, however, a general algorithm, but present a specialized solution for the modified CRC with the generator polynom $g = x^{16} + x^{15} + x^2 + x$. Looking for an incremental algorithm that computes the modified CRC not bit for bit, but one byte at a time, we have the following situation:

Assume we have a bit string, or polynom p, and we know already the modified CRC for p, that is, we know r such that for some q, we have $p \cdot x^{16} = qg + r$.

$$\underbrace{0101001000\cdots010111011}_{p}\,00000000\,00000000 = p \cdot x^{16} = qg + r$$

To make the representation as bytes and 16 bit words explicit, we use in this section the variables p and q for bit sequences of arbitrary length, the variables r and s for sequences of 16 bits (words) and the variables a, b, and c for sequences of 8 bits (byte). The remainder r, for instance, has a maximum degree of 15, and hence fits into a 16 bit word. Because we will need bytewise access to r, we write r as $r = a \cdot x^8 + b$, splitting it into a high-byte a and a low-byte b.

To continue with the problem at hand, we assume that we read in an other byte c and want to know the modified CRC of the bit sequence obtained by appending c to the end of p.

$$\underbrace{0101001000\cdots010111011}_{p}\,\underbrace{10110011}_{c}\,00000000\,00000000 = (px^8 + c)x^{16}$$

Now we use some elementary algebra to obtain

$$
\begin{aligned}
(px^8 + c)x^{16} &= px^{16}x^8 + cx^{16} \\
&= (qg + r)x^8 + cx^{16} \\
&= qgx^8 + rx^8 + cx^{16} \\
&= qgx^8 + (ax^8 + b)x^8 + cx^{16} \\
&= qgx^8 + ax^{16} + bx^8 + cx^{16} \\
&= qgx^8 + (a + c)x^{16} + bx^8
\end{aligned}
$$

If we now have a table to look up the modified CRC for any possible byte value, then we can look up in that table for $a + c$ a 16 bit value s such that

$$
(a + c)x^{16} = q'g + s
$$

Using this equation, we can continue the above computation and have

$$
\begin{aligned}
(px^8 + c)x^{16} &= qgx^8 + (a + c)x^{16} + bx^8 \\
&= qgx^8 + q'g + s + bx^8
\end{aligned}
$$

From the last line, we can read off the new modified CRC as $s + bx^8$. We summarize the algorithm:

To compute the modified CRC of c appended to p, from the modified CRC r of p alone,

- take the high-byte a of r and compute $a + c$;
- look up the modified CRC s for the byte $a + c$;
- take the low-byte b of r and shift it left by 8 bits to obtain bx^8;
- and add bx^8 to s.

This algorithm fits on a single line, taking the next byte c directly from the bit stream as $*byte\_pointer$. In addition the $byte\_pointer$ gets advanced to the next byte.

$\langle$ compute the CRC for one byte $_{441}\,\rangle \equiv$ (441)
$\quad crc = (crc \ll 8) \oplus crc\_table\,[(crc \gg 8) \oplus *byte\_pointer\,{+}{+}]$ Used in 100, 101, and 214.

The table, that contains all the modified CRCs for all bytes from 0 to 255 is generated using the $bitcrc$ function.

$\langle$ print element $_{132}\,\rangle \mathrel{+}\equiv$ (442)
$\quad$ **void** $crc8\,($**int** $i)$
$\quad \{\ printf\,($`"0x%04x"`$, bitcrc\,(0, ($**unsigned short int**$)\, i, 8)); \ \}$

$\langle$ print table $_{135}\,\rangle \mathrel{+}\equiv$ (443)
$\quad print\_array\,($`"static unsigned short const crc_table"`$, 256, crc8\,);$

C Equalization

Equalization is based on scaling the 32 subband frequencies for each channel by individual factors provided as an option with the *mp3_open* call.

⟨ options $_{20}$ ⟩ +≡ (444)
unsigned char (*equalizer*)[32];

The *equalizer* option should be either NULL, in this case there is simply no equalization, or it should be the address of $2 \cdot 32$ unsigned 8 bit values. (For example "**unsigned char** *equalizer*[64];" and "*options.equalizer* = *equalizer*;"). Using these values, the subband samples are scaled just before they enter the IMDCT.

⟨ equalize $_{445}$ ⟩ ≡ (445)
if (*s*→*options.equalizer* ≠ NULL)
{ **int** *sb*;

 for (*sb* = 0; *sb* < SUBBANDS; *sb*++)
 { **int** *m* = *s*→*options.equalizer*[*ch*][*sb*];
  if ($m \equiv 0$) $\boldsymbol{y}[i][ch][sb] = 0.0$; **else** $\boldsymbol{y}[i][ch][sb]\mathrel{*}= 2^{(m-210)/32}$;
 }

}
Used in 70.

As can be seen, the scaling factor is not linear. It is similar to the layer III scaling operation discussed in Section 11.7. By dividing by 32 instead of 4, we trade a smaller range for finer steps. The range as well as the position of the unit gain at $m = 210$ was determined experimentally.

⟨ public declarations $_{15}$ ⟩ +≡ (446)
#**define** MP3_EQ_UNITGAIN 210

Choosing the unit gain at 210 looks like a quite unsymmetric arrangement. Why not use 128? First, one should be careful with gain factors greater than 1. An amplification might cause clipping at the point where the PCM samples are converted into the **mp3_sample** type. This is not the case with factors less than 1. So there is some inherent unsymmetry that is reflected by this choice.

By now, it should be clear how to compute $2^{(m-210)/32}$: we make a table.

⟨ print element $_{132}$ ⟩ +≡ (447)
void *power132* (**int** *i*)
{ *printf* ("%.16e", *pow* (2.0, (i − MP3_EQ_UNITGAIN)/32.0)); }

⟨ print table ₁₃₅ ⟩ +≡   (448)
  print_array("static␣const␣double␣power132", 256, *power132*);

⟨ private declarations ₁ ⟩ +≡   (449)
#**define** $2^{(m-210)/32}$ *power132*[m]

The equalizers gain factor for the value m is $2^{(m-210)/32}$. The dB scale is a logarithmic scale, to get the gain factor in dB we compute $10\log(2^{(m-210)/32})$.

Equalizer	0	1	210	255	Step size
Gain	$-\infty$	-19.66 dB	0 dB	$+4.23$ dB	0.094 dB

Tab. 31: Dynamic range of equalizer values

The center frequency of subband i is determined by the ith row of the analysis matrix, $v_i = \big(\cos((k-16)(2i+1)2\pi/128)\big)$ (see Section 10.6). The formal frequency of $(2i+1)/128$ must be multiplied by the actual sample rate. So if the sample rate is f, the center frequency of the ith subband is $(2i+1)f/128$.

Sample	Center Frequency										
Frequency	0	1	2	3	4	5	6	7	8	9	10
48 kHz	0.375	1.125	1.875	2.625	3.375	4.125	4.875	5.625	6.375	7.125	7.875
44.1 kHz	0.345	1.034	1.723	2.412	3.101	3.790	4.479	5.168	5.857	6.546	7.235
24 kHz	0.188	0.563	0.938	1.313	1.688	2.063	2.438	2.813	3.188	3.563	3.938
22.05 kHz	0.172	0.516	0.859	1.203	1.547	1.891	2.234	2.578	2.922	3.266	3.609

Sample	Center Frequency										
Frequency	11	12	13	14	15	16	17	18	19	20	21
48 kHz	8.625	9.375	10.125	10.875	11.625	12.375	13.125	13.875	14.625	15.375	16.125
44.1 kHz	7.924	8.613	9.302	9.991	10.680	11.370	12.059	12.748	13.437	14.126	14.815
24 kHz	4.313	4.688	5.063	5.438	5.813	6.188	6.563	6.938	7.313	7.688	8.063
22.05 kHz	3.953	4.297	4.641	4.984	5.328	5.672	6.016	6.359	6.703	7.047	7.391

Sample	Center Frequency									
Frequency	22	23	24	25	26	27	28	29	30	31
48 kHz	16.875	17.625	18.375	19.125	19.875	20.625	21.375	22.125	22.875	23.625
44.1 kHz	15.504	16.193	16.882	17.571	18.260	18.949	19.638	20.327	21.016	21.705
24 kHz	8.438	8.813	9.188	9.563	9.938	10.313	10.688	11.063	11.438	11.813
22.05 kHz	7.734	8.078	8.422	8.766	9.109	9.453	9.797	10.141	10.484	10.828

Tab. 32: Center frequencies in kHz of the 32 subbands

D Testing Compliance

The standard ISO/IEC 11172 has a part 4 that specifies how to test a decoder for compliance with the specification[2]. Sample input and output files for layer 1 and layer 2 are given as text files with hexadecimal numbers. It is an easy exercise to produce a program using mp32pcm that will read, decode, and write files in this format:

⟨hex2hex.c 450⟩ ≡   (450)

```
#include <stdio.h>
#include <ctype.h>
#include "mp32pcm.h"
  int hex_read(int id, void *buffer, size_t size)
  {   char hex[3];
    int c, i = 0;
    unsigned int b;

    hex[2] = 0;
    while (i < (int) size)
    { do if (EOF ≡ (c = getchar())) return i; while (¬isxdigit(c));
      hex[0] = c;
      hex[1] = (char) getchar();
      sscanf(hex, "%x", &b);
      (((unsigned char *) buffer)[i++]) = b;
    }
    return i;
  }

  static unsigned
      mask = ((unsigned) −1) ≫ ((sizeof(unsigned)−sizeof(mp3_sample))*8);
  void hex_write(mp3_sample *buffer, int size)
  { int i = 0;
    while (i < size)
      printf("%0*X""\n", (int) sizeof(mp3_sample) * 2, buffer[i++] & mask);
  }
  int main(void)
  {   int id, size;
    mp3_sample buffer[MP3_MIN_BUFFER];
```

```
    if ((id = mp3_open(hex_read, NULL)) < 0) return 1;
    while ((size = mp3_read(id, buffer, MP3_MIN_BUFFER)) > 0)
        hex_write(buffer, size);
    if (mp3_close(id) < 0) return 1;
    return 0;
}
```

To judge the quality of the decoder output, we have to compare sample by sample the decoder output with the reference output, as provided by the standard. If there are two channels, both channels shall be tested.

Samples are again interpreted as m bit binary fractions. Where $m_s = 24$ for the standard samples and $m_d = \textbf{sizeof}(\textbf{mp3\_sample}) * 8$ for the mp32pcm decoder.

If $m_s > m_d$, the standard requires that the shorter samples are padded with zeros. If $m_s < m_d$, the standard does not say anything. Here, we just pad again the shorter samples with zeros. To simplify things, this program converts all samples to 32 bit binary fractions, that are stored in plain signed **int** variables. To convert such a variable into its fractional value it is multiplied by $scale = 2^{-31}$.

After the differences are computed sample by sample, we square the differences, add them up, divide by the number of samples, and take the square root. The result of this operation is called the "rms" value (root mean square).

The decoder under test may be called an ISO/IEC 11172-3 audio decoder if the rms is less than $1/(2^{15} * 12^{0.5})$ and if the maximum absolute value difference for two samples is less than or equal to $1/2^{14}$. The last requirement is equivalent to at least 15 bits precision (14 plus one bit for the sign bit).

The standard provides the reference output as plain text files, with one sample value per line, and the above program can generate plain text files of the same format from the reference input files. So all we need to test the decoder quality for compliance is a program that compares the two text files:

⟨ rms.c   451 ⟩ ≡   (451)
```
#include <stdlib.h>
#include <stdio.h>
#include <ctype.h>
#include <math.h>
    int main(int argc, char *argv[])
    { FILE *f1, *f2;
        char l1[80], l2[80], *r1, *r2;
        double s0 = 0.0, s1 = 0.0;
        int maxsample1 = 0, maxsample2 = 0, ch = 0, maxdiff = 0, channels = 0,
            diffcount = 0, count = 0, maxcount = 0;
        double diff_limit = 1.0/(1 << 14);
        double scale = 1.0/((1 << (sizeof(int) * 8 - 2)) * 2.0);
        double rms_limit = 1.0/((1 << 15) * sqrt(12.0));

        if (argc < 3) return printf("use␣rms␣file1␣file2\n");
```

```
    if ((channels = atoi(argv[1])) < 1)
      return printf("number␣of␣channels␣expected␣%s\n", argv[1]);
    if (NULL ≡ (f1 = fopen(argv[2], "r")))
      return printf("unable␣to␣open␣%s\n", argv[2]);
    if (NULL ≡ (f2 = fopen(argv[3], "r")))
      return printf("unable␣to␣open␣%s\n", argv[3]);
    while (r1 = fgets(l1, 80, f1), r2 = fgets(l2, 80, f2), r1 ≠ NULL ∧ r2 ≠ NULL)
      ⟨compute results 452⟩
    ⟨print results 453⟩
    return 0;
  }
```

⟨compute results 452⟩ ≡   (452)
```
  { int i, x1, x2, diff;
    if (r1 ≠ NULL)
    { sscanf(l1, "%x", &x1);
      for (i = 0; isxdigit(l1[i]); i++) continue;
      x1 = (x1 ≪ (sizeof(int) * 8 − i * 4));
    }
    else x1 = 0;
    if (r2 ≠ NULL)
    { sscanf(l2, "%x", &x2);
      for (i = 0; isxdigit(l2[i]); i++) continue;
      x2 = (x2 ≪ (sizeof(int) * 8 − i * 4));
    }
    else x2 = 0;
    diff = x1 − x2;
    if (fabs(diff * scale) > diff_limit) diffcount++;
    if (abs(diff) > maxdiff)
    { maxdiff = abs(diff); maxsample1 = x1; maxsample2 = x2;
      maxcount = count; }
    if (ch ≡ 0)
    { s0 = s0 + (diff * scale) * (diff * scale);
      count++;
    }
    else s1 = s1 + (diff * scale) * (diff * scale);
    ch = (ch + 1) % channels;
  }
```
                                                                  Used in 451.

⟨print results 453⟩ ≡   (453)
```
  { double rms0 = sqrt(s0/(double) count), rms1 = sqrt(s1/(double) count);
    if (r1 ≠ NULL) printf("WARNING:␣file␣%s␣is␣shorter!\n", argv[2]);
    if (r2 ≠ NULL) printf("WARNING:␣file␣%s␣is␣shorter!\n", argv[1]);
```

$printf$ ("rms␣channel␣0\t%e\n", $rms0$);
if ($channels > 1$) $printf$ ("rms␣channel␣1\t%e\n", $rms1$);
$printf$ ("limit\t\t%e\n", rms_limit);
$printf$ ("maximum␣difference␣%08X␣!=␣%08X␣in␣sample␣%d,\n"
    "difference␣%d␣=␣%e,␣limit:␣%e\n", $maxsample1$, $maxsample2$, $maxcount$,
        $maxdiff$, $maxdiff * scale$, $diff\_limit$);
if ($rms0 < rms\_limit \wedge (channels < 2 \vee rms1 < rms\_limit) \wedge diffcount \equiv 0$)
    $printf$ ("encoder␣is␣compliant!\n");
else
{ $printf$ ("encoder␣is␣not␣compliant!␣%e/%e/%d\n", $rms0$, $rms1$, $diffcount$);
    return 1;
}

}
                                                                            Used in 451.

As an example, we apply `hex2hex` to the file `layer1/fl8.mpg` and then use `rms` to compare its output to the file `layer1/fl8.pcm` (both files are part of the standard). The result looks as follows:
with 16 bit output (**mp3_sample** set to be a **short int**):

```
rms channel 0    8.721587e-06
rms channel 1    8.726953e-06
limit            8.809666e-06
maximum difference 07EA0000 != 07E98000 in sample 702,
difference 32768 = 1.525879e-05, limit:   6.103516e-05
encoder is compliant!
```

with 32 bit output (**mp3_sample** set to be an **int**):

```
rms channel 0    3.434708e-08
rms channel 1    3.442370e-08
limit            8.809666e-06
maximum difference FFFFF480 != FFFFF500 in sample 406,
difference 128 = 5.960464e-08, limit:   6.103516e-05
encoder is compliant!
```

The rms values are below the limit, even with 16 bit output. One should note the maximum absolute difference: In the 16 bit case this is [#]07EA0000 versus [#]07E98000. It means that in the 24 bit value the 17th bit was set and the value was correctly rounded to 16 bits, changing the 9 to A. In the 32 bit case, the value [#]FFFFF480, rounded to 24 bits, gives exactly the reference value of [#]FFFFF500.

In conclusion, the maximum error is limited to rounding errors in the last bit. To obtain a decoder that reproduces exactly the 24 bit output given by the standard, all we have to do is produce 32 bit output and round the results to 24 bit precision. I wonder whether to some audiophile ears dithering the output to 24 bits, which commonly will produce superior sound quality, will still make an audible difference.

References

[1] ISO/IEC 11172-3. *Information technology—Coding of moving pictures and associated audio for digital storage media at up to about 1,5Mbit/s, Part 3: Audio*. ISO/IEC, 1993.

[2] ISO/IEC 11172-4. *Information technology—Coding of moving pictures and associated audio for digital storage media at up to about 1,5Mbit/s, Part 4: Compliance Testing*. ISO/IEC, 1995.

[3] ISO/IEC 13818-3. *Information technology—Generic coding of moving pictures and associated audio information, Part 3: Audio*. ISO/IEC, 1998.

[4] Yukihiro Arai, Takeshi Agui, and Masayuki Nakajima. A fast DCT-SQ scheme for images. *Transactions of the IEICE*, 71(11):1095–1097, December 1988.

[5] Marina Bosi and Richard E.Goldberg. *Introduction to Digital Audio Coding and Standards*. Kluwer Academic Publishers, 2003.

[6] K. Brandenburg, B. Edler, E. Eberlein, and J. Herre. Comparison of filter banks for high quality audio coding. In *IEEE International Symposium on Circuits and Systems*, pages 1336–1339, San Diego, CA, May 1992.

[7] James W. Cooley and John W. Tukey. An algorithm for the machine computation of complex fourier series. *Mathematics of Computation*, 19:297–301, 1965.

[8] Bernd Edler. Aliasing reduction in sub-bands of cascaded filter banks with decimation. *Electronic Letters*, 28(12):1104–1105, June 1992.

[9] Bernd Edler. *Äquivalenz von Transformation und Teilbandzerlegung in der Quellencodierung*. PhD thesis, University of Hannover, 1995.

[10] Matteo Frigo and Steven G. Johnson. FFTW: An adaptive software architecture for the FFT. In *Proc. 1998 IEEE Intl. Conf. Acoustics Speech and Signal Processing*, volume 3, pages 1381–1384. IEEE, 1998.

[11] Matteo Frigo and Steven G. Johnson. The design and implementation of FFTW3. *Proceedings of the IEEE*, 93(2), 2005. special issue on "Program Generation, Optimization, and Adaptation".

[12] GCC: The GNU compiler collection. `http://gcc.gnu.org/`.

[13] Werner Greub. *Linear Algebra*. Springer Verlag, 1975.

[14] William M. Hartmann. *Signals, Sound , and Sensation*. Springer Verlag, 2000.

[15] D.A. Huffman. A method for the construction of minimum redundancy codes. *Proceedings of the IRE*, 40:1098–1101, 1952.

[16] ICC: The Intel C compiler.
`http://developer.intel.com/software/products/compilers/`.

[17] Donald E. Knuth. *Literate Programming*. CSLI Lecture Notes Number 27. Center for the Study of Language and Information, Stanford, CA, 1992.

[18] Trevor Lamb and Janine Bourriau, editors. *Color: Art &Science*. Cambridge University Press, 1995.

[19] Byeong Gi Lee. A new algorithm to compute the discrete cosine transform. *IEEE Transactions on Acoustics, Speech, and Signal Processing*, 32(6):1243–1245, December 1984.

[20] Florence Jessie MacWilliams and Neil James Alexander Sloane. *The Theory of Error-Correcting Codes*, volume 16 of *North-Holland Mathematical Library*. North-Holland, 1996.

[21] MAD: MPEG audio decoder. `http://www.underbit.com/products/mad/`.

[22] mpg123: Version 0.59r, a real time MPEG audio player for layer 1, 2, and layer 3. `http://www.mpg123.de`.

[23] MSVC: The Microsoft visual C compiler. `http://msdn.microsoft.com/visualc/`.

[24] Alan V. Oppenheim, Ronald W. Schafer, and John R. Buck. *Discrete-Time Signal Processing*. Prentice Hall, 1999.

[25] A. Perez. Byte-wise CRC calculations. *IEEE Micro*, pages 40–50, June 1983.

[26] W. W. Peterson and D. T. Brown. Cyclic codes for error detection. *Proc. IRE*, 49:228–235, January 1961.

[27] Tenkasi V. Ramabadran and Sunil S. Gaitonde. A tutorial on CRC computations. *IEEE Micro*, 1988.

[28] Wolfram Research. Mathematica: A mathematical reasoning tool.
`http://www.wolfram.com`.

[29] Martin Sieler and Ralph Sperschneider. MPEG layer 3—bitstream syntax and decoding. 1997.

[30] SPIRAL: Automatic generation of platform-adapted code for DSP algorithms.
`http://www.ece.cmu.edu/~spiral`.

[31] A.S. Tanenbaum. *Computer Networks*. Prentice Hall, 81.

[32] Bartel Leendert van der Waerden. *Algebra*. Springer Verlag, 1930.

[33] Mark Allan Weiss. *Data Structures and Algorithm Analysis in* C. Addison Wesley, 1997.

[34] Ross N. Williams. A painless guide to CRC error detection algorithms.
`ftp.adelaide.edu.au/pub/rocksoft/crc_v3.txt`, August 1993.

[35] Eberhard Zwicker and Hugo Fastl. *Psychoacoustics, Facts and Models*. Springer Verlag, 1999.

Index

www.ingramcontent.com/pod-product-compliance
Lightning Source LLC
Chambersburg PA
CBHW080634060326
40690CB00021B/4933